Palgrave European Film and Media Studies

Series Editors

Andrew Higson
University of York, UK

Ib Bondebjerg
University of Copenhagen, Denmark

Caroline Pauwels
Vrije Universiteit Brussels, Belgium

Aim of the Series

Palgrave European Film and Media Studies is dedicated to historical and contemporary studies of film and media in a European context and to the study of the role of film and media in European societies and cultures. The series invite research done in both humanities and social sciences and invite scholars working with the role of film and other media in relation to the development of a European society, culture and identity. Books in the series can deal with both media content and media genres, with national and transnational aspects of film and media policy, with the sociology of media as institutions and with audiences and reception, and the impact of film and media on everyday life, culture and society. The series encourage books working with European integration or themes cutting across nation states in Europe and books working with Europe in a more global perspective. The series especially invite publications with a comparative, European perspective based on research outside a traditional nation state perspective. In an era of increased European integration and globalization there is a need to move away from the single nation study focus and the single discipline study of Europe.

More information about this series at
http://www.springer.com/series/14704

Tobias Ebbrecht-Hartmann • Derek Paget
Editors

Docudrama on European Television

A Selective Survey

Editors
Tobias Ebbrecht-Hartmann
Hebrew University of Jerusalem
Jerusalem, Israel

Derek Paget
University of Reading
Reading, UK

Palgrave European Film and Media Studies
ISBN 978-1-349-69862-2   ISBN 978-1-137-49979-0   (eBook)
DOI 10.1057/978-1-137-49979-0

Library of Congress Control Number: 2016941774

Cover illustration: © Image Source / Alamy Stock Photo

Printed on acid-free paper

This Palgrave Macmillan imprint is published by Springer Nature
The registered company is Macmillan Publishers Ltd. London

CONTENTS

NOTES ON CONTRIBUTORS

Åsa Bergström is a PhD student in Film Studies at Lund University, Sweden. Her dissertation analyses how Sweden has addressed and represented the Holocaust in moving images. The project involves archival research, primary source material consisting of newsreels, documentaries, docudramas, and fiction films from the Second World War up until today. Her current research includes projects and publications on factual theatre, children's film, newsreels, media representations of humanitarian organisations, and Swedish docudrama on screen, stage and television. She has a professional background as an actress, and extensive experience in contemporary drama, musical theatre, children's theatre, and improvisational theatre.

Milly Buonanno is former Professor of Television Studies at the University of Roma La Sapienza (Italy). Currently she is Director of the research programme on Gender and Media at the Department of Communication and Social Research at La Sapienza, and the Observatory of Italian TV Drama. She has researched and written extensively on television, television drama, journalism, gender and media, and is the author and editor of more than 50 books. She has co-edited the *Sage Handbook of Television Studies* (2014) and is the editor of *Women Behaving Badly*, a collection on female leads in contemporary crime and prison drama (forthcoming 2016).

Tobias Ebbrecht-Hartmann is Lecturer in Film and German Studies in the Department of Communication and Journalism and the DAAD Center for German Studies at the Hebrew University in Jerusalem, Israel. He was formerly Senior Researcher at the Filmuniversity Babelsberg KONRAD WOLF, and a Postdoctoral Fellow in the programme 'Media of History—History of Media' at the Bauhaus University Weimar. He has presented his research at the Film and History, NECS and Visible Evidence international conferences and is the author of several articles and books on cinematic memory, the appropriation of archive footage, docudrama, and historical event-television.

Georges Fournier is Senior Lecturer and Researcher at the *Institut d'Etudes Transtextuelles et Transculturelles* (Lyon 3 University, France), as well as an Associated Researcher at the *Axe Civilisation Britannique* (Rennes 2 University, France). His research interests are in British media and the cinema of the English-speaking world. He is a member of *InMédia* for which he has published articles and edited issues. He has also written articles for the *LISA e-review* and for foreign publishers. A member of the *European Network for Cinema and Media Studies*, he has given several presentations at conferences around Europe and is part of a project on European TV screens.

Wiesław Godzic is Full Professor in Film and Media at the University of Social Sciences and Humanities in Warsaw, Poland and Head of the Audiovisual Department. His many publications include *Television as Culture* (1999), *Understanding Television* (2001), *Television and Its Genres: After Big Brother* (2004), *'Known for his Well-knownness': Celebrities in Tabloid Culture* (2007), and *Kuba and Others: Faces and Masks of Pop-culture* (2013). He also edited the first analysis of reality television in Poland, *Watching Big Brother* (2001), and a noted Polish media studies text book *Audiovisual Media* (2011). He is a member of the Polish Academy of Science.

Derek Paget is Visiting Fellow in the Department of Film, Theatre and Television at the University of Reading in England. He is the author of the monographs *True Stories: documentary drama on radio, television and film* (1990) and *No Other Way to Tell It: Docudrama on Film and Television* (1998, 2011), as well as many chapters and articles on docudrama and documentary theatre. A member of *Studies in Theatre and Performance*'s Editorial Board, he was a founding Associate Editor of *Studies in Documentary Film*. He was Principal Investigator for the Arts and Humanities Research Council of England's research project 'Acting with Facts' (2007–2010).

Victoria Pastor-González is Senior Lecturer at the Institute of Languages and Culture at Regent's University London. Her research interests include docudrama in Spanish television, and the work of the directors Krzysztof Kieślowski and Benito Zambrano. She has collaborated on a special edition of the journal *Studies in Documentary Film* (2010) with an article on religious iconography in Spanish docudramas, and with the *Directory of World Cinema: Spain* (2011) with an entry on Zambrano's film *Solas*. Her work on Krzysztof Kieślowski appeared in the book series *New Studies in European Cinema* (2005).

David Rolinson is Lecturer in Film and Television at the University of Stirling. He is the author of *Alan Clarke* (2005) and co-editor of a collection of Dennis Potter pieces, *The Art of Invective: Selected Non-Fiction 1953–1994*

(2015). His work has appeared in journals including *Critical Studies in Television* and the *Journal of British Cinema and Television* and books including *British Social Realism in the Arts since 1940* (2011) and *Shane Meadows: Critical Essays* (2013) and DVD releases including *Red Shift* (2014). He edits the website www.britishtelevisiondrama.org.uk.

CHAPTER 1

Introduction: A New Europe, the Post-Documentary Turn and Docudrama

Derek Paget

A Genre Made for New Times

This book is predicated on the idea that the screen genre docudrama became ubiquitous during the latter part of the twentieth century. It argues in general that the genre was made for new times. Fact-based art burgeoned during this period, part of a millennial zeitgeist. It is tempting to relate this to Francis Fukuyama's controversial 1992 concept of the 'End of History', which posited a new world order at the close of a century in which the capitalist system seemed triumphant. While the coming of this order seems less likely in the second decade of the new century, it is clear enough that Greater Europe has been radically reconfigured in the past quarter-century, and that more change must come. Initially, the new era was heralded by striking workers in Poland, by Gorbachev's glasnost policy in the USSR, and, crucially, by the fall of the Berlin Wall in 1989. Even before the fall of the Wall, the forests of aerials pointing westwards in East Germany, remarked by many visitors from the West during the long Cold War period, were testament to many things, including the desire for a 'free' media in the East that would open up proscribed subjects.[1] The extent to which any medium can actually be free will, of course, always be debatable. But the Wall and its collapse became a powerful symbol of contrasting desires arising from opposed political systems. If keeping some things out was uppermost on one side of the Wall, letting

© The Editor(s) (if applicable) and The Author(s) 2016
T. Ebbrecht-Hartmann, D. Paget (eds.), *Docudrama on European Television*, Palgrave European Film and Media Studies,
DOI 10.1057/978-1-137-49979-0_1

1

some things in was surely the aim of those aerials. On both sides was a consciousness of a Europe still troubled by its twentieth-century past and becoming confused by the looming twenty-first-century future. The ramifications of the break-up of an uneasy Pan-European postwar settlement that had seemed for two generations to be set in stone, the emergence of a new, and unsettled, Europe, triggered many things—as the subsequent two-and-a-half decades have shown.

By 2000, the 'old' Cold War had (effectively) ended, the former Eastern European power bloc had (apparently) collapsed, and its organising ideology had (again apparently) become discredited. It was not just that 'satellite' nations formerly sealed into an alliance with the Soviet Union could suddenly secede from the previous union (for example, Poland, Romania, East Germany); the USSR itself also quite rapidly fragmented into its constituent parts. A New Europe seemed to be, if not born, at least emerging as the old millennium tipped over into the new. Docudrama—at its investigative journalistic best a profoundly democratic screen genre—offered, we will argue in the chapters that follow, a means in many European countries of supplying a real need for information, explanation, and reflection at this time of uncertainty and dizzying instability. The genre's history is embedded in anglophone and Western European television cultures, and its development is inevitably inflected by British and American influences. But the subject of this book is the emergence of docudrama elsewhere in Europe. The genre's spread can even be detected in countries from the old Eastern Europe, as Chaps. 2 and 3 will show.

In an article in 2000, John Corner identified what he called a 'post-documentary' turn in screen culture, occurring as millennial events played out. Indeed, 'docu-hybridity' has played a major role in representing these times to film and television audiences. Much inventive mixing of formerly discrete television genres has been evident. The 'intermateability' of factual and imaginative ways of seeing (literally, the mixing of separate components) has been viewed with much suspicion in the past, being seen as an unnecessary and confusing 'blurring of boundaries'.[2] But in the new era it has become almost de rigueur, and fact-based approaches have been evident across the performing and expressive arts.[3] Docudrama began as a distinctively post-World War II televisual genre (as I argued first in my 1990 book *True Stories?*). The tectonic shifts of the late twentieth century fuelled a new interest in facts and information that was altogether different from the earlier, post-Enlightenment 'faith in facts' that had spawned early docudrama. Improved technology, too, has had a role in widening access to information.[4] Screen docudrama's newfound status served to bracket the genre off from the excesses of other forms of fact-based (some would say 'dumbed-down') television, such as 'reality TV'. With status came increased production activity, and instead of being, as I stated in 1990, an 'occasional' feature of broadcast television scheduling, docudrama's presence became frequent as well as significant. This has made the form more difficult to attack for lacking the heavyweight, 'discourse of sobriety' claims of documentary.[5] Indeed, its range of generic possibility has been hugely expanded as the result of synergies between the formerly rival film and television industries. Thus the 'biopic' and the 'based-on-fact' areas of the film industry, each with their own traditions of practice, have fed off television docudrama to emerge as more and more important parts of the modern cinema industry too. The pace of these changes was remarkable, and in my later *No Other Way to Tell It*, I proposed the idea of a 'continuum' of docudramatic practice to account for the burgeoning spectrum of fact-usage. And I attempted to highlight all this by using the phrase 'screen drama' to reflect the fact that docudramatic strategies were now at play in both film and television (2011, p. 3).

By the time the team that has produced this book were working together in the early twenty-first century, docudrama had established sufficient levels of industrial production, broadcast visibility, audience loyalty, and even academic respectability within the spectrum of hybrid fact/fiction television and film practices to demand further examination and analysis. This book seeks to explore docudrama's emergence and importance in a number of European television ecologies, and to examine the ways in which the genre has adapted to particular national sensibilities and interests. It seeks simultaneously to be an introduction to a potential research area (for there are more exclusions than inclusions in our 'Selective Survey'), and a blueprint for further investigation. It appears at a time when the precise contours of European re-alignment seem every bit as problematical as they have been at any time since the end of World War II; a time when the 'New Europe' is a place of doubt and difficulty rather than a stable point at the End of History. Geopolitical alignments and realignments, complicated further by religious extremism, population diaspora from within and beyond Europe's frontiers, and global economic uncertainty have added to the historical problems already evident in the very concept of 'Europe'. It seems more than likely that fact-based screen drama will continue to be a means of trying to make sense of social, political, cultural, and indeed geographical, change within the continent well into the future.

The 'Selective Survey'

Selection is the inevitable result of two pragmatic factors. Firstly, the core of the team that has produced the book came together at various international conferences through a common scholarly interest in the dominant screen traditions of Anglo-American docudrama.[6] Distinctively British (investigative journalistic) and American (entertainment-led) traditions of docudrama have been influential since at least the 1960s. Anglophone co-production has caused these traditions to dovetail since at least the 1980s, and international 'co-pros' with channels and production companies in Europe have extended the form's reach and grasp. It is important in this Introduction to acknowledge the hegemonic implications of anglophone screen culture. For all the contributors to this book it was a necessary—but manifestly insufficient—first step in the work that followed. The transfer of our common interest in anglophone docudrama to the screen cultures of each person's home nation was a more important step towards conference presentations that sought to gauge to what extent, if any, the distinctive features of the 'two traditions' could be traced in indigenous production in France, Germany, Spain, and Italy, and to what extent, if any, there were 'local', nuanced, differences—evidence, perhaps, of distinctive national concerns and senses of identity. The core group, then, already represented five major language communities of old Western Europe. The nations represented in the panels could in addition be claimed as hosting the continent's earliest, most highly developed, and sophisticated television systems and cultures. The docudramatic models of British and American practitioners have been both available and influential almost from the inception of these European nations' television systems. This has been ratcheted up by international co-production, and the influence of Arte and Canal+ in Europe is also an important factor. Our 'compare and contrast' approach in conference presentations offered an early opportunity to open up the subject further, to try to establish what might be distinctive about each nation's approach to docudrama, and to speculate on what this might mean for the wider European culture.

Secondly, we felt we had not only to acknowledge the fissures—hegemonic and otherwise—in our coverage, we had also at least to have a policy towards those gaps. A comprehensive survey taking in all European nations was highly tempting for 'completists' (myself included). But it had to be recognised as impossible in practical terms—no publishing house would wish to finance such a large volume. Having said all this, it was still logical to try for as broad a base as possible. We wanted at least some coverage from outside the nations already represented. To this end, we sought out fellow academics elsewhere in Europe, and succeeded in drawing perspectives from Sweden and Poland. Thus there is at least some limited consideration of situations obtaining in countries outside the dominant language groups; one from a country formerly part of the old Communist bloc, and one from a Scandinavian country newly emergent as a 'player' on the European television scene thanks in particular to the rise of so-called 'Nordic noir' TV drama.

This book, then, argues only for representative potential within a directed but partly serendipitous selection. Collectively, we accept that some aspects of this must have the appearance of 'tokenism', but with a study that is, effectively, the first of its kind, this has the kind of operational inevitability that is regrettable but unavoidable.[7] Our hope is that this collection is a first step in encouraging academic studies of all kinds across the continent—theses, articles, books—because we are convinced that the docudramatic mode has been, is, and will continue to be vital to the representation, narrativisation, and understanding of difficult times. The best examples of docudrama have always gone beyond print and broadcast news and documentary; they possess a reach and grasp unavailable to other modes of public address. The worst examples—so-called 'disease of the week' docudramas, or those featuring tabloid crime, for example—furnish another kind of perspective on mass culture that is also potentially valuable. Examples from across the spectrum will be found in the chapters that follow, all have a relevance to the future potential of the genre and the future trajectory of its study (and I will return to this subject in the final section of this Introduction). Partial, then, our coverage is, but we hope that the selection we have made, the approach we have taken, and the examples of practice on which we focus will serve to point the way.

OUR APPROACH: AN ACADEMIC BACKSTORY

Docudrama's generic characteristics have been formed via traditions in theatre as well as film, and its claims to documentary authenticity are additionally underscored by practices in both film and print journalism. Television networks throughout Europe have used and are using docudrama to examine key events in national histories, and to review the lives of individuals central to unfolding national histories. At the lower end of the scale, there is what might be seen as a pandering to the kind of tabloid culture that has bedevilled an industry somewhat in thrall to the quick fix of reality TV and 'celebrity'. The celebrity biographical docudrama could be an element of this, but it need not be—as some writers show in their chapters. Worthy, serious docudrama—with something new to say about history, current affairs, and the place of important people in them—is the aspect of the genre to which many academics are drawn. But we do not avoid commentary on the tabloid just because it is tabloid.

At this particularly crucial point in a perennially troubled European history, screen docudrama is one of the means cultures have to work through issues, including difficult, even traumatic, elements of experiences shared both within national borders and in a pan-European context. The burgeoning of the genre across the 'quality-of-subject' spectrum is a good indication that it has a part to play in the task of making sense both of complex current events, and of cultural obsessions. Its inherent exploration of representational boundaries as creatively permeable in wholly new ways is one of the many reasons why we claim docudrama as a 'genre for the times'. This book's overarching theoretical position, then, is one grounded in the surveying of specific national contexts and practices, but one always alive to those relational issues that offer nuanced points of departure towards wider, international perspectives. To some extent the approach taken to docudrama is a common one; it is an approach founded on a distinctive academic backstory which, I hope, will partially excuse the personal tone of this Introduction.

If much of the history and tradition of docudrama developed via an anglophone screen culture that has somewhat dominated the genre—largely because of American/English-language screen hegemony—something similar is true of the academic attention that docudrama has received. This too has been dominated by British and American scholars. Work mainly from the last half of the twentieth century established the distinctiveness of the genre as residing in a combination of 'head' and 'heart' treatments of 'events that really happened'. The 'head' approach derives from forensic, investigative journalism, and legalistic applications of the notions of 'research', 'evidence', and 'proof'. The 'heart' approach stems from the emotional and behavioural dimensions available through performance—dramatic writing and structuring, realist film technique, and actor skill. Drama's capacity to offer second-order experience can never be discounted (see Paget 2011, pp. 287–289). Study of docudrama has emerged from many academic paths—studies in theatre, film, television/media, history—all with distinctive approaches. But in the early days of commentary on the form, things were rather different. Beginning work on docudrama more than a quarter of a century ago, I was primarily interested in two things about the writing on the subject that irritated me. The first was a tendency to regard docudrama as either bad documentary, bad drama, or both those things. Critics would routinely condemn films and programmes on the basis that the facts were wrong (or inadequate), or the drama lame (or overly didactic). In the former case, as more than one maker of docudrama told me, the tendency was to think 'if they got *that* wrong, what about everything else?'[8] In the latter case, realist drama's problems in exposition—in supplying basic information (vital or otherwise) were always seized upon gleefully.[9]

A further assumption back in those days concerned the relative status of the different performative arts. An unspoken but very obvious hierarchy obtained, and to some extent still does. So film and (it almost went without saying) theatre were always seen as having the inherent potential to be art of the highest order. Television, and again it almost went without saying, was intrinsically inferior—a mass medium prone always to lowest common factor logic. Then as now, newspaper reviewing of television featured coverage of a range of programme categories unheard of for reviewing theatre and film. It was rather as if film reviewers had had to comment on the whole of the programme available to 1950s cinemagoers ('B' feature, a documentary, a cartoon, advertisements, main feature). For many early television commentators it became a given that docudrama could never claim either the 'truth' of documentary or the exalted degree of 'excellence' available in real dramatic art. In those days hybridity was an impure, mongrel element in an already mongrel medium. Times have changed to some extent as far as this attitude goes, and as the film and television industries in Britain and America have synergised there is now far more acknowledgement of the artistic possibilities available to television drama in particular.

In former times, it was easier for practitioner, newspaper critic, and academic alike to sustain the notion of a 'hard border', to coin a phrase, between documentary and drama. But hybridisation has always been the medium's strong suit in comparison with other media; it just took a long time to acknowledge it. Sophisticated systems have accelerated invention within television formats, and recognition of a 'soft border' between documentary and drama has become more evident as a result. Even in the academy, where many disciplines are in the business of categorising and defining, hybridisation has been recognised as a benefit, not a curse, through work in emergent disciplines such as media and television studies. Docudrama has even been welcomed (if cautiously) into the field of documentary studies itself, and prominent historians have become involved both practically and theoretically.[10] In the present dispensation, 'long form' mini-series television drama in particular has increasingly claimed artistic status through the nuanced complexities of theme, plot, and character available to writers, the challenges available to actors, directors, and their co-workers in production, and to the audiences receiving the finished work. Writers, actors, and (to a lesser extent) directors now actively seek work in a medium no longer technologically confined to one timetabled broadcast and the possibility of repeats.

Television drama's stepping out of the long shadow of theatre and film has everything to do with industry synergy, technical innovation, artistic brilliance, and entrepreneurial awareness, and rather less to do with academic recognition. However, my 1990 *True Stories?* and *No Other Way To Tell It* (1998, 2011), along with Steven N. Lipkin's 2002 *Real Emotional Logic* and 2011 *Docudrama Performs the Past*, have marked out some of the ways this 'border territory' can be discussed positively. These remain the only current academic monographs specifically dealing with British and American docudrama. Ideas deriving from them will be found quite often in the chapters that follow.[11] In my own books, I was responding to Alan Rosenthal's still-pertinent question 'Why Docudrama?', and I attempted to do three things. I sought first to analyse docudramas in and for themselves, trying to determine what was distinctive in the genre—consciously opposing the bad documentary/bad drama argument. By means of this kind of enquiry I hoped to establish the hallmarks of successful docudrama, recognising that the form, like any other, manifests a wide range and variable quality of practice. I believed, too, that it was possible, occasionally, for a TV film/programme to aspire to the value-laden condition of Art. This led to my 1990 contention that there were 'two traditions' of docudrama, an entertainment-led American one ('docudrama'), and a British TV tradition founded upon investigative journalism ('dramadoc'). I also, along with many other commentators, drew distinctions between 'documentary drama' (invented plot and characters plus factual base) and 'drama-documentary' (real names and situations, with some authentic, some speculative, dialogue).[12]

As British and American film and television industries synergised, I subsequently (1998, 2011) argued that a merging of the two traditions has become evident especially in international 'co-pro' docudrama, beginning with the American HBO and the British BBC and ITV channel Granada in the 1980s, and now involving major European players such as the BBC, Arte, and Canal+. For me, it became imperative to simplify terminology in order to focus on wider issues of content and motivation (Why this subject? Why a docudramatic approach?). There are understandable fears that continue to exist about the 'watering down' of the British investigative drama-documentary through a kind of contamination with American 'movie-of-the-week'-style docudrama. I have however contended that the best examples still contain enough facts and information for documentary credibility and enough dramatic quality to reach beyond the purely rational. I also believe that less exalted examples continue to tell us something about the wider world, and the individual cultures, within which we live.

Another idea for which I take some responsibility, and which also drives some of the nation-based accounts that follow, is the proposition that there have been identifiable 'phases' in the development of anglophone docudrama, and that these correspond to wider developments in television itself. These range from early periods of relative dearth (where the medium was limited in output and forced to compensate for technological inadequacies), through to the current period of plenty—in terms of digital channels, multiplicity of platforms, and greater quality.[13] Always a medium driven to hybridise, television can now claim to lead the way in formal dramatic innovation. Facts now shadow a good deal of dramatic and imaginative activity on all kinds of screen in the current dispensation.

Finally, I have recently opposed the very notion of 'blurred boundaries', not because it is without foundation, but rather because it has resulted in lazy commentary. This kind of commentary normally comes in two forms: either the writer subscribes unproblematically to the bad documentary/ bad drama thesis, or they take the line that a mass audience of a mass medium is incapable of recognising the difference between fact and fiction. This argument often concludes that docudrama is thus socially 'dangerous'. I have sought instead to encourage the notion that borders are about meetings as well as separations—or about 'entanglements', as my co-editor Tobias Ebbrecht-Hartmann terms it. For me, the Benjaminian concept of 'porosity' is preferable—because less judgemental—to the idea of 'blurring' (see Paget 2011, p. 273). Here, perhaps, is the real significance of the idea of placing something—whether it is drama, film, opera, novel, popular song—on the 'based on fact' continuum signalled by the prefix 'docu'. This is why, having worked to define terms in 1990 and 1998, I now prefer to use the word 'docudrama' to cover the full spectrum of screen drama underpinned by fact. This is bound to irritate some academics, but definition rarely precedes form in any artistic practice; it is generally a reaction to change in form. Definition is the colander in which we academics try to catch the practices of creatives. Therefore, this book freely co-opts the 'biopic' as itself a form of docudrama, and we use the term 'biographical docudrama', as something on the docudrama's 'continuum of practice'.[14]

However, the academic backstory is just as much about Steven N. Lipkin's contribution. His ideas in relation to film melodrama, his concept of docudrama's 'arenas of representation', his establishing of the 'warranting' of docudrama's claims of fact, and—especially—his production executive-based "'rootable", "relatable" and "promotable"' mantra constitute the other controlling arm of theories that drive the accounts that follow.[15] Importantly, these theoretical ideas provide points of departure as well as organising principles. There have also been hugely important contributions specifically on docudrama from, for example, John Corner, John Caughie, Gary Edgerton, Hoffer et al., and Alan Rosenthal. Taken altogether, the academic backstory has gone a long way towards defining the terms for discussion of docudrama, mapping its history, and analysing its practices.[16]

THE CHAPTERS

The seven contributors to this book focus on the wider significance of the usage of facts and information in dramatic formats, rather than on further attempts to pin down the vagaries of form. In the second chapter, Tobias Ebbrecht-Hartmann makes the important point that the contemporary turn towards fact-based drama across Europe indicates a contemporary re-evaluation of the complex relationship between personal memory, historical memory, and nationhood. All this is part of, and goes beyond, the docudrama. The ongoing process of what he terms 'making Europe' is manifestly a site of contestation as established and emergent European nations struggle to define who and what they have been, are, and may become in what is still a very new century. Docudrama is a significant means of both the attempt to harmonise and to dispute the valency of 'memory'—personal and collective—in the public sphere of screen representation. So the best docudrama disputes received histories and hypostatised memory. It does this in two ways: either via its fact-base (often introducing new facts, highlighting neglected facts, and/or realigning well-known facts); or via insights into human behaviour within events embedded within the dramatic frame of historical events. When it works to counteract hegemonic narratives, I see docudrama as part of a cultural immune-system response, seeking to heal the body politic by its intervention into the public sphere of broadcasting. The events depicted can in their origins be significant, provocative, contentious, prurient, celebratory. Responses across the board of quality scale the heights and plumb the depths of that 'ethical uncertainty' which Steven N. Lipkin has observed 'beset[s] a post-9/11 world' (Lipkin 2015, p. 52). Docudrama is in part a cultural admission that rationality alone is never enough. The rational seeks to explain, but can never be the sole repository of explanation of human activity, endeavor, and—particularly—frailty. Offering as docudrama does 'history in the present tense' (Lacey 2015, p. 36), television experiences a pre-eminence over film, which necessarily operates within the markedly different timescale of cinematic 'release'. The very words 'broadcast' and 'transmission', used about television, carry conceptually different connotations to 'release'. Television, even in the new age of multiple platforms, retains the ability for rapid response to crisis, noteworthy events, and the lives (and deaths) of significant individuals. Docudrama is one of the medium's key rapid-response options.

Each of the chapters that follow offers an account of the history of the TV industry in a particular country, and an account of docudrama's place in it. This includes an account of characteristic subject matter, and the wider social and political contexts in which docudramatic material appears. Case studies then take closer looks at specific material, with a view to bringing out similarities and differences inherent in national practices when compared to overarching genre characteristics as defined in the leading books and articles that have established docudrama as a genre to be reckoned with. Some chapters deal with terminology, some with its absence; some chapters focus on individual practitioners, some on characteristic approaches. As co-editors, Tobias Ebbrecht-Hartmann and I have adopted a particular policy with regard to presentation of the basic unit of information on case studies: we have asked for Title/Title Translation/ Broadcaster/Year of Transmission. However, occasionally the name of a particular director or writer can assume an importance to which it is worth drawing attention. So, to take the UK example, it is important to mention directors such as Peter Kosminsky or Ken Loach, producers such as Tony Garnett, writers such as Peter Morgan, precisely because of their past record (and often, it should be said, because of their film as well as television backgrounds). In some countries (Poland, for example), connections with a well-established and honourable documentary film tradition are significant factors. But in so much industrial TV production, director and writer tend to be 'hired hands', working without the resources and without the influence that an established name can virtually guarantee. The hard economics of television production determine that channels and production companies are often of more significance. As editors, we have left decisions about whether to go beyond the basic information unit to individual contributors. A select list of films and programmes is available, however, in the Filmography to this book.

In Chap. 2, Tobias Ebbrecht-Hartmann is available significantly to his own 2007 concept of 'historical event television' in his examination of recent tendencies in the 'long tradition of the genre on German television'. In that long tradition, he shows that Germany, like Britain, has its specialists: Heinrich Breloer and Egon Monk being German equivalents of Loach and Kosminsky in their frequent recourse to the genre and in their target topics. The Third Reich and German reunification are especially important periods in his account of German history and analysis of practice. Docudrama's potential to turn formally inwards (and here the influence of Brechtian theatre is strong) and conceptually outwards (into what I have termed the 'extra-textual'—2011, pp. 117–118) is illustrated in his account. His analysis of German docudrama post-reunification demonstrates how the 'competing memories' of Greater Germany's problematical past have been represented both in the separated old Germanys, and in the new Germany.

Borders of any kind connect fully as much as they divide, and in making this point Ebbrecht-Hartmann's case study material seems particularly important to the project of the book as a whole, being focused as it is on representations of the division and reunification of Germany. The historical event of the fall of the Wall returns in the anniversary schedule he examines at the beginning of his chapter, the whole day's television virtually, in his words, 'an extended docudrama'. Ebbrecht-Hartmann's citation of de Certeau in his chapter also seems foundational in terms of this book's angle on those 'borders' that docudrama, according to many commentators, allegedly transgresses. De Certeau, like Benjamin, reminds us that borders (whether literal or metaphorical) are unfixed. Inevitably they betoken 'entanglement', and this, as he shows, is a far more complex matter than separation. The entanglement of West with East Germany leads to a renewed search for 'Germanness' in the new, post-1989 dispensation—amongst a new generation seeking truth from its forbears.

The first two chapters analyse contrasting vectors following the fall of the Wall. The event resonated very differently in Wiesław Godzic's Poland. Journalistic input even in an age of entertainment-for-entertainment's sake gives the docudrama greater claim to documentary's originary power. Any attenuation of the directly documentary (and parallel increased accommodation to drama—with and without a capital 'D') in modern practices has tended to be seen as 'dumbing down'. As Godzic remarks in Chap. 3, the kind of detail in terms of facts and information made available in the best examples of the genre 'requires time and reflection'—for makers and audience alike. These are qualities not always available in the meretricious era of reality television, particularly as it has been foisted on post-Communist Poland. Polish television came very late to docudrama, part result of a culture forced to re-veal through artistic con-cealment. It was possible, as he shows, to comment on the absurdities of life under Communism, but full disclosure was not just impossible, it was positively dangerous. Reading his chapter, I was reminded of Jan. Kott's counterintuitive remark about Polish theatre in the Cold War: 'When we want fantasy, we do Brecht. When we want realism, we do Beckett' (Whitaker 1977, p. 19).

With the economic volte-face that followed the events of 1989, the full force of Western capitalism brought Poles the dubious benefit of tabloid television. This was, for Godzic, the most remarkable result of the reorientation of Polish television, and he laments its effects on serious work. But the rise of tabloid television and culture in his country has not entirely offset the potential docudrama possesses to revisit the past. And this is a past that has hitherto been more hidden then openly declared. Godzic examines, for example, the way the exalted nature of previous depictions of Poland's 'heroic' liberators has been recast, and focuses on key moments in Polish history such as the Warsaw Uprising. New treatments of a World War II and Cold War history heavily (and understandably) inflected by Poland's powerful eastern neighbour and its ideology, seek to rewrite this history. 'Television Lies!', the Polish street graffito of the Communist years, is sufficient indication that no political ideology can fool all the people all the time. In 1998, Poland even created a new state institution, 'The Institute of National Remembrance', to try to manage national memory and readjust the misremembering that results from skewed history. The authorities' propaganda, especially of the 1970s, left a need for the residue of those 'Lies' to be counteracted. As Godzic observes, there is always a danger that such organisations as the Institute will substitute the lies that reinforced an old regime with lies that buttress the new one. What is certain is that the burden of conscience has determined that adjustments to the body politic become as vital as adjustments to the historical narratives that determine nationhood. Godzic's phrase 'the unrepresented world' is a telling one for any assessment of what can and cannot be treated by docudrama. In the case of Poland, it refers to those subjects proscribed under Communism. For Western observers, it resonates in a different way—where, for example, are the docudramas on political corruption and corporate fraud? Manifestly, they are not as easy to make as 'Disease of the Week' or 'Headline' docudrama.

Milly Buonanno, writer of Chap. 4, is a scholar who has already written extensively about what she calls Italy's '"return to the past"' (2012a p. 199). In the present dispensation, she fears the attenuation of docudrama production as the twenty-first century progresses in Italy. Like Godzic and other contributors, she notes how the serious is always so much more challenging and difficult to produce than the trivial. For Buonanno, the slowing-down of previously buoyant docudrama production is more a matter of Italy running out of the heroes through whose biographical docudramas the nation can reassess (and in some cases, radically rewrite) national history. While figures from the long past feature in historical docudramas discussed in her chapter, once again the guilt of the totalitarian past in World War II forms a focus for docudramatic treatment. Her case study hero, Giorgio Perlasca, was a kind of Italian Schindler. His biographical docudrama, she writes, was 'a high point' in the development of the form in Italy, and that was broadcast in 2002.

Rod Carveth, writing in 1993, observed that contemporary American docudrama came in two basic forms: 'the historical docudrama' and what he terms 'the headline docudrama' (p. 121). Buonanno's assessment of Italian historical and biographical docudrama as using fictive means to exploit an audience's prior knowledge of the events depicted fits well with Carveth's categories. The Italian form derives directly from historical film and biopic, but Buonanno remarks how the 'lack of a proper name' for docudrama in Italian critical discourse has held discussion back. Her chapter is one of several to call for further research, hugely complicated in the Italian case, she notes, by significant absences in the TV archive. She believes that the lack of interest in definition of terms has had serious consequences for the wider historiography of television in Italy. The void has been filled instead with a reliance on what she calls 'umbrella terms' that are particular to Italian culture and convenient to use (she cites *sceneggiato* and *originale televisio*). Beyond the recent focus on historical figures, treated in biographical docudrama, she identifies stories about family (involving challenges to traditional patriarchal models) and the Catholic Church as being significant foci for docudramatic treatment. Here also is potentially fruitful ground for further study and comparison; across a whole range of nations the influence of established religions on society, as dramatised in docudrama, would surely be worth investigating (see also Chap. 6 on Spain in this regard).

In previous work in 2012, Buonanno noted the power of fact-based films to encourage 'national reconciliation'(p. 223), and Georges Fournier pursues a similar line in Chap. 5 on French docudrama. Seeking a more positive line on the genre, he makes a not dissimilar point to Buonanno concerning the nation-building potential inherent in the stories of a country's great and good (as well as its more notorious) from the past and the near-present. So often, and in so many countries, this is fundamental to fact-based storytelling—especially if the subject's story also touches a sore spot in the national consciousness. In the course of his discussion, he coins the term 'patrimony television' to encapsulate the intention of such programming. His phrase denotes television production that seeks to bind together or to question notions of nationhood. Another of Fournier's important coinages is 'embedded biopic', through which he extends the notion of the biographical docudrama discussed often in these pages. We have become familiar with the notion of the 'embedded journalist' thanks to the military policy of effectively 'licensing' the reporting of recent wars both in Europe (the Balkans) and in the Middle East (Iraq and Afghanistan). Much ink, academic and journalistic, has been spilt on trying to establish the degree (if any) of compromise to the journalistic project inherent in the kind of 'privileged' access granted by the modern military to the modern journalist (see, again, Lacey 2015 on this). At times, this has made for fascinating collisions of intention (as represented in, for example, the 2008 HBO television mini-series *Generation Kill*, based on an embedded US journalist's 2004 book).[17]

Fournier's case study to illustrate the nature of the embedded biopic is about a significant but still controversial French politician—François Mitterrand—and a subject that has obsessed France for many years, namely the part played by the Resistance in World War II. The biographer with privileged access depicted in the docudrama, in Fournier's account, grows dangerously close to his subject—to the extent that his ability to assess Mitterrand is threatened and compromised. Fournier's analysis of the significance of this 2005 film, *Le Promeneur du Champ de Mars* (The Last Mitterrand), traces the ramifications of this situation. In the course of his chapter, Fournier also remarks on the significance of a 2000 French High Court judgement that released some of the restrictions on docudrama. There is an obvious connection here both to Poland's Institute of National Remembrance, and to Victoria Pastor-González' citation, in Chap. 5, of Spain's 2006 *Ley de la Memoria Histórica* (Law of Historical Memory). This law, too, was one designed to reinstate that which was formerly occluded in Spanish history. The part often played by law and regulation is key to understanding docudrama, because television is more susceptible to interference (political and legal) than any other medium using drama. This is a direct result of its wide accessibility. Docudrama in turn is more vulnerable than almost any other kind of dramatic representation because of its factual claim.[18] The fascist past of Spain looms over the passing of this law, and Pastor-González notes that Spain was also what she calls a 'latecomer' to docudrama precisely because dictatorship militated against similar sorts of broadcast freedom to those which Godzic writes about in Chap. 3.

Pastor-González identifies different modes of address that obtain in Spanish public service compared to its commercial channels. Several of the teleplays she singles out for discussion bring to mind once again the headline docudrama: 'based', according to Carveth, 'on events that have occurred much closer to their airing'. Crime dramas, as was the case in Fournier's account (and as is the case again in Bergström's Chap. 7) feature strongly—sometimes permeated not just by the tabloid but also with distinctively Catholic religious overtones (see again Buonanno's Chap. 4). While Pastor-González takes the view that the current Spanish television ecology has an unfortunate predisposition towards the tabloid, she also focuses on docudramas dealing with arguably the most important recent shift in Spanish culture, the transition from dictatorship to democracy. Following the death of the dictator Francisco Franco in 1975, Spain became both a constitutional monarchy and a democracy with a new constitution (1978). But arguably the most significant event after Franco had gone was a failed right-wing coup in 1981 (which led to Spain's first fully democratic election in 1982). Pastor-González' version of 'patrimony television' consists in the analysis of docudramas that review '*la Transición*' and give accounts of its significance. Some of the chosen case studies concentrate on the Spanish Royal Family's contribution to the event, and especially their handling of the attempted coup of 23 February 1981. One of the films is titled *23F*, and '23F', Pastor-González notes, has become a shorthand rather as '9/11' references the 11 September 2001 destruction of the Twin Towers in New York. Additionally, Pastor-González analyses docudramas that feature an outstanding female protagonist—an illustration of Meryl Streep's pertinent observation that, unlike film, the television industry 'has understood that there's a women's audience' (Collins 2015, p. 39).

The headline docudramas considered by Åsa Bergström in Chap. 7 tend to rely on what she describes as 'tales of adversity' as well as 'tales of crime'—tales told 'usually within five years' of the events they portray. They mimic headline news stories that are their principal source. Everyone who writes on the anglophone form comments on the increasing speed (and associated dangers) of the docudramatic response to news (see, for example, Rosenthal 1995, pp. 3, 10–11). Three kinds of ethical danger, again according to Carveth, attend headline docudramas: they can 'compromise the legal positions of the principals'; they often 'ignore the social and political forces surrounding an event'; and, 'adapting an event to standard narrative formulas changes reality in the process' (pp. 123–125). Where Pastor-González has cause to lament the fact that Spanish docudrama is mired in Carveth's second point, Bergström finds more promising material, especially in regard to crimes based in Swedish social problems, and in the kinds of emotional totalitarianism that tend to find roots in cult-like religion. She shows, too, that Sweden also has its key practitioners of docudrama in Olle Häger and Hans Villius. Perhaps the most significant of her case studies examine docudramas tackling Swedish political corruption. This subgenre, so common in the British tradition, tend often to be missing elsewhere in Europe.

Åsa Bergström is another contributor to point out that the naming of the form constitutes something of a prerequisite for adequate academic discussion of docudrama, and she argues like Buonanno that the absence of a language to talk about it has retarded progress in making sense of docudrama in her country. She applies my segmentation of docudrama history into 'phases of development' to the Swedish context, and Lipkin's concepts of 'warrants' and 'arenas' of authenticity as the foundation stones for charting docudrama's take on Swedish history and current affairs. 'Warranting', in Lipkin's analysis of US film and television docudrama, refers to the means by which filmmakers seek to persuade their audiences that the fact-base for their drama is both necessary and sufficient for the purpose not only of belief, but also to satisfy at least the legal requirements that surround the form. Warrants 'connect' filmmakers' claims of authentic presentation to the evidence (such as it is) that supports those claims.

Belief, then, inheres both in the pre-production work of establishing facts to underpin the drama, and—crucially—in what Bergström calls the 'performative warrants' that enact this research and convince audiences. 'Docudrama', Lipkin remarks, 'exists to create conviction' in order to achieve 'persuasive practice' (2002, p. ix). Performative elements—script, acting, filming technique—supply (or attempt to supply) credibility to the action of the docudrama. Bergström adds to Lipkin's arenas of 'noteworthy events, people and war' the arenas of crime and judicial process, and shows how important this arena is in the Swedish context.

In Chap. 8, David Rolinson concentrates on recent British docudrama, its latest developments extending what is a particularly rich tradition of practice. Having given a brief account of British docudramatic tradition and its links with the history of British television, he defines the most recent post-documentary turn that has led to practices that can be characterised as postmodern and reflexive. These not only rest on a long docudramatic tradition and history, they presuppose a highly sophisticated audience—one with a long memory for history itself, for the history of British television, and even for the history of British docudrama. There are knowing references to heroes, but these are not the heroes of national identity that feature in so many other chapters—they are instead the 'sad clown' heroes of postwar British light entertainment and comedy. The dramatis personae in his case studies are drawn in the main from another popular tradition, one inherited by British television. The long history of theatre-based popular entertainment, stretching back to nineteenth-century music hall, taking in 'end-of-the-pier' seaside entertainment, and culminating in twentieth-century 'variety', shadows early British television entertainment. Developing then into sitcom frameworks, this tradition recently became the focus of some thoughtful docudramas shown mainly on BBC4, and these form the subject of Rolinson's analysis. The biographical docudramas bring to life not only long-dead entertainers, but also particular aspects of British cultural life and cultural history. They additionally illuminate docudramatic treatment.

The other important recent postmodern tendency analysed by David Rolinson in Chap. 8 is the 'What If?' conditional/subjunctive tense docudrama that projects the legitimate fears of modern industrialised nations into researched dramatisations that enact those fears. Such docudramas deal in a variety of projected disaster scenarios, but scenarios that like much of docudrama content are to be regularly found in national discourse on television and radio and in newspapers. Anxieties about 'rogue' states and their capacity to mount fatal attacks, worries about resource dearth and ecological meltdown—all are potential arenas of representation for 'What If?' docudramas that come both in single play and in series form. The tradition of the 'What If?' docudrama stretches back at least to Peter Watkins' celebrated (and banned) film *The War Game*. Made for the BBC in 1965, this docudrama was considered so dangerous it was not screened on television until 1985—even though in the 1966 the American Academy of Motion Picture Arts and Sciences was prepared to award the film an Oscar as 'Best Documentary'. Rolinson's analysis of some recent variants of the 'What If?' demonstrates the potential for reflexivity at the heart of contemporary British docudramatic practice.

In the Conclusion to this book, co-editor Tobias Ebbrecht-Hartmann draws together some of the threads emerging from this book's individual chapters, his own included. He highlights similarities in what I have called the 'spectrum of practice' that constitutes modern docudrama—a praxis very largely innovated within and extended by the television industry. If the history of docudrama is dominated by American and British practice, as I have argued in this Introduction, a twenty-first century of transnational co-production, involving ever more complex patterns of distribution, has changed the landscape forever. Not least, the capacity of television to air important debates both within and amongst individual European nations has entered a new phase and created a new landscape—one involving both the 'old', public service and commercial broadcasters of Europe, and the 'new', multi-platform digital media.

What Next?

In the second edition of *No Other Way to Tell It*, I concluded by acknowledging that the left pessimism of the first edition, which led me to fear for the future of docudrama, was mistaken. I failed to take account of the innate creativity of film and programme makers. It seems to me now that this creativity is undiminished. Amongst the 'disease-of-the-week' and 'murder-of-the-month' tabloid docudramas that continue to supply a basic need for TV channels and audiences ('basic' often being the operative word), there are sufficient new forms to justify confidence, and enough serious practitioners to justify a guarded optimism. From an audience point of view, the Internet, I also observed, enables the curious viewer to investigate further the factual background of docudrama so often doubted by commentators in the past, and thus to take their own view of the degree of accuracy in any given treatment. Clearly, the use being made of the form in the film industry and on television means that docudrama has graduated in a big way from its former status as an occasional television form. And as I have already said, it is unlikely that the taste for factuality in drama will diminish in troubled times. Indeed, all I will venture in the way of prediction is to say that long-form series docudrama has great potential. I am struck currently by the number (and quality) of long-form docudramatic series from Europe that have found their way onto British television. All the examples below were broadcast in the UK in 2015, and three of them come from nations not covered in our selection. Their arenas of representation have clear associations, too, with much of the material examined in the seven chapters of this book.

Two series deal with their countries' World War II past. *Kampen om Tungtvannet* (The Heavy Water War, NRK, 2014—seen on More4 in Britain as *The Saboteurs*) is a Norwegian/British/Danish six-part series about the sabotage mission of 1943 that sought to destroy a heavy water plant in Norway vital to Nazi efforts to develop an atom bomb. *Résistance*, a six-parter produced for TF1 in 2014 (broadcast on C4 in Britain) is about the World War II resistance movement and, in the words of its producers, focuses on 'young Resistance fighters … relatively unknown to the general public'.[19] The Danish *1864*, about the disastrous Second Schleswig War (1 February–30 October 1864), is an eight-part series (DR1, 2014). This historical docudrama features many of the actors who gained international recognition for their roles in exported 'Nordic noir' dramas such as *Borgen* (The Castle, DR1, 2010–2013). It caused a good deal of controversy amongst Danish historians, who disputed its use of history, but fundamentally it is about the way politics drives idealistic young people into war. Finally, there is the Belgian Flemish-language series *Cordon* (vtm, 2014), shown on BBC4 in 2015. This, a 'What If?' ten-part series, concerns the escape into the city of Antwerp in an imagined future of a killer virus from a science laboratory. This leads to the sealing-off of part of the city, and to devious political cover-ups that stretch the emergency services to breaking point. Thus it has in common with all 'What If's the exploration of the bleak ramifications of modern, metropolitan nightmare scenarios. The production company behind this dystopian drama was Eyeworks, Amsterdam-based but part of the Time Warner conglomerate. Here we see the shape of things to come industrially in European production and international co-production. All four series are the result of a coming-together of interests national and international; all four demonstrate the common interests in past, present, and future that continue to drive docudrama.

I am altogether less tentative about suggesting the legitimate areas in which I believe the academy could (and should) pay attention to docudrama. I take my cues here directly from the various emphases to be found in the chapters of this book. Firstly, then, I repeat that it would be fascinating to read research about docudrama from the countries not included in this 'selective survey'. Secondly, there are two substantive areas that pertain to production and performance that require further thought (not to say new thinking). They are the ethics and the aesthetics of docudrama. The former, of course, must involve an account of the effects intentional and otherwise deriving from each producing nation's legal and regulatory systems for screen representation, and an assessment of how these factors influence production, performance, and reception. Legal systems across Europe have important differences that would surely repay investigation. My books have attempted to do this for the British, and to an extent the American, systems, and in this book several contributors make reference to systems that obtain within their own countries. But necessarily they are not in a position at this point to go into detail, nor to explore consequences, given the limitations of the book's brief.

Where aesthetics is concerned, it is somewhat easier where there is previous docudrama history and practice. Both Ebbrecht-Hartmann and Rolinson have more opportunity to deal with this than colleagues for whose television ecologies docudrama is relatively new. As Ebbrecht-Hartmann makes clear, the influence of anglophone practice in Germany has been substantial; as Godzic, Fournier, and Pastor-Gonzalez make equally clear, coming late to docudrama makes for its own difficulties. It is not too much to say that commentary on aesthetics is easier if the tradition is established (hence Rolinson's focus on what he establishes as postmodern British docudrama is pretty well impossible elsewhere, other than in Germany). Establishing the aesthetics of the form will enable escape from the lockstep of 'blurred boundary' commentary and 'failed drama/failed documentary' dismissal. It should also enter, in my view, the vexed territory of 'value'. I have claimed that docudrama at its best is profoundly democratic—this is my belief, but the testing of this claim is a work in progress.

Thirdly, much academic work in individual European countries remains to be done on the terminology that pertains to docudrama (the 'word-search', as I term it in the opening section of Chap. 4, Paget 2011). Buonanno in Chap. 4, Pastor-Gonzalez in Chap. 6, and Bergström in

Chap. 7 make this point. There have, of course, been several academic interventions on the intermateability of fact and fiction in other counties. Pastor-Gonzalez cites Jaime Barroso's 2005 contribution to the Ortega collection *Nada es lo que parece. Falsos Documentales, hibridaciones y mestizajes del documental en España*. And in France, Isabelle Veyrat-Masson published *Télévision et histoire, la confusion des genres* in 2008. In 2009, French filmmaker François Viney published *Le documentaire et ses faux-semblants*. But, as the very titles of these books indicate, whatever the excellence of their contribution to the debate, the works take on the whole a rather dim view of docudrama, one that accords to some extent with the negative account of docudrama that obtained in the UK in earlier times. An absence of critical terminology is part-consequence of the absence of theses, articles, and monographs and is, perhaps, an indicator of early practical development in a country. Godzic, Buonanno, and Pastor-Gonzalez all see this as a direct comment on the way their respective country's attitude to the past is framed. The very different views of the fields of fact and fiction themselves within a culture would present, I suggest, opportunities for academic enquiry.

Several chapters refer to 'the extra-textual' in docudrama—those elements associated with discrete productions that reinforce an argument, add to the stock of information conveyed, ensure an 'afterlife' for a docudrama (see Paget 2001, pp. 117–119 and *passim*). Much remains to be done to establish the function and significance of this dimension. In their accounts of docudrama in the 'old' East, both Godzic and Ebbrecht-Hartmann are concerned with that which is elided in docudramatic presentation in any given country. There were clear ideological barriers to some subjects in East Germany and Communist Poland—both declared and undeclared. Pastor-González too notes key absences in Spanish docudrama's account of Spain's past. Godzic's concept of the 'unrepresented world' marks this out as an area for potential exploration. It is not only in former dictatorships that the unrepresented world shadows the worlds represented. Western absences in docudramatic subjects include many apparently 'no go' areas: corporate capitalism's predisposition to fraud, exploitation, bribery, corruption, for example. Stories about 'black capitalism' such as human trafficking exist, but then such stories are sufficiently sensational (and permit realist drama's wish to focus on individual characters) to be more viable.[20]

Several chapters refer to what I want to call the 'Rise of the Eyewitness' in modern culture. Increasingly, this figure has acquired a special warranting function in docudrama (and this is true for theatre and film as well as television). The witness phenomenon carries both legal and religious overtones in a time when trust in public offices has diminished. It also has implications for memory both in terms of 'testimony' and in terms of the belief engendered in audiences by that testimony. Docudrama incorporates and performs features of human recollection; it communicates images from and versions of history, negotiating the nature of memories and understandings in ways more difficult to achieve than in formal history. This also offers fertile ground for future research.

This brings me back finally to the idea of 'hard' and 'soft' borders. It seems particularly apt to be discussing this in relation to a Europe itself currently troubled by its inability to mark out with any degree of precision the areas where its West and East meet and where its individual borders can be clearly established. Europe-wide, we can see in history as in the present day how the centripetal and centrifugal forces of different senses of nationhood cause boundaries to coalesce and fragment across the region. As Tobias Ebbrecht-Hartmann has said elsewhere: 'historical docudrama plays a significant role in shaping [national] cultural memory and identity' (2007a, p. 35). Reading recently a book on an iconic marker for cultural memory and identity—the formerly German city Breslau, now the Polish Wroclaw– it occurred to me that the book's concept of 'The Lands Between' (see Davies and Moorhouse 2003) was relevant to docudrama. Davies and Moorhouse use the phrase to express the nature of this provocatively uncertain European region. It is, and remains, indeed a 'Land Between', a place where religious and political ideologies met and clashed, a place where two contrasting modes of expressivity meet, a place where borders are both fluid and porous.[21] This is what makes docudrama such a challenge to research, such a resource for understanding events and individuals, and such a means of analysing their representation.

NOTES

1. See Chap. 2, where Tobias Ebbrecht-Hartmann points out the 'asymmetrical viewing habits' evident during the period of the two Germanys.
2. The word 'intermateability' derives from the modern fibre-optic industry. Here there are huge advantages to be gained from physically coupling together products from different sources. The word is practical; it signals that this can be done without mechanical damage to the components, and without compromising safety or functionality. The co-editors of this book

see it as another term which is potentially useful in a positive, affirmative, assessment of docudrama.

3. One manifestation of the rise of fact-based discourse in dramatic art is 'verbatim theatre'—briefly, theatrical performance derived from testimony. This form has become popular across the world—see Forsyth and Megson (2009).

4. Although, counter-intuitively, it must be said that the more access to information has been made available, the more a kind of scepticism has become a default audience response. One clear witness of this is the proliferation of conspiracy theories in the modern period. See, for example, my Chap. 1 in the 2015 Lacey/Paget collection, where I discuss conspiracy theories centred on 9/11 documentary footage.

5. See Nichols (1991, pp. 3–4 and *passim*) for more on 'the discourse of sobriety'. Nichols' phrase became key to academic discussion of documentary film. Through this phrase, he situated documentary discourse with the serious, rational areas of human social and legal activity, and thus bracketed it off from (for example) the less sober discourses of entertainment modes.

6. The core group presented panels at a number of international conference series such as 'Visible Evidence' and NECS (2007–12).

7. Åsa Bergström pointed out to her editors that the decision to standardise chapter titles meant that it was possible to infer from her subtitle (formerly her title) that Sweden itself was a 'borderland' in terms of its place in Greater Europe. It is one thing, we acknowledge, to be aware of language-group hegemony, quite another to eliminate it!

8. Docudrama producers Tony Garnett, Ian McBride, and Sita Williams all told me versions of what I think of as the 'tunic button' story. In Garnett's case he was referring to his experience on *Days of Hope* (BBC1, 1975), the classic British documentary drama of the between-the-wars period (produced by him, written by Jim Allen, and directed by Ken Loach). Someone spotted that the tunic buttons on one of the military costumes were from the wrong regiment, and, according to Garnett, concluded from this that nothing in the series could be trusted. Sita Williams called it the 'slippery slope argument' by which one mistake condemned everything (see Paget 1998, 2011).

9. The writer Clive James (*Observer* television critic in the 1970s) was particularly cruel on this kind of fault. He was among the first English television critics to remark the creaking nature of much plot exposition in docudrama. Here he is on the 1975 BBC1 historical docudrama *Churchill's People*: 'Since [character King Edward the Confessor] was the centre of the action, he was occupied full time not only with telling people what they already knew, but with being told what he knew in return' (1977, p. 117). Clumsy exposition is not just the curse of docudrama, however; it is the curse of a good deal of TV dramatic realism.

10. Bill Nichols, among other documentary scholars, acknowledged my 1998 addressing of the 'specific case of docudrama' in his *Introduction to Documentary* (2001, p. 182). Also see Brian Winston's 2013 collection—called *The Documentary Film Book*, it none the less includes my piece on docudrama. While many historians adopt the 'false history' accusation against docudrama, there are now many who engage with it more productively. Robert Rosenstone stands out not only as a writer on fact-based film but also as an on-set historical advisor (see especially Rosenstone 2006). Vivien Sobchack's 1996 collection is another important book addressing the use of history in film.

11. Alan Rosenthal's crucial contribution must be acknowledged here. As well as editing collections of writing about docudrama (1999a, 2005), he has written practical guidance on the genre (the latest was published in 2007—see pp. 288–293; 296–300 on docudrama).

12. The key intervention in drawing a distinction between the two approaches to dramatising facts was John Caughie's. His seminal 1980 *Screen* article is reprinted in Bennett et al. (1981). See Part 1, #1.7 in Winston 2013 for a digest of my distinctions between 'docudrama' and 'dramadoc'.

13. See Ellis 2000 for more detail on the developmental phases of television itself.

14. Biopic, of course, is another relatively under-researched area. For many years, there was only George Custen's seminal 1992 monograph, but there has been valuable recent input from Dennis Bingham (for example, see Bingham 2010) and also the 2014 Brown/Vidal collection. In her 'Introduction' to the latter, Bélen Vidal notes that the collection seeks:a rethinking of the biopic's generic limits, by proposing the genre as a hybrid form that changes in contact with other genres, such as the docudrama' (p. 10).Her Chap. 7 in the collection explores this thought in further detail. It is worth pointing out how often these books (and the ones by historians such as Rosenstone) tend to refer specifically to 'film' in their titles. The synergies between film and television industries, and the technological improvements in televisions, make this academic distinction more and more difficult to sustain in my view.

15. Briefly, 'rootable' refers to audiences identifying with characters, 'relatable' refers audience connection to story (for example, knowing a story from the news), and 'promotable' means that channels can advertise and promote the docudrama by means of the audience's prior knowledge. See Lipkin (2002, Chap. 5) for more detail.

16. This is not, of course, to bracket out equally important contributions by writers on documentary film, theatre, and television drama.

17. Evan Wright was the embedded journalist/book author in question.

18. See Paget (2011, Chap. 2) for more detail on legal and regulatory matters as they pertain to British and American docudrama.

19. See TF1 International's website, where a 'Producers' Intent' section outlines the scope of the series: www.tf1international/int_fiche.php? Film=1004&Type=2 – accessed 31 August 2015.

20. *Sex Traffic* (C4, 2004) is one example of this. A British-Canadian two-part series, with script by writer Abi Morgan (also writer of the 2011 cinema feature *The Iron Lady*, in which Meryl Streep played Margaret Thatcher), it was about the trafficking of young women from Eastern Europe to become sex workers in Britain. A notable exception to the failure to deal with capitalist misconduct is the financial sector docudrama *The Man Who Broke Britain* (BBC2, 2004—see David Rolinson's Chap. 8).

21. In this connection, Tobias Ebbrecht-Hartmann has drawn my attention to Randall Halle's 2014 book *The Europeanization of Cinema: Interzones and Imaginative Communities* (Champaign, IL: University of Illinois Press), which examines boundary-crossing spaces in European cinema. See also his Conclusion to this book.

CHAPTER 2

German Docudrama: Aligning the Fragments and Accessing the Past

Tobias Ebbrecht-Hartmann

INTRODUCTION

On 9 November 2014 Germany celebrated the twenty-fifth anniversary of the fall of the Berlin Wall in 1989 and the advent of German unification in 1990. In a public ceremony that could be interpreted as a symbolic re-enactment, around 8000 illuminated balloons marked the length of the former wall and were later released as a citywide commemoration, allowing them to rise in the night sky. This public event re-enacting the past in and for the present was created by light artist and designer Christopher Bauder and his brother, filmmaker Marc Bauder.[1] The installation included several video screens with cinematic collages from archival material and presented documentary footage portraying the previously divided city. Additionally visitors could listen to around 100 personal anecdotes and stories recollecting the former wall, at mobile sound stations across the route of the former border. The installation combined symbolic re-enactment, archival footage, personal memories from the past and testimonies, thus 'forming a collective landscape of memories of Berlin' (Hausen 2014)—a kind of a 'real life docudrama' that was broadcast nationally and around the world.

It was not only communicated globally, but also turned into a media event. Such events, in Daniel Dayan's and Elihu Katz's definition, 'have given shape to a new narrative genre that employs the unique potential of the electronic media to command attention universally and simultaneously

© The Editor(s) (if applicable) and The Author(s) 2016
T. Ebbrecht-Hartmann, D. Paget (eds.), *Docudrama on European Television*, Palgrave European Film and Media Studies,
DOI 10.1057/978-1-137-49979-0_2

in order to tell a primordial story about current affairs' (1992, p. 1). Media events, they suggest, 'create and integrate communities larger than nations' (p. 23). In November 2014, the installation on the one hand re-echoed the real historic events and on the other hand recreated them in a televised memory, thus shaping both personal and collective recollections into a communicable narrative.[2]

Television docudrama is an important transmitter for such mediated history, which then turns into a new media event. It is especially suited for such a purpose due to its porous and intermateable form. By assembling fragments from the past, such as archival footage and eyewitness accounts, and arranging them according to a narrative structure, illustrated by (partly fictitious) re-enactments, the genre is situated in between different sections of the programme flow. Merging documentary and fiction, report and dramatization, debate and interpretation docudrama performs the past according to present patterns of interpretation and thus connects private and public as well as national and global perspectives. Furthermore docudramas are interlinked with, often extensions of, other parts of the TV schedule. Most important in this context is docudrama's extension through 'extra-textual events' such as additional documentaries or reports, round table discussions or newspaper coverage preceding or following the broadcast (Paget 2011, pp. 117–118). In the case of the anniversary ceremony in Berlin such mediation of the past, and the genre of docudrama in particular, served as a model for the new real-life event. In turn this event was broadcast and framed by extra-textual events. Spread through news reports, the illuminated recreation of the German-German border, as well as recollections and memories of visitors, entered television broadcasting that day and affiliated with other parts of the schedule related to televised memories of 9 November 1989 and of the GDR (German Democratic Republic).

This can be illustrated by a closer look at the programming of the second German public broadcasting station ZDF (Zweites Deutsches Fernsehen) on that day. ZDF reported on the light installation in the evening edition of its news show *heute journal*, which dedicated parts of the broadcast exclusively to the twenty-fifth anniversary of the fall of the Wall. This news programme in turn linked that day's primetime movie, the melodramatic television drama *Zwischen den Zeiten* (Between the Times, ZDF, dir. Hansjörg Thurn), to an additional documentary *Zwischen den Zeiten—Die Dokumentation* (Between the Times—the Documentary, ZDF, dir. Florian Hartung and Anja Kühne), which provided, as an extra-textual event, a historical background to the drama. Both *Zwischen den Zeiten* and *Zwischen den Zeiten—Die Dokumentation* addressed the aftermath of the GDR and focused on the collaborative work of scientists and historians in finding proper ways to reconstruct destroyed Stasi files in order to make them usable for historical research.[3] Thereby the drama as well as the documentary related the present (reconstruction of historical documents) to the past (encounter with personal fates) within the fictional narrative of a border-crossing East–West love story based loosely on historical facts.

Thus the core television event on ZDF that day provided a connecting link on several levels. It echoed other programmes, such as reports on the historical events (*Heute: Die Leute fallen sich um den Hals*/ Today: The People are Celebrating; *Berlin direkt: Der Tag, an dem die Mauer fiel*/Berlin Direct: The Day the Wall Collapsed) and historical docudramas like *Das Wunder von Berlin* (The Miracle of Berlin, ZDF, 2008, dir. Roland Suso Richter), produced for a previous anniversary and again broadcast in the afternoon schedule. It also referred to other commemorative broadcasts—*Freiheit—25 Jahre Mauerfall*/Freedom—Twenty-Five Years after the Wall; *Heute: 25 Jahre Mauerfall – Feier und Gedenken*/Today: Twenty-Five Years after the Wall—Celebrations and Commemoration; *Heute: Politiker gedenken der Maueropfer*/Today: Politicians Commemorate the Victims of the Wall; *Lichtspur der Freiheit*/ Illumination of Freedom—and beyond that to programmes tracing the significance of the GDR's heritage (such as an environmental report by the series *planet e* titled *Biotop im Mauerland*/Biotopes Replacing the Wall, on nature reserves created in the no man's land at the former borderline). In a nutshell, the ZDF output from 9 November 2014 not only illustrates that docudramas and historical event movies are an important cornerstone of German television's historical programming, it also indicates that docudrama and its different formats need to be analysed in the context of programme flow in order to understand the interplay with other formats addressing and commemorating past events.

The following chapter will focus on recent tendencies in docudrama as inflected by German television practice. As indicated above, the term docudrama is therefore used in a broader sense. According to Derek Paget, 'docudramas *re-tell events* from national or international histories, reviewing and/or celebrating these events (often at a suitable "anniversary" point in history) [,...] portray *issues of concern* [,...] focus upon *ordinary citizens and their stories* [... and] provoke questions about form' (2011, pp. 94–95). This concentrated definition can be applied to all the manifold forms of television docudrama, television drama and dramatized documentaries that constituted the evolution of this genre on West as well as East German television. Furthermore it highlights key aspects that interrelate prototypical docudramas (television films that merge documentary footage with eyewitness accounts and dramatic re-enactments), and historical event movies that compress past events into mostly melodramatic personal narratives that resonate with other, mostly documentary, extra-textual events in the context of programme flow.

These recent tendencies are based on a long tradition of the genre on German television. To situate contemporary modes of television docudrama, the chapter will therefore also discuss its historical context, shedding light on the specific tradition of the genre in East and West Germany and emphasising the particular role docudrama played in communicating competing memories of the German past in the Cold War period. Following this overview the analytical focus of this chapter will be on its most popular topics and generic modes. Aspects considered will include stylistic as well as narrative elements (for example, the embedding of archive footage and its recreation, the function of witnesses and oral history, the tensions between private and public history as well as the impact of extra-textual events and public debates). Thus the chapter will aim to show how far the representation of the GDR also shapes public memory of this specific part of German history.

TRADITIONS AND PHASES: EVOLUTION AND INFLUENCES

In its first phase of development, the newly established public television in both West and East Germany communicated images of the past, as well as perceptions of each of the other Germanys—mainly in the form of dramatized documentaries and television dramas. From the 1980s, in a second phase, many of the foremost West German directors developed a particular form of television docudrama, which extensively merged fact and fiction, documentary footage and re-enactments. According to Werner C. Barg such television docudramas, mainly linked to the work of Heinrich Breloer and Horst Königstein, examined the story beyond news reports and historical facts and tried to fill 'gaps in reality' (*Wirklichkeitslücken*) in order to reflect the fabrication of historical narratives (2012, pp. 285–287). After German unification, in a third phase during the mid-1990s and early 2000s, these mainly journalistic docudramatic attempts slowly turned towards more dramatic forms and began to generate particular television events by commemorating central historic incidents from the German past, often related to '"anniversary" moments in history' (Paget 2012, p. 245). Thus docudrama on German television transformed into what I term elsewhere 'historical event television' (Ebbrecht 2007a, b). This historical event television increasingly affected its programme environment. As mentioned in the introduction we may therefore face a further transformation of docudrama on German television, with docudramatic structure shaping the whole programme context. Historical event movies address huge audiences who are then also drawn to additional documentaries based on eyewitness testimonies and personal memories, talk shows and news reports, thereby virtually turning the whole television schedule into an extended docudrama.

As part of the culture of everyday life, television played an important role in communicating German history and its perception in German postwar culture and society. In so doing it became an important social and political agent, particularly in Germany as a border zone of the Cold War. Indeed, the special situation in Germany also turned television with its competing images into an instrument of Cold War politics. As an institution, it therefore helped the Federal Republic (FRG) and the GDR to construct two distinct national identities. The first public television broadcaster was founded in the British Zone in northern Germany, and copied the organizational structure of the BBC. West German public service television was closely linked to the federal constitution of the newly founded state and based on a cooperative network of regional broadcasting stations (ARD), founded in 1950 and first broadcasting in 1952. In 1963 a second public service broadcasting station, the ZDF, was created, and that was not based on a federal structure. Meanwhile, the GDR launched its first television station, also in 1952. From 1956, the Deutsche Fernsehfunk (DFF, later DDR-TV) broadcast on a regular basis. In October 1969 a second station was created in East Germany, marking the twentieth anniversary of the establishment of the socialist state. Both East German television stations worked according to a centralized and state-controlled organizational structure.

In the 1960s and 1970s both German states used television to represent and to communicate competing images of history against the background of current political issues. But the contrasting institutional constitution of public service broadcasting television in West Germany and state-controlled television in East Germany had a fundamental effect on how the two states portrayed events of the past. Furthermore it must be kept in mind that the production of national narratives never occurs in a linear and automatic process. First of all, television dramas in particular were often uncomfortably prone to criticize, and sometimes even undermine, official versions of events. Furthermore television consumption in Germany was shaped by asymmetrical viewing habits on either side of the Iron Curtain. East Germans, in particular, regularly watched both their own as well as West German television. Another significant factor, particularly regarding the evolution of a specific German form of docudrama, was parallel methodological and stylistic influences, and similarities in background, of programme makers in East and West. Paradoxically, directors of television docudramas in East and West had similar political and aesthetical roots, stemming largely from the tradition of proletarian theatre associated with Bertolt Brecht.

Television drama in general and historical documentary drama in particular was a dominant form, used for the shaping of historical consciousness, with a clear focus on education. West German public television's mission was, inevitably, influenced by the British model with its 'classic BBC Charter aspiration to "inform, educate and entertain"' (Paget 2012, p. 241). Within this framework scriptwriters and directors had the freedom to develop more abstract and allegorical aesthetical forms when representing the recent past. As Knut Hickethier observes, the critical preoccupation with the German past played a significant role in television dramas of the 1960s, especially those made by the NDR (Norddeutscher Rundfunk— North German Broadcasting Corporation) and its department of television drama, headed by Egon Monk from 1960 to 1968 (1979, p. 59). Monk, born in 1927, had worked as an assistant to Brecht at the Berliner Ensemble. After the war he co-developed a new aesthetic for the television drama, strongly influenced by Brechtian theatre. It became the foundation for a German style of docudrama. These television dramas avoided the use of naturalistic décor and combined fictive scenes with documentary material that served to interrupt the narrative and disrupt the illusion for the spectators (p. 61). Similarly, East German programme makers were influenced by the proletarian theatre tradition and the concepts of Brecht (who had re-emigrated to East Berlin in 1949).

Historical programmes, often categorizable as docudramas, were part of German television broadcasting from the 1960s onwards. Docudramas were either influenced by British drama-doc aesthetics, presenting 'based on facts' stories which combined re-enactments and a sober narrative to recreate the past, or adopted elements from the German docu-theatre tradition of Peter Weiss, Rolf Hochhuth and Heinar Kipphardt. This theatre style was based on 'actual events, generally recent, to explore a concern for guilt and responsibility in public affairs and morality' (Hoffer et al. 1985, p. 183). In West Germany the interest in such political theatre—and with it an interest in Brecht—was a response to the political stagnation of the Federal Republic during the Adenauer era. The Eichmann trial in 1961 in Jerusalem and the trial of Auschwitz guards in Frankfurt in 1963–65 shaped the ways in which theatre and then television used documents and elements of courtroom drama to deal with the German past and empower audiences to make judgments about social and political questions (Hickethier 1979, p. 50). Weiss's canonical play *Die Ermittlung* (The Investigation) (1965) even became part of the multi-layered television drama *Mord in Frankfurt* (Murder in Frankfurt, WDR, 1968, dir. Rolf Hädrich) informed by the Auschwitz Trials.

ENTANGLEMENT: DOCUDRAMA IN EAST AND WEST

Committed to the postwar educational remit of West German public service television, Monk acknowledged the task of furthering coming to terms with the past by representing the history of the Third Reich (Hickethier 1998, p. 110).[4] One of his most impressive works in this regard was the television drama *Ein Tag—Bericht aus einem deutschen* (Konzentrationslager 1939) (One Day—A Report from a German Concentration Camp 1939, NDR, 1965), which was clearly influenced by Brecht. Monk believed that television had a responsibility to become a moral institution communicating liberal and democratic values to the Germans (p. 244). During the 1960s he thus intended to 'strengthen the audience's loyalty to the new state' by educating them in democracy and tolerance (Hickethier 1979, p. 58).

This educational focus intensified during the 1980s and developed into a critical and investigative journalistic approach. This type of television docudrama was characterized by a hybridization of documents, testimonies and re-enactments and was strongly influenced by a critical perspective on television and media. Hence Christian Hißnauer described this mode as 'journalistic polit-television' (2008, p. 258). Although directors and scriptwriters such as Heinrich Breloer and Horst Königstein are linked to the tradition of Monk and others they developed their own, very specific, mode of docudrama (Barg 2012, p. 279). It transformed a basically educational focus into a critical perspective, depicting controversial topics and reconstructing images and scenes omitted by the selective perspective of television news broadcasting and approved historical narratives (Hißnauer 2008, p. 259). The influence of Brecht and docu-theatre was still visible, but in even more radical form. In combination with interviews and eyewitness accounts, re-enactments in a docudrama like *Die Staatskanlei* (The State Office, NDR/WDR, 1989, dir. Heinrich Breloer) functioned similarly to Brechtian theatrical alienation effects (Barg 2012, p. 283). As I argued elsewhere, in an analysis of his *Kollege Otto die Coop Affäre* (Colleague Otto, the Coop Affair, NDR/WDR, 1991, dir. Heinrich Breloer):

> Breloer's aim is not to reconstruct or imitate the past. He wants to highlight the fragmentary nature of docudramatic construction. The actors do not need to look like their historic models, and do not have to imitate them but study their behaviour and manners. They should not become imitators but interpreters. (2010, p. 215)

In contrast GDR television turned into a largely uncritical governmental instrument to communicate official party lines and state-socialist views of the past and present. However, even to the end, historical programmes played a vital role as they were singled out as projects of political prestige. An early, although more challenging, example of this tendency in political prestige films is the East German television adaptation of Bruno Apitz's famous Buchenwald novel, *Nackt unter Wölfen* (Naked among Wolves, DFF, 1960). Indeed, GDR party officials speedily realized that television—if thoroughly controlled—was almost ideal for their propaganda purposes thanks to its boasting a much broader circulation than cinema films. To control the relatively new mass medium, the GDR founded a State Committee for Television (Staatliches Komitee für Fernsehen) in 1968. One of its most important sections was the Department for the Art of Television (Hauptabteilung Fernsehkunst) with its sub-department for television drama. These departments were given the task of getting political and ideological topics into emotional and dramatic stories. An important part of this mission was to present the virtues of the socialist GDR over the Federal Republic and to expose the failures of the 'class enemy' personified by the competing West German state (Schwab 2007a, p. 15).

In this regard, historical topics, especially the history of fascism, became a central element of television in the GDR, and dramatic formats were the most powerful tool with which to present them. These television dramas were characterized by a focus that shifted between the socialist present, the interrogation of the legitimacy of the West German state in the context of the Cold War and the struggle to come to terms with Germany's past. An example of this ambivalent status of television drama in the GDR, partly also taboo-breaking, was the mini-series *Die Bilder des Zeugen Schattmann* (The Images of the Witness Frank Schattmann, DDR-TV, 1972), based on the novel by Auschwitz survivor Peter Edel. This series, the first historical drama to explicitly address Jewish suffering during the Nazi period was broadcast on East German television several times and once even competed with the canonical American mini-series *Holocaust* (USA 1979, dir. Marvin Chomsky) when it was broadcast on West German television. But reflecting the state-controlled politics concerning depictions of the past, such television dramas mainly supported the GDR's anti-fascist self-perception. Therefore retrospectively the programmes have to be seen in the context of specific ideological efforts in GDR politics during the Cold War, and in the case of *Die Bilder des Zeugen Schattmann*, also in context of the GDR's relationship to the State of Israel, shifting between indifference and hostility.

German political and geographical division, especially after the establishment of the Berlin Wall in 1961, fundamentally shaped the dramatization of past and present on German television on both sides. I will be discussing the GDR dimension and giving examples of its use of docudrama later in the chapter, but to take West German docudrama practice first, in 1963 Egon Monk and Gunther R. Lys collaborated on the television drama *Mauern* (Walls, NDR/SFB, 1963). In depicting the fates of two families during the construction of the wall Monk not only reconstructed recent political events, he also related them to previous political conflicts. Five years earlier, *Besuch aus der Zone* (Visit from the Eastern Zone, SDR, 1958, dir. Rainer Wolffhardt) had already depicted the issue of East and West German entanglement in a television drama. Although many viewers (mainly from West Germany) praised the film it caused a controversy among West German lawmakers (Hickethier 1998, p. 154).[5] During a debate in the federal parliament on 28 February 1958, five days after the broadcast, Friedrich Zimmermann from the governing CDU/CSU accused *Besuch aus der Zone* of spreading anti-Western resentment. He interpreted the film solely within the framework of Cold War competition, and saw television mainly as an instrument for pro-Western propaganda (Bundeszentrale für politische Bildung 2012 p. 1).[6] In contrast, Heinz Kühn from the opposition Social Democratic Party praised the film and criticized the use of binary-coded attitudes in the dispute between East and West (p. 1).[7]

The representation of West Germany on East German television was, in contrast, always related to the ideological concepts of the ruling socialist party (Hickethier 1994, p. 344). East German television drama often focused on continuities with the Nazi past in the FRG. In the early phase East German television drama depicted the aftermath of the World War II mainly as an anti-fascist struggle, and thereby tried to connect to the ambivalent state of mind (of both German peoples) over the depiction of the Nazi past and its aftermath. This became increasingly schematic after the consolidation of television as an important instrument of propaganda and object of control in the GDR. Following the construction of the Wall in 1961, television dramas such as *Eine Nacht und kein Morgen* (Night and No Morning, DFF, 1962, dir. Wolfgang Luderer) or *Er ging allein* (He Went Alone, DFF, 1967, dir. Hans-Joachim Hildebrandt) increasingly contributed to this controversial subject of the East and West German propaganda war. Other East German films, mainly in the late 1970s and 1980s, referred to current political topics (such as nuclear weapons and armament) or generally presented life in West Germany as miserable (pp. 343–344).

MEMORY AND IDENTITY: DOCUDRAMA AFTER UNIFICATION

After the fall of the Wall, television programme makers aspired to merge both German traditions into what Gunter Witte, then head of the television drama department at the WDR, called the 'new German television drama' (Hickethier 1994, p. 344). Until the end of 1991, when GDR television was finally turned off, several scripts, that could not been realized before because of political censorship, were filmed in East Berlin's television studios, and broadcast in West Germany as well. Unification and life in the GDR itself now became subjects of what was evolving into the genres of historical television docudrama and historical event movies during the 1990s and especially in the new millennium. Partly also absorbing dramatic approaches from the East German tradition, West German docudrama was constantly inclined to recreate the past 'as it was', telling generic, mostly melodramatic, stories 'based on facts' that carried a warrant of 'authenticity' as well as special effects and event-orientated entertainment. This turn had already been prepared for by tendencies in West German historical television programming of the late 1980s. In order to compete with increasingly popular private (commercial) broadcasting stations, German public service television makers favoured television dramas and mini-series on German and European history with high production values (Hickethier 1998, p. 451). From 1993, on the other hand, private broadcasters also started producing dramas in the form of highly emotionalized TV movies partly based on 'true stories' (p. 459). Meanwhile the Brecht-influenced and porous tradition of docudrama, as practised by directors such as Heinrich Breloer and Horst Königstein, in many cases transformed into an indiscriminate montage of different historical sources and structural layers merging re-enactments, historical images and testimonies into a smooth narrative.

This transformation of explanatory television into a much more visually narrating form during the 1990s was often seen as the result of concessions to popular taste, and has to be seen against the background of the steady erosion of public service broadcasting in many European countries. But this dramatization of history not only makes complex entanglements from the past easy to consume; it also has consequences for the understanding of the past and therefore for the way historical events enter into the collective memory of a society. In this case public service broadcasting was leading the way in representing historical events in narrative form, when compared to private commercial broadcasters. These developments were the result of an interplay between several factors. First, the post-reunification context was a changed one, fuelling new senses of national identity and self. Contemporary history played, and continues to play, a key role in this process of redefining Germanness in the wider context of European unification. As a mediator of memory, television docudrama became an important tool, in first framing and then generating national and transnational commemorative events and debates about public memory. Second, producers of historical television encountered the increasing impact of new ways of communicating the past. A main factor that had already fundamentally shaped the character of docudrama on German television in the second half of the 1980s was the valorization of oral history. Interviews with ordinary people who had witnessed past events had already been interwoven into experimental docudramas as well as historical documentaries during the 1970s and 1980s. But now the eyewitness was awarded a special warranting function. In accordance with commemorative events (such as those marking the end of World War II in 1995 and 2005) such testimonies began to be an increasingly important element of historical television documentaries and later would even form the basis for generating new stories from the past. The increasing impact of personal stories from the past corresponded with a third aspect: a production practice that aimed to assure high-end cinema standards (use of stars, special effects, digital animation) to create a popular television event. Well-known German actors re-enacted the memories of ordinary people who had lived through history. Special effects and high production values guaranteed a re-experience for an audience that thereby were given the chance to live through the past while watching the movie. Finally, the cast as well as the (younger) audience were engaged in a televised transgenerational dialogue, a mode of perceiving the (national as well as family) past. This would have increasing influence over time.

I made the point some time ago that historical docudrama plays a significant role in shaping cultural memory and identity (2007a, p. 35). This is true for both national and transnational contexts, particularly because docudrama assembles, aligns or re-enacts documents as well as memories from the past, producing interpretation patterns and transmitting images of history. Furthermore docudrama, as a transmitter of cultural memory through a genre of popular television, corresponds to significant shifts in attention of contemporary memory studies 'from high culture to popular culture' and to 'space-bound media of circulation, which can reach large audiences almost simultaneously' (Erll 2008, p. 390). Television in general, and historical event television in particular, generates the gathering of audiences. Docudramas participate in creating a sense of community and historical belonging, and post-unification docudrama thus became an important tool in initiating memory processes, at the level of both national and personal memories. It intensified a transgenerational dialogue about the past; at the same time it imitated particular elements and narrative structures from this 'family conversation' (Ebbrecht 2011, p. 69). Such family conversations about the past are characterized by active forms of editing and realigning the story-fragments that are passed down by older generations: '[m]oving down the generations, stories become so altered that in the end they undergo a complete change of meaning' (Welzer 2005, p. 7).

This is of particular significance for German perceptions of World War II and the Holocaust. In the case of German wartime memories 'this reconfiguration generally functions to turn grandparents into people of constant moral integrity, according to today's standards and normative appraisal' (pp. 7–8). Although there is no doubt among the younger generations about the historical reality and cruelty of Nazism, this very knowledge 'rather evokes the subjective need to assign one's grandfather or grandmother the role of the "good" German in everyday life under the Nazis' (p. 8). The crucial effect of this revaluation of grandparents' experiences is a 'restoration of the belief, thought to be long uprooted, that "the Nazis" and "the Germans" were two different groups; thus it follows that "the Germans" can be seen to have been seduced, abused, and robbed of their youth, and they can see themselves as victims of Nazism' (p. 17). Contrasting such a consensual narrative, based on excluding Nazi perpetrators as 'the Others' and reconfiguring one's own position, is also typical for contemporary German historical television in general and television docudrama in particular. Numerous documentary series, especially on the Nazi period and the war, fabricated a harmonized image of a shattered German past based on multiple interviews with ordinary people, archival film footage and illustrative re-enactment. Docudrama advanced this consensual narrative further with the specific adoption of the framework of the family conversation. The docudrama *Speer und Er* (Speer and Hitler: The Devil's Architect, WDR/BR/NDR, 2005, dir. Heinrich Breloer), for instance, situates the re-evaluation of the relationship between Hitler and the architect and minister for armaments Albert Speer in this way. Speer's children turn into eyewitnesses and report their memories and experiences. Their ambivalent feelings and fragmented memories are then visualized through re-enactments with well-known actors (Sebastian Koch as Speer, Tobias Moretti as Hitler) that explore the relationship between these figures from history. The techniques of the docudrama thus help to fabricate a particularly skewed version of the past, in this case corresponding mainly with Speer's self-perception as a victim both of Hitler and of Nazi ideology. Interestingly, the fragmented character of the docudrama narration intensifies this. The merging of documentary images and drama does not have the effect of disrupting the re-enactments and thus disputing the fabrication of history 'as it was'. On the contrary, archival films and documentary images from different sources (Nazi propaganda as well as Allied news reports) are realigned during the opening sequence into a subjective dream and memory sequence evolving from Speer's miserable situation as imprisoned war criminal. Thus the 'factual images' turn into 'memory images' in this particular montage (Ebbrecht 2011, p. 140).

Finally, contemporary German television docudrama and historical event movies also reflect the increasing tendency to re-evaluate the relationship between memory and nation (Fortunati and Lamberti 2008, p. 127). More and more situated and produced in a transnational and especially European framework, television docudrama plays an ever more active part in a the process of making Europe. It contributes to the negotiation of contesting national memories and therein often attempts to harmonize conflicting perspectives within the narrative framework of the docudrama. Within this transnational European context docudramas can facilitate 'processes which select and filter the past' (p. 127). But they can also initiate an 'interactive act' by bringing contesting memories into the public sphere and thereby prevent the 'fixing and hypostatizing [of] memory' (p. 128).

The docudrama *Unsere Mütter, unsere Väter* (Generation War, ZDF, 2013, dir. Philipp Kadelbach) presents an interesting final case for this section. It had consequences unintended by its makers that relate to the broader context both of docudrama's ability to initiate debate by aligning 'extra-textual events' beyond a particular broadcast and its transnational reception. A prime-time historical event series, it was quite deliberately based on the structure of German family conversations, but the series did not try to disavow German war crimes, cruelty and the Holocaust. However, its effect was still to make clear distinctions between Nazis and the seduced German youth. It contrived to turn those later to be the mothers and fathers of postwar Germans into 'people of constant moral integrity' (Welzer 2005, pp. 7–8). Elsewhere in Europe, however, this aspect of the series caused controversy. Eastern Europe (in this particular case Poland) offered competing memories that disputed the German version. The *Unsere Mütter, unsere Väter* case illustrates how different national perceptions in reactions to a fact-based drama.[8]

HISTORICAL EVENT TELEVISION: TOPICS AND NARRATIVES

Docudrama and historical event television play a crucial and important role in historical broadcasting on German television today. I have distinguished in this chapter two different formats of contemporary television docudrama, which are connected through a specific mode of production and programming. The first format is the prototypical television docudrama, characterized by a mixture of documentary and drama elements and techniques. Such television docudramas visibly constitute a "hybrid of fact and fiction" (Hoffer et al., 1985, p. 182), in which the different elements (archival footage, interviews, commentary, captions, re-enactments) are still visible, audible and traceable. In contrast to the more experimental forms referred to earlier (Hißnauer's 'journalistic polit-television'), more recent and high-quality docudramas have been programmed as prime-time broadcasts and were therefore intended as television events. The tendency in such programmes is either to harmonize conflicting perceptions of the past or to fabricate a version of history 'as it was'. However, because of their porous narrative structure, these docudramas are potentially able 'to encourage a reflective, critical response' (Kilborn and Izod 1997, p. 149) and 'provoke questions about form' (Paget 2011, p. 95). I think of the second format as the 'historical event movie' because it mainly avoids archive footage and other visible documentation in favour of telling a thrilling and emotional story through the effects of dramatization. However, this format still corresponds to the significant characteristics of the docudrama genre. Paget notes that in this kind of format: 'dramatisation causes the film to look and sound more like a fiction film, but a claim is nevertheless made for its documentary status' (2012, p. 243). This claim corresponds to the attempt to '*re-tell* events from national or international histories', often in the context of anniversaries and public commemoration events (Paget 2011, p. 94). Furthermore they 'focus upon *ordinary citizens and their stories*' (pp. 94–95) and therefore correspond to the dominant orally based approach that relies on interviews, testimonies and witness accounts. These invisible sources can be interpreted as 'indexical roots' coded by the dramatization, as Steven N. Lipkin points out; such docudramas, he goes on, 'replace indexical "unstaged" images with a quasi-indexical narrative' (1999, p. 370). In order to trace the docudrama heritage of such historical event movies it is even more important to analyse them in the context of programme flow. This context defines the docudrama structure because it juxtaposes the drama with extra-textual news and documentary formats, shedding light on the historical background as well as on the making of the films. Thus the different docudrama elements (documentary, interview and drama) are separated in different formats with different strategies for addressing the audience, but they still correlate and respond to each other in the wider context of the schedule.

Owing to certain significant elements and features characterizing both formats, the prototypical television docudrama and the historical event movie, I suggest both should be considered as part of historical event television. The latter phenomenon is characterized by the personalization and individualization of history, popular history-telling, and the use of dramatic strategies—all aimed at high audience ratings. One of its basic principles is the use of oral history and the presentation of ordinary people, either as eyewitnesses in the film or as its fictionalized protagonists (Ebbrecht 2007b, p. 225). In summary, historical event television in its different shapes is characterized by: a merging of fact and fiction, either visibly or by dramatizing historical facts and personal experiences; a focus on personal lives in political conflicts; the dominance of the witnesses' perspective; transnational encounters that refer to the increasing impact of European memories and identities; and finally, extra-textual framing of the broadcasting within the programme flow or in and through other media.

The representation of everyday life during the Third Reich and suffering during wartime became a key reference for such historical event television in Germany. But the country's shattered past, mainly comprising those events from the twentieth century that have significantly shaped German and global memories, offers a rich reservoir of potential topics and especially tragic and conflictive stories even beyond the Nazi period. Matthias Steinle has identified three dominant topics that characterize docudrama on German television today: the history of the Third Reich; the history of the Federal Republic; and the history of the GDR 1949–90 (2012, p. 306). These historical subjects also reflect German social memory and historical awareness, which is still characterized by two different, and sometimes conflicting, cultures of memory shaped by the 40-year division of the country (p. 305). Seen from this perspective, the history of the Third Reich functions as a common and connecting past, while the perception of the Federal Republic and of the GDR is characterized by competing patterns of interpretation and sometimes conflicting personal experiences.

Steinle also provides a useful attempt at relating particular narrative strategies to the main historical topics. Similar to the family conversation about the Nazi past presented above, recent docudramas about the period of the Third Reich are often characterized by a tendency towards exculpation. They focus on situations of suffering and existential threats for the German population, such as falling victim to the cruelty of warfare (*Unsere Mütter, Unsere Väter*), the last days before Berlin's defeat (*Die letzte Schlacht*/The Last Battle, ZDF, 2005, dir. Hans-Christoph Blumenberg), British bombing raids (Dresden, ZDF, 2006, dir. Roland Suso Richter), or the expulsion of Germans from the Eastern territories at the end of the war (*Die Flucht*, or March of Millions, ARD Degeto, 2007, dir. Kai Wessel). *Die letzte Schlacht* turned the focus from political and military decision-making to the experiences of ordinary people, thus providing a kind of reverse shot to the internationally successful movie *Der Untergang* (Downfall, Germany 2004, dir. Oliver Hirschbiegel). In *Die letzte Schlacht* 'the witnesses—especially the German ones—become characters to identify with, because they act as the audience's own mirror image' (Ebbrecht 2007a, p. 42). Similarly *Dresden* is focused almost solely on German suffering, as personified by the nurse Anna. A subplot about a Jewish family, as well as the additional storyline depicting the British military, are put on the margins of the thrilling and highly emotional central plot. On the other hand the film draws a clear distinction between ordinary Germans and Nazis, something also true for *Die Flucht* (Ebbrecht 2007b, p. 229). However, the experience of the Nazi past is also narrated as a struggle to overcome the negative past in both films—German docudrama significantly re-enacts wartime suffering because it is a redemptive starting point for the postwar period. This corresponds with Steinle's observation that docudramas about West German history mainly focus on community-building, miracles and founding myths (2012, p. 306). *Die Luftbrücke—Nur der Himmel war frei* (Berlin Airlift, Sat. 1, 2005, Dror Zahavi) turns a crisis—coming from outside—into a founding myth of the postwar German, Western-oriented, new political order. Challenges occur mainly through catastrophes and accidents as shown in *Das Wunder von Lengede* (The Miracle of Lengede, Sat. 1, 2003, dir. Kaspar Heidelbach) and *Die Sturmflut* (The Storm Flood, RTL, 2005, dir. Jorgo Papavassilou). Steinle observes that these crises are always faced collectively and create a new sense of community (p. 306). Thus such films present the Federal Republic as a success story, evolving from ruins and based on a mutual sense of social responsibility and collective solidarity.[9]

In contrast most docudramas and historical event movies referring to the GDR follow a narrative of crisis (p. 307). The main historic events that are depicted by these films are the uprising of East German construction workers in June 1953, the construction of the Berlin Wall in 1961 and the collapse of the GDR following the incidents of November 1989, a development which then, according to Steinle, merges with the West German success story narrative, which is already indicated through the title of the prototypical unification docudrama, the 2008 ZDF *Das Wunder von Berlin* (The Miracle of Berlin). The vast majority of docudramas and historical event movies that depict incidents from East German history are based on German-German entanglements and are accordingly centred on characters from both parts of the divided Germany. The border becomes the most significant symbol in nearly all of the films—dividing, but also connecting, the country. Usually borders are understood as a symbolic entity, which turn into a material barrier aimed at dividing and separating. But paradoxically, exactly because of this ability to disconnect, a border also creates points of entanglement and even sites of transition, as

Michel de Certeau has emphasized through his observation that a border is 'created by contacts, [because] the points of differentiation between two bodies are also their common points. Conjunction and disjunction are inseparable in them' (1988, p. 127).

In German television docudramas the German-German border constitutes just such a point of entanglement. Although it is mainly framed as historical mistake and thus interpreted from the post-unification perspective of overcoming the GDR, the border also serves as a dramatic catalyst for thrilling stories of the Germanys' actual entanglement. Thereby the mischief, the moral injustice incorporated by the wall as political symbol, turns into a dramatic playground for, mostly genre-bound, rescue and escape stories. This again contributes to the intertwining of the geopolitical and the personal as well as the historical and the experiential levels that constitute the multi-layered form of docudrama. *Der Tunnel* (The Tunnel, Sat. 1, 2001, dir. Roland Suso Richter) portrays a rescue attempt following the construction of the wall. *Die Mauer—Berlin '61* (The Wall—Berlin '61, WDR/Arte/RBB, 2006, dir. Hartmut Schoen) depicts the historical incident within the framework of a family melodrama about separation, loss and trauma. Similarly *Die Frau vom Checkpoint Charlie* (The Woman at Checkpoint Charlie, MDR/BR/RBB/Arte, 2007, dir. Miguel Alexandre), this time not situated in context of the events from 1961 but in the 1980s, focuses on the border as a point of blocked transition—the border post at Checkpoint Charlie—within the genre of a family drama. *An die Grenze* (To the Border, ZDF, 2007, dir. Urs Egger) also tells a story from the aftermath of 1961. It focuses on Alexander, recalcitrant son of a famous GDR professor, who is serving his military duty at the German-German border. This coming-of-age drama reveals a complex micro-cosmos of ambivalent feelings, conformity, dissent and crisis that illustrates the East German dilemma. In contrast *Böseckendorf—Die Nacht, in der ein Dorf verschwand* (Böseckendorf—The Night when a Village Vanished, Sat. 1, 2009, dir. Oliver Domenget) depicts the borderland within the genre patterns of an entertaining event movie. This film shows that private broadcasting companies have also adopted the structure of historical event television set by public service broadcasting. Critics even stated that this depiction of a historic incident, when a majority of inhabitants of an East German village planned a last-minute escape before the borders were finally closed, marked a harking-back to the earlier event-movie culture, which was mainly based on stereotypical narratives and genre patterns (Buß 2009). However, even this example, as well as those broadcasts that depicted the fall of the Wall, from early docudramas such as *Das Deutschlandspiel* (The Germany-Game, ZDF/Arte, 2000, dir. Hans-Christoph Blumenberg) to event movies such as *Das Wunder von Berlin* and even comical dramas such as *Bornholmer Strasse* (Bornholmer Street, RBB/MDR, 2014, dir. Christian Schwochow) use the border and its transition as the main narrative element to access the history of the GDR as German-German entanglement.

This is even true for films that clearly focus on incidents from East German history such as the events of June 1953 that led to an uprising in the GDR (finally broken with the help of Soviet tanks and military). Unquestionably the June 1953 events also had a German-German dimension and involved protagonists from both sides of the, then still open, border. But the events generated two completely different memories in the two Germanys. In West Germany the uprising was transformed into a national myth and reference point for unity. This was illustrated by the fact that 17 June, the date of the uprising, became a national holiday in the Federal Republic. The GDR, in contrast, officially deleted the date from national memory, in spite of the fact that large parts of the population were actually involved in the protests. It must also be said many of them were the 'workers' more usually celebrated by the state as models for the new socialist society. Nevertheless, any reference to these incidents became a taboo and memories remained only on a personal level for those who had participated in or experienced the events.

In 2003, the fiftieth anniversary of 17 June 1953 was turned into a national commemoration event that was intensively mediated by various television stations. Two historical event movies and one docudrama marked the anniversary. The East German public broadcasting station MDR produced *Tage des Sturms* (Stormy Days, MDR, 2003, dir. Thomas Freundner), a local view on the occurrence of protests in the industrial city Bitterfeld. Broadcast earlier in May on ARD in the run-up to the anniversary, *Tage des Sturms* reached 4.24 million viewers (Müller 2003). Written by the famous dissident East German author Erich Loest (imprisoned in the GDR, he left the state in 1981), the film, in contrast to other depictions, presented East Germans as much more sympathetic and also assembled well-known East German actors, such as Peter Sodann (who had started his career at East Berlin's Berliner Ensemble). Steinle notes that *Tages des Sturms* was also exceptional in its patterns of interpretation because it framed the events of 1953 within the broader context of Germany's twentieth-century history (2012, p. 316). A week after *Tage des Sturms* ARD broadcast another historical event movie on the same incidents, this time set in Berlin. *Zwei Tage Hoffnung* (Two Days of Hope, SWR/WDR, 2003, dir. Peter Keglevic) was made by famous producer Nico Hoffmann (*Die Luftbrücke; Dresden; Die Flucht; Unsere Mütter, Unsere Väter*) according to the basic principles of historical event television. The film tells a thrilling and suspenseful border-crossing story against the background of the uprising and increasing measures of repression. The narrative unfolds as family drama, adopting the structural motif of two brothers, one who had escaped to West Berlin, and who in the film's present works for the American radio broadcasting station RIAS; the other, meanwhile, has made a career in the East German state. The brothers thus function as symbols of the two Germanys whereby a complex historical context is condensed into a personal conflict. Furthermore *Zwei Tage Hoffnung* repeats a canonical constellation found in many historical event movies by having the brothers compete for the same woman, the nurse Angelika.[10] The historical storyline, depicting the economic misery and increasing conflicts at the construction sites at Stalinallee, is thus moved more and more to the margins. The uprising as depicted mainly consists of a chaotic and increasingly violent environment for the action-driven drama, culminating at the iconic point of entanglement, the German-German border. Nikolaus von Festenberg observes that the story's tempo, however, illustrates an important aspect of the historical event, the notion that the course of history can become increasingly dramatic and even rousing (2003, p. 94). Steinle emphasizes a different aspect, the iconic framing of the events. Towards the end of the film, when the RIAS secret informer, a construction worker and colleague of the East German brother, is arrested by the GDR's secret service police secret service police the camera suddenly focuses on his arm—on which is a tattooed number. By signifying the victim of East German repression as a former survivor of Nazi concentration camps both chapters of German history are easily blended together. According to Steinle, this provides a pattern of interpretation that constructs Germans as victims of the GDR and Third Reich alike (2012, p. 316).

The third television event, ZDF docudrama *Der Aufstand* (The Uprising, ZDF/Arte, 2003, dir. Hans-Christoph Blumenberg), contains several 'classical' attributes of docudrama narration: archival footage, interview sequences, dramatic re-enactments, a voiceover commentary and captions. Within this well-known framework the actors perform the memories of eyewitnesses:

> The recreated scenes illustrate the testimonies. One effect of this narration is that the stories, which are told and presented to the audience, neither have specific historical value nor follow a dramatic structure. They just double the narrated stories. (Ebbrecht 2007a, p. 42)

But in this dramatic repetition individual memories are also codified and collectivized through the mediating potential of historical event television.[11] Indeed, the film team interviewed 150 people who had been involved in, or witnesses of, the events. Sixty of these interviews are incorporated into the film. The re-enactments that illustrate these testimonies were then shot using old cinematic techniques in order to make them look like amateur colour footage from the 1950s. Furthermore, most of the scenes were shot at the original locations in order to emphasize an 'authentic look' (Blickpunkt: Film 2002). This corresponds to the tendency of historical event television to create a notional authenticity and attempt to present history 'as it was' with codified images and narratives.

In contrast to that notion, the interview sequences constantly interrupt the docudrama, rendering its structure porous. These sequences serve also to thwart the narrative tension created by the dramatic re-enactments. As a result the film creates a fragmented narrative that implicitly echoes the historical experience of contingency, closely related to the actual events. Furthermore, by re-enacting not only testimonies but also written documents, such as the protocol of an assembly of East German heads of state, Der Aufstand also adopts strategies of investigative alignment derived from the docu-theatre tradition and does more than fill the gaps left in the visual archives (Müller 2003). Finally the docudrama creates a multi-vocal dialogue about the events, which are depicted from four different perspectives: those of ordinary people (construction workers, a medical doctor, a young FDJ woman,[12] secretaries), the heads of state (Walther Ulbricht, Otto Grotewohl and others), Soviet generals and political leaders, and staff members and journalists from the West Berlin-based radio station RIAS.

Historical events are thus constructed from differing, even competing, perspectives, which illustrate: the inner East German conflict (dissatisfaction, miscommunication and mistrust between leadership and citizens); the German-German relationship (the engagement of American-run RIAS and the indifference of the Federal Government); the transnational framework of the Cold War and the conflicts and tensions within the Soviet leadership; and finally (by referring to McCarthy) also the attitudes within the US administration. This reflects the fact that the East German workers' struggle for better working conditions also had a transnational impact.[13] Additionally *Der Aufstand* is structured by constant border-crossing, thus reflecting not only the historic context but also the conventions of the genre and the aesthetic techniques of television docudrama. Besides German-German border-crossings at the level of the plot, as when East German construction workers visit the RIAS radio station in Berlin and West Berlin journalists report from protest marches in the East, the drama also bridges social and generational borders. But beyond its plot, *Der Aufstand* also uses editing to virtually cross national borders by relating diverging perspectives, especially the German and Soviet view of the events. This also indicates the constant blurring of aesthetical borders, signified in the merging of disparate materials from different sources and especially by a time-bridging montage that interlinks the past (archival footage and re-enactments) and the present (interviews). This alliance of the dominant narrative of crisis and the dominant symbol of the border are significant characteristics of docudramas and historical event movies depicting the GDR and its heritage on German television. Both elements—crisis and borders—are also significant characteristics of the docudrama genre itself. Thus the history of the GDR poses a constant challenge to the dominant German national narrative of overcoming the traumatic Nazi past and transforming it into a West German success story. Docudrama's inherent porosity meets this challenge.

CONCLUSION

Docudramas and historical event movies remain a dominant and successful part of German television broadcasting. Evolving from a long tradition, historical television dramas in Germany have shaped the perception of history and enabled some negotiating of a troubled past. Experimental forms as well as critical attempts at challenging dominant modes of perception and historical narratives have never vanished, although historical event television has increasingly tended towards harmonizing images of the past. But a closer look at the representation of the GDR within the framework of historical event television has shown the potential of conflict-driven narratives within the fragmented and porous form of television docudrama. The challenging and crossing of borders is one of the main effects of the hybridization of fact and fiction within the parameters of historical docudrama. And an additional constitutive element is the assembling of fragments, memories, leftovers and remnants remaining from the past. Therefore docudrama works in a similar way to historiography— collecting, assembling, aligning and readjusting. Today these operative techniques do not only characterize the single broadcasting event, either in the form of a docudrama or a historical event movie. The process of assembling and aligning the fragments of the past can affect the whole television schedule.

The disparate but nevertheless interwoven formats that commemorated the twenty-fifth anniversary of the fall of the Wall indicated this development. This historiographical aspect of docudrama was perfectly illustrated by the melodramatic historical event movie *Zwischen den Zeiten*, broadcast on ZDF on the evening of 9 November 2014. The female protagonist, working on a project that attempts to digitally realign fragments from shredded Stasi files, is forced to investigate her own past. This results in a fateful blurring of the borders between past and present that symbolically re-enacts an earlier crossing of the German-German border. Her shattered life, falling apart, mirrors the broken pieces of history, which need to be gathered, analysed, re-assembled and re-edited. Documents, files and photographs appear in this film mostly in fragments. Thus the scanning machines as well as the protagonist who turns into an investigator of her own life operate according to the rules of docudrama: realigning fragments, bridging past and present and adjusting different national, European and global perspectives on the past.

NOTES

1. Marc Bauder and Dörte Franke directed *Jeder schweigt von etwas anderm* (Last to Know, Germany 2006), one of the first documentaries dealing with the impact and aftermath of repression and imprisonment of dissidents during GDR times. This was mainly based on interviews with witnesses from that time.
2. This kind of media event can thus be interpreted as a significant moment of transforming communicative into cultural memory. Jan Assmann has described the forms of collective memory in the following terms: while communicative memory is still based on living experiences and is thus 'based exclusively on everyday communications' that are 'characterized by a high degree of non-specification, reciprocity of roles, thematic instability and disorganization' (2008, p. 126), cultural memory 'has its fixed point; its horizon does not change with the passing of time.' It is therefore 'main-

tained through cultural formation (texts, rites, monuments) and institutional communication (recitation, practice, observance)' (p. 129). Docudrama, especially in its more fragmented form, assembling documentary and fictional components, can be characterized as a significant mediator in this process. As I have argued elsewhere, media can organize the exchange of memories and the perception of history between individual, social (communicative) and cultural memory (2011, p. 39).

3. All translations into English from the original German are mine. The Stasi (*Staatssicherheit*) was the East German State Security Service. One of its main tasks was to spy on the population and collect reports and other materials that could be used to counter any form of political opposition or cultural deviation.

4. The necessity of confronting the recent German (Nazi) past has to be seen as one of the most important reference points for political and cultural activities in both parts of Germany. Docudrama significantly contributed to this development, and was regarded as a work of *Aufarbeitung*, of 'coming to terms with the past', which of course always also included attempts of 'overcoming the past'. While, following the GDR's claim of being an 'antifascist state', in East German television and film the German Nazi past was transformed into a particularly promoted genre, the discourse on *Aufarbeitung* in the West also became a significant part of civil protest movements in general and the student movement of the 1960s in particular. Television docudrama played an important, but often overlooked, role in this transformative process.

5. In letters to the West German television magazine programme *Hörzu* some viewers from Braunschweig, Schweinfurt and Helmstedt stated that they were deeply impressed by the excellent drama, which they interpreted as a denunciation of dullness and thoughtlessness (Hörzu 1958, p. 49).

6. Interestingly the debate on *Besuch aus der Zone* started in the context of a parliamentary session on the need for a second West German nationwide television station to compete with a 'new network of broadcasting stations' popping up in the 'occupied Soviet zone' of East Germany (Bundeszentrale für politische Bildung 2012, p. 1).

7. West German television directors and authors regularly turned to the topic of East and West German relations as demonstrated by films such as *Preis der Freiheit* (The Cost of Freedom, NDR, 1966, dir. Egon Monk) and *Die Dubrow-Krise* (The Dubrow Crisis, WDR, 1969, dir. Eberhard Itzenplitz), which was already illustrating a certain amount of distance towards the, now ironically, depicted German-German subject (Hickethier 1998, p. 245). In 1979 ZDF broadcast *Flugversuche* (Attempts to Fly, ZDF, 1979, dir. Rainer Wolffhardt), a television drama about an unfortunate love story between the daughter of a high-ranking East German official

and a sensitive boy written by a dissident East German author. Wolffhardt, director of *Besuch aus der Zone*, made this film for the West German national television ZDF, which was the object of the debate in Germany's Federal Parliament in 1958. Interestingly the broadcast of *Flugversuche* (26 November 1979) was followed by an interview with Friedrich Zimmermann, the same politician who in 1958 so vehemently opposed Wolffhardt's film *Besuch aus der Zone* (Der Spiegel 1979, p. 287).

8. For more on the Polish reaction to *Unsere Mütter, unsere Väter*, see Chap. 3 of this book.

9. One exception to this depiction of postwar history in Western Germany is the appearance of left-wing terrorist groups in the 1970s following the student protest movement. The actions of the 'Red Army Faction' (RAF) during their so-called 'German Autumn', for example the kidnapping of the president of the German employers' association Hans Martin Schleyer, and the hijacking of a Lufthansa passenger plane by a Palestinian commando, were presented in Heinrich Breloer's *Todesspiel* (Play of Death, ARD, 1997) and *Mogadischu*, ARD, 2008, dir. Roland Suso Richter). The fortieth anniversary of the hostage crisis during the 1972 Olympic games in Munich was covered by two German docudramas, *Vom Traum zum Terror—München 72* (From a Dream to the Terror—Munich 72, ARD, 2012, dir. Marc Brasse, Florian Huber) and *München 72—Das Attentat* (Munich 72—The Attack, ZDF, 2012, dir. Dror Zahavi).

10. This constellation is also the basic narrative in films such as *Die Luftbrücke*, *Dresden* and *Die Flucht*.

11. Steinle feels that the scenic re-enactments of these statements and interviews tend towards an iconographic fixation of individual memories and they therefore construct a codified image of the past instead of identifying the constructed nature of history (2012, p. 313).

12. The Freie Deutsche Jugend (FDJ—Free German Youth) was the official youth organization of the ruling party SED in the GDR. Membership in the FDJ was voluntary but social pressure and the fact that certain areas of education and social mobility (such as access to universities) were linked to membership of the FDJ led a majority of East German youth to join the organization.

13. Although mainly a local and regional GDR phenomenon (workers' strikes appeared all over East Germany) these events correlated with the global ideological conflicts of the Cold War and internal crises within other countries (in the Soviet Union, for example, and in McCarthyite America). There was arguably a knock-on effect on the global framework of the Cold War.

CHAPTER 3

Polish Docudrama: Finding a Balance Between Difficult and Easy Pleasures

Wiesław Godzic

POST-1989 POLISH TELEVISION: CHALLENGE FOR REALITY?

A history of television docudrama in Poland begins with the Round Table Talks and the fall of the Berlin Wall in 1989. Those historical events, bringing freedom and self-determination to Central and Eastern European nations, were decisive in the shaping of a completely new concept of television. Studies of the medium up to the 1990s by Andrzej Kozieł and Jarosław Kończak (published in 2003 and 2008), acknowledge the breakthrough in the political system as crucial to television programming, but neither of them cites any examples of docudrama produced before that time. The genre is not recognized by the academic history of television (Pokorna-Ignatowicz 2003), nor is it discussed in the critical guide *30 najważniejszych programów TV w Polsce* (The 30 most important TV programmes in Poland, Godzic ed. 2005). In the following chapter, I will investigate the reasons for this, and will try to account for the scarce presence of docudrama in the first 40 years of Polish television. I will argue that the situation was caused by political and social factors, and not by factors within the medium itself. The turn of the twenty-first century marked a short-lived eruption of docudrama, when there was some bewilderment about the 'play with reality' offered, or indeed, provoked by the genre.

That brief golden age of docudrama was generally characterized by a focus on war subject matter and a very serious approach. As Reality

© The Editor(s) (if applicable) and The Author(s) 2016
T. Ebbrecht-Hartmann, D. Paget (eds.), *Docudrama on European Television*, Palgrave European Film and Media Studies, DOI 10.1057/978-1-137-49979-0_3

TV spread alongside entertainment genres with the prefix 'docu', the popularity of docudrama deteriorated, since the genre demanded more complicated preparation. TV viewers can still find its classic examples in the schedules—and by classic I mean docudramas produced with a high degree of skill, encouraging reflection (rare enough in Polish television practices today). However, the docudrama genre is now increasingly dominated by fake-documentary/mockumentary, the more aggressive contemporary forms, which maintain a playful and ironic contact with reality. This competition will continue, but it is to be feared that the poorer forms are likely to prevail.

Docudrama is a special genre, given that any detailed, investigative and historical perspective requires time and reflection. In Poland, the 'Institute of National Remembrance—Commission for the Prosecution of Crimes against the Polish Nation' (Instytut Pamięci Narodowej—Komisja Ścigania Zbrodni przeciwko Narodowi Polskiemu, or IPN) was established in 1998. It has been in charge of dealing with grey areas of recent history (though it has often been criticized for shaping historical policy excessively and one-sidedly). The opening of the archives, the abolition of censorship, and the post-revolutionary atmosphere pointed the way for both filmmakers and TV producers. Initially, documentary films mostly depicted the events of the recent past. In these films many scores were settled with Poland's communist past, but an equally strong influence was an infatuation with newly gained access to the photographed and recorded past. During the last 25 years, films have been made about key incidents in Poland's troubled twentieth-century history: the massacre at Katyń, the Warsaw Uprising, the Polish-Bolshevik War, and the deportation of Poles to Siberia. With a clear line still evident between the 'docu' and the 'drama' components, it was not a good time for the development of docudrama.

I will in this chapter describe the contexts (political, social, and aesthetic) of the transformation in Polish television, highlighting the role that documentary film in particular played in audiovisual culture. Documentary had an important role as a result of the social context in Poland. I will also comment upon the post-1989 emergence of commercial television genres aiming at a play with reality. It was in the context of this phenomenon, or quite often in opposition to it, that docudrama functioned. I will then focus on analyses of particular examples of docudrama and genres closely related to it, the most important components of which involve discussing how the language of documentary has been used and adapted in Polish docudrama.

The Background: 'Television Lies'

From the very beginning the development of the television medium was less about reaching individual viewers than reaching families in their households. However, public TV-watching was the dominant form for a certain time because of political-propaganda reasons, cultural reasons, or simply financial ones. In the early 1950s, the so called 'golden age' of American television, the basic model of commercial television became popular, which meant that one serial programme (such as the news, a game show, or a sitcom) was sponsored wholly by one company that would impose its requirements on the programme. As the advertising revenue increased, television stations began to produce or commission their own programmes, leaving space for sponsors and advertisers in-between. This is how advertising 'spots' emerged in the West, combined into larger blocks. The producers felt considerable freedom: they had money and also the opportunity to (almost) freely decide on the shape of their programmes. That opportunity was sometimes used to create the stuff of many contemporary cultural animators' dreams; namely, great television dramas. American public television (PBS—Public Broadcasting Service) grew out of civic and educational initiatives. The European model was shaped according to a completely different principle, its background and essence being the state public broadcasting stations that began to emerge in the early 1950s, with commercial broadcasting developing later. It would take some time for numerous commercial stations—on radio and television—to be established through new technologies in Western Europe; most of these appeared in the 1980s. For political reasons, none of this would be possible in Eastern Europe until the final decade of the twentieth century.

Postwar television in Poland functioned first as an educational and artistic novelty. Regular broadcasts began in the mid-1950s, and the flood of Soviet-made television sets resulted in the Poles developing a new kind of cultural activity, watching their one and only TV channel (from 1952 until 1970, 'TP' was the abbreviation universally used for this). A second channel only became available in October 1970, so from 1970 to 1992 there was 'TP1' and 'TP2'. The situation became much more complicated, of course, following changes in the 1990s when many more channels emerged. TP, as it then was, offered the first Polish talk show—original and ambitious in form—hosted by Irena Dziedzic, an icon of early Polish television. It also offered satirical-entertainment programmes, and drama series of various kinds. The Polish audience was particularly enthusiastic about *Stawka większa niż życie* (More Than Life at Stake, TP, 1967–68) a series depicting the wartime adventures of 'our man in a German uniform', Lieutenant Hans Kloss. This character, played by popular actor Stanisław Mikulski, was a real Polish Abwehr secret service officer who was a spy for the Russians and Poles. The original 18 episodes were first broadcast in 1968, but are still re-broadcast from time to time. Another series that dealt with World War II was *Czterej pancerni i pies* (Four Tank-Men and a Dog, TP, 1966–70). It told the story of a tank crew and their T-34 tank called 'Rudy 102'. It was, of course, full of references to certain documentary wartime realities. At the same time it must be noted that the series distorted history, especially when it came to Polish-Russian relations. For example, there was no mention of Stalin ordering the murder of Polish prisoners of war at Katyń, nor of the numerous acts of rape and looting committed by the 'liberating' Red Army. Instead there was a great deal of emphasis on Polish-Russian comradeship in arms, mutual bravery, and friendship.

As this example shows, unless the documentary element in docudrama comes equipped with an unrestrained freedom in both the interpretation and the evaluation of historical phenomena, the project cannot work properly, whatever the skills of dramatist, actor, and director. If the reference to historical events proves fundamentally false, as it does here with the invader and the rapist presented as benefactor and friend, the docudrama loses credibility. Indeed, it begins to be seen as fundamentally false to the kind of viewer (and there were many) who saw the series as pure Communist propaganda. Some public television managers even tried to cancel the programme because of this. They failed to do so mainly because just as many viewers found the series amusing, entertaining, and well-informed; up to the present day, viewers still want to see it.

It must be emphasized that the Communist authorities only began to use television for propaganda on a large scale as late as the 1970s, and this particularly affected the journalistic and informational aspects of television. The main news programme, *Dziennik Telewizyjny* (Daily TV News) became synonymous with corrupt news or things that had to go unsaid. The liberating success of the Solidarity movement (founded August/ September 1980) contributed to the fact that television, associated as it was with authority structures, provoked social dissatisfaction because of its role in the machinery of propaganda. The numerous inscriptions on walls saying 'Television Lies' were a clear sign that the medium was expected to take a particular government line, thus threatening its ability to comment truthfully on events. As a result of this situation, the 1980s was something of a lost decade when we consider the development of television in Poland in general (and especially so for docudrama). Martial law, declared in December 1981, interrupted countless artistic projects, with many active artists being dismissed from their posts. Television became a militarized institution, managed by a commissioner. A bright spot on the otherwise murky landscape was the TP1 comedy series *Alternatywy 4* (4 Alternative Street) directed by Stanisław Bareja—completed in 1983, but not broadcast until 1986 because of censorship difficulties). It depicted the lives of tenants in a newly built block of flats in the Ursynów district of Warsaw. Its satirical portrait of life combined all the nonsense and ills of the socialist economic system, and reflected the collapse of traditional values in postwar Poland. Many of the characters' sayings permeated into everyday language. The series continued for many years and was popular thanks to its uncompromising humour and its jeering at the system—all this happening despite censorship and its numerous interventions.

Another bright spot on the 1980s map was the exceptionally successful Brazilian soap opera *Isaura, the Slave Girl*. Produced in 1976, it was transmitted on TP1 in 1984, the year in which George Orwell had set his dystopian novel. The story of the beautiful slave who is oppressed by her wicked owner, Leoncio, was a schematic abolitionist story, and it was distant in time and space from 1980s Poland. Nonetheless it appealed to Poles on a metaphorical level, and was recognized as something very much needed at that time. Isaura's (mis)adventures were followed by more than three-quarters of Polish TV viewers.[1] It even became a fashion for parents to name their newly born children after the characters in the series. One of the reasons for this hungering after a simple plot that inspired strong emotions (empathy in particular) was that Poles sympathized with the state of enslavement; the audience read *Isaura* metaphorically. Under martial law Polish people felt just as the slave girl did, bereft of human or civil rights, oppressed by others.

The 1989 breakthrough in Eastern Europe meant new challenges, both political (the first partially free elections) and economic (fundamental, indeed revolutionary, changes in the economic system), as well as the promise of a free media. All these factors had a strong impact on television, which by 1992 was subject to a new media law and new audit institutions, including the National Broadcasting Council (KRRiT). The 1990s was thus a decade characterized by a great deal of chaos, especially in terms of the television aesthetic. Viewers quickly learned to read new and highly codified genres, especially since their Polish counterparts emerged quickly (sitcoms, game shows, various TV series, and satirical variety shows). In a sense, Poles became the ideal consumers, associating regained political freedom with freedom of consumption—they liked commercials and even wanted to watch special cinema screenings of them (*Night Feeding with Commercials*). This cyclical event for lovers of ads has now been running for 23 years. It was as if, after the dull years of mediocrity, Poles felt they were now entitled to a pinch of luxury—luxury provided by newly-available American light entertainment programmes and numerous TV drama series.

Two commercial stations, POLSAT (established in 1994) and TVN (1997), were an influence by 2000; they began to establish standards of production, which manifestly affected modes of reception. At this time, the concept of screened reality became corrupted and appropriated by the reality show, the first of which appeared in March 2001. This was the Polish edition of *Big Brother*, which caused a great deal of scandal. Hosted by TVN, it was the first ever season of the show in Eastern Europe. From the very beginning *Big Brother* was not limited to the television medium, pushing the boundaries of media convergence and re-shaping reception.[2] In some ways television seemed to come closer to reality than ever before; indeed, but for television this kind of everyday reality might well have remained undiscovered. There is no question that *Big Brother* caused an earthquake, because Poland was unprepared for this kind of programme. The show inspired other trash TV clones in the form of, for example, docusoaps and talent shows. Media reality ceased to be what it had been before. This huge change has been summarized thus:

> All the 'techie' talk, changing business models, new interactive formats, new ways of delivering content and getting people to pay for it—all of this is fine. But there is still a constant principle which is that people want entertainment. They like to be told stories. (Moran 2009, p. 58)

This has troubled Polish intellectuals, who study this lesson with a certain reluctance knowing that it is unfair to criticize the audience for responding to the artistic and aesthetic values of contemporary society, however meretricious that society's cultural products may be. But the media themselves are in many ways happier in the company of admirers of light (or even primitive) entertainment. All too often now, the notion of 'difficult pleasures' seems to be disappearing in favour of 'easy' ones. The balance of difficult and easy pleasures seems particularly important as it gets to the heart of the issues surrounding docudrama in Poland.

THE 'UNREPRESENTED WORLD' IN THE POLISH DOCUMENTARY TRADITION

Poland after World War II was not only a mutilated, devastated country, subject to Soviet domination in terms of both its politics and its economy; it was also undergoing a demographic revolution. Hundreds of thousands of families moved from poor villages to industrialized cities that were developing quickly. In this situation, and with new leaders, the perception of documentary film as a genre shifted markedly. It was not seen as being in the service of a Griersonian civic and educational ideal, as in the UK for example, but simply as propaganda vehicle for the postwar socialist authorities. Before the war, Polish documentary had been the domain of an artistic, avant-garde expression, but this was somewhat lost in the new dispensation. It is important to understand this Polish context because docudrama emerges in Poland, as it does elsewhere, from a distinctive documentary film tradition, reshaped in postwar Poland by the new medium—and reshaped further both postwar and post-fall of the Wall.

Of course, there were several interesting exceptions. Kazimierz Karabasz (born 1930), one of the seniors of contemporary documentary and renowned for portraying the inhabitants of small towns and hamlets, was also known for empathizing with his characters. The viewer of his films feels that the director not only sympathizes with his characters whenever they find themselves in difficult situations or when they cannot make a decision, but also roots for their efforts to adapt to the new social conditions. He does not, however, cross the border separating the object filmed from the filming subject. From a formal perspective, his film *Rok Franka W.* (A Year in the Life of Franek W., 1967) was unusual as a psychological-observational documentary. A man approaching 20 asks for admission to the Voluntary Labour Corps (OHP), a partly militarized educational institution, popular after the war. The filming took over a dozen months and was divided into the seasons of the year. Our protagonist goes through the process of getting used to the camera which follows him during his various activities. It is by no means an intrusive camera; in fact, we do not feel its presence. The sphere of its influence stretches between observation (we gradually forget about this basic function) and the creation of a character. The protagonist Franek's position changes from that of object of investigation to the subject of man's interaction with the camera. Franek reading fragments of his diary offers viewers an in-depth subjective view on, for example, his dating of a girlfriend; not only is he seen as a main character reacting to on-screen events, he is heard in voice-over, offering interpretation and evaluation of his personal life. Semantic collisions happen in the film, as in the cases when the viewer's interpretation of the event based on the image might differ from that based on Franek's voice.

Forty years later the director sought Franek out again for his 2006 documentary *Pan Franciszek* (Mr. Franciszek). It tells the story of Franek's later life, and shows him working in a bakery, gardening, and maintaining his large family (four daughters and a son). This time, however, the plot is illustrated by numerous photographs and videos of family celebrations, and not by fragments of his diary. The aged director also finds himself in a new reality, which makes him humbly contemplate the mission of a documentary director today—he considers what he should talk about and how. He feels that the director must constantly choose between what is too complicated and what seems banal.[3] It is important to note that this structure, with its core of repetition (the same person but older) reveals a fundamental principle of docudrama. If we regard the initial event as a historical source, and the subsequent act of using the same, non-professional, social actors to build a new interpretation around it as a form of creating a plot, then the shaping and framing of the 2006 film has similarities with fictional narrative arcs and structures. If the 1967 documentary represents 'experienced reality', then the later film is a kind of 'dramatized squared' documentary.

The Polish approach to the problem of 'truth' in documentary consisted also in the fact that this was inseparably tied to politics. The new generation of filmmakers, including Krzysztof Kieślowski, Marcel Łoziński, Marek Piwowski, and Grzegorz Królikiewicz, were very important in Poland. In their statements, the directors would voice a somewhat idealistic desire to express the truth about Poland in their times. They also imposed on themselves the duty (which they considered to be their social mission) to research and describe all the areas of contemporary life, even the most painful ones. This was, in fact, a 'political kind of idealism', resulting directly from the tragic events at the Gdańsk shipyard in 1970, when the militia shot unarmed striking workers. To demand the right to make movies about such phenomena was indeed both a privilege (in the prevailing system) and a symptom of the film community's determination. It also testified to the perception of the documentary medium as a tool in fighting for values, rather than as the instrument of an emotionally detached description of reality. Among the popular notions of that time was the idea of 'the unrepresented world'. Taken from the title of a book written by two poets, Adam Zagajewski and Julian Kornhauser, this phrase drew attention to that vast area of the world which, for political reasons, could not be the subject of any artist's reflection.

In attempting to represent the unrepresented world, filmmakers took their place in the first ranks of those fighting for high quality and ethical values in social life. They had to accept that direct access to the world of politics was denied them, and they knew they most probably never would be able to present politics accurately. One of the shortcuts to the unrepresented world which they adopted was to make the most of the presence of non-professional, social actors in their films. This enabled them to be creative in their filming of real-life events. The resulting films revealed scarcely any interference from their directors, yet the method could not be called objective. In Marcel Łoziński's *Próba mikrofonu* (Microphone's Test, 1980), for example, a journalist who operates a radio station in a factory is conducting a survey, trying to record the workers' opinions on the management of the institution. As it turns out, the vast majority of his interlocutors are opportunists with no opinion of their own. In the end, the viewer is not sure of how authentic the young journalist's behaviour actually is (though it seems authentic). The suspicion arises that the director has suggested—maybe even rehearsed—the scenes and this dramatic element undercuts the surface meaning. Krzysztof Kieślowski's film *Z punktu widzenia nocnego portiera* (From a Night Porter's Point of View, 1977) was made at roughly the same time, its interpretative frame is both sophisticated and persuasive, while maintaining the appearance of objectivity. The undercutting of an apparent message by creative means is evident also with regard to Wojciech Wiśniewski's documentary *Wanda Gościmińska. Włókniarka* (Wanda Gościmińska, a Textile Worker, 1975), in which the female protagonist is seemingly allowed to speak about anything she wants, in her distinctively taciturn way. In front of the camera, Gościmińska describes what seems to be her successful career as a hero of socialist labour. However, framing and structure once again cause the viewer to distil something very different from her monologue: her life seems rather to have been wasted and devoid of deep satisfaction, despite the words that she utters.[4]

Paradoxically, one of the most important films in the Polish documentary tradition is *Człowiek z marmuru* (Man of Marble, 1976), a Polish *Citizen Kane* directed by Andrzej Wajda and award-winner at Cannes. There are four diegetic layers in the film, signalled by the colour/black-and-white opposition:

1. A colour sequence presenting the basic diegesis: a story of a young student who is making a film about a 1950s hero, set in the 1970s;
2. A colour sequence presenting fictional events set in the 1950s;
3. A black-and-white sequence presenting the events of the 1950s;
4. Reconstructed, simulated documentary photographs;
5. An authentic black-and-white sequence, a chronicle of the years 1949–56.

This structure creates confusion with regard to reliable cognitive evaluation. It turns out that the black-and-white events that seem like documentary are not documentary at all (even if film history seems to indicate they should be). They are staged, whereas the colour shots (insofar as they belong to the plot) show 'what it really was like'. Wajda's film was seen partly as expiation for the sins of opportunism committed by many filmmakers during the Communist period. Wajda himself was confessing that he too fitted into the category of those who, in order to work at all, had failed to tell the truth.

Andrzej Wajda, the most eminent Polish authority in film directing, is also a fine example of an artist who is a master in creating a genial mixture of fable and reality in a work of art. His *Kanal* (1957) is based on the true story of soldiers in the Polish Home Army who decided to escape from the Germans during the Warsaw Uprising in 1944. Enterprisingly, they used the underground sewage system to get around the city, but their defiance of the Nazis ended in tragedy. Wajda has a genius for creating a highly intensive dramatic aura within a very realistic (true) narrated story. In *Kanal* he uses voice-over commentary to build tension between the framing narration and the world represented visually. The spectator is compelled to ask questions arising from the nature of that tension, because s/he—as a viewer—is deprived of certainty in belief: a 'realistic' story is artfully packed with emotions, and step by step, symbols of light start to dominate the global sense of the film. At the end some of the Home Army soldiers literally and metaphorically approach 'the light'—the metaphor of freedom contrasted to the darkness of the sewer system. But it is an illusion of freedom: the sewer's gate is closed—and light means death not freedom. The viewer of *Kanal* (and other Wajda films) is forced to differentiate between three layers: what could be true (in the physical sense); how emotions create another kind of truth, namely the truth of feelings; and finally how realistically the story is narrated. This is the case in the abovementioned *Man of Marble* (1977) as well as in *Man of Iron* (1981). The latter film was realized during 'the sixteen months' festival of Solidarity' (1980–81), when the Communist regime (and its censorship) was about to fall.

Wajda has always been conscious of the possibility inherent in layering and mixing levels of reality in his films. This strategy was made complete with the addition of a highly rhetorically composed story, making the world represented close to the world characteristically represented in documentary. What this master proclaimed to be possible, other directors/documentary makers attempted. For instance, Marcel Łoziński made the creative documentary, *Ćwiczenia warsztatowe* (Workshop Exercises, 1987), in which a television crew carries out a survey at a university campus, asking students about the typical features of the young generation. In the middle of the film, the camera rotates 180 degrees, and the images previously selected are now shown again with slightly different background music. The soundtrack is 'practically the same', only it goes a little ahead of the image or is delayed. This reverses the previous sequences and changes the interpretative frame: the young people are in fact happy and look at the world with optimism.

Documentary, perhaps, always comes with such creative, or dramatic, input—but this was especially necessary in a country subject to censorship. Krzysztof Kieślowski was once asked if he had actually made everything up in an interview about his film *Personel* (Personnel, 1975). This film depicts difficult, unclear relationships within a group of workers. Kieślowski replied:

> No, I'm sorry, actually I didn't make anything up. All this had already happened somewhere, I'd seen such people, heard the intonation, I only had to gather it all somehow. (Zawiśliński 2005, p. 153)

The production of documentaries also underwent a very important change at this time, with the transition from film to television aesthetics marking an industrial shift towards television. This meant that documentary made by and for television tended towards genre hybridity, a tendency accelerated by the 1990s birth of consumerist ideology and practice. This was ironically depicted in the films made for television by Maria Zmarz-Koczanowicz, Marcel Łoziński and Paweł Łoziński, or Andrzej Fidyk (the latter director also being TVP's Head of Documentaries). The fundamental question that haunts documentary theory—'Can the camera lie?'—became sharply relevant in the new, television-dominated and 'free market' world, a world in which post-modernism has long established the idea that the camera should never be unproblematically trusted. Such thinking paved the way for feature films deconstructing both fiction and non-fiction film, such as *The Truman Show* (1998), and *EDtv* (1999). The Polish equivalent, *Show* (2003), similarly stripped away, or threw into question, the illusion that the TV camera can 'speak the truth'. This is the new world into which new formats, such as docudrama and reality TV, have entered.

AN EARLY EXAMPLE OF DOCUDRAMA

While only a few native docudramas were made before the 1990s, it is important to pay attention to productions that come close to the format. *Epilog norymberski* (The Nuremberg Epilogue) started life as a teleplay produced for and broadcast by TP in 1969 by Jerzy Antczak and a group of the most famous Polish actors. A new, revised version was filmed and broadcast the following year—25 years after the end of World War II and the actual events of the war crimes trial. It was a thrilling fact-based piece, the actors playing the roles of real victims in emotionally charged scenes. The narrator (played by Andrzej Łapicki, the most popular actor at that time) occupied on-screen space as one of the characters in the courtroom, while additionally addressing the audience directly in order to underline various points. At the time this was a most original way to present and to comment upon a 'real show'. However, decades later the essential false-hood of this account was revealed. For instance, the film reduced the number of judges, and while American motives and arguments were only partially presented, the Russians' contribution was glorified and also falsi-fied. Historians argued that this Polish version of the Nuremberg trials did not cover the fact that 'Russian criminals pronounced judgement on German criminals'.[5] But there are sections in the film, a long part on the subject of Auschwitz, for example, with good documentary provenance. Modern Polish culture was created in the shadow of the war—and this is very evident in *The Nuremberg Epilogue*.

From 1983 to 2005 Polish television transmitted Bogusław Wołoszański's *Sensacje XX wieku* (Sensations of the Twentieth Century) on TVP1. The massive popularity of the series led to its being repeated in 2013 on the National Geographic Channel as well as on TVP Historia. This popular historical series, concerned with historical detail and the aura of the times which it presents, started production under martial law and the all-powerful censorship of the time. It was therefore propagandist and pro-state material, yet viewers received it with enthusiasm, accepting to some degree the distortion of historical facts. More important was its unconventional way of presenting historical processes and events. The subjects included reports of intelligence officers as well as, for example, the story of Himmler's astrologer. Wołoszański, the editor, created a unique rhetorical relationship with the audience: his opinions were based on sensational facts, but at the same time the narrative provoked historiographical questions: examining what history might mean in the life of a nation, and asking questions about both responsibility for successes and failures, and the role of the individual. A further ten episodes were announced in 2015. Wołoszański became something of a Polish docudrama institution as a result of the 13 episodes of *Tajemnicy Twierdzy Szyfrów* (The Secret of the Ciphers' Fortress, TVP1, 2007). This spectacular production depicts the battle fought by special agents in the Lower Silesia region of Poland during World War II. Made on a grand scale, and set in beautiful locations such as Silesian castles, the experience of watching the series can be compared to that of watching an exciting war movie—with lots of spectacular action. But for the spectator the experience is often interrupted, as the journalist Wołoszański interprets what has been watched as fact or comments on what is to come. The easy pleasure, as it were, is followed by the difficult.

While the last 15 years have seen less in the way of World War II-related topics, they are still popular—especially among the older members of the television audience who experienced the period. *Historia Kowalskich* (The Story of the Kowalski Family, TVP 2, 2008) was a shocking reconstruction of events in December 1942, when the 34th SS Division burned villagers alive for hiding Jews in Ciepielów, near Radom. New dramatizations of social and political events began to appear, which until then had been the domain of investigative journalism. For instance, the still unsolved tragic death of a government minister, Barbara Blida, was reconstructed in 2010 (*Wszystkie ręce umyte. Sprawa Barbary Blidy* (All Hands Washed. The Case of Barbara Blida, TVP2).[6] Away from the subject of the war, *We Will Be Happy One Day* (2011, TVP HD) consisted of a series of microreportages about young people's dreams in contemporary Poland, and created the rhetorical form of a film within a film, also including many frames of reference. In consequence, the viewer is not sure as to which frame of reference to reality is being reconstructed. It is difficult also to disentangle who is a real social actor and who is a professional playing an amateur actor. Marcin Koszałka's *Takiego pięknego syna urodziłam* (Such a Beautiful Son I Gave Birth To, 2000, TVP1, produced by Wytwórnia Filmów Czołówka and premiered at Krakow's Film Festival in May 2000) and Grzegorz Pacek's *Jestem zły* (I'm Bad, 2001, TVP1, produced by Telewizyjna Agencja Produkcji Teatralnej i Filmowej, premiered at Krakow's Film Festival in May 2001) are both examples of bio-documentary, which allows amateurs to film freely and thus plays an uncompromising game with the realism of the world presented. While content remains documentary, the controlling narrative principles derive from melodrama and/or investigative journalism.

In Poland there has been a strong tradition of respect for the military uniform, and an interesting phenomenon has been the emergence of historical reconstruction groups consisting of young people who re-enact battles in authentic uniforms and with proper military equipment. In a fictionalized documentary about the defence of the Post Office in Danzig (Gdańsk) on the first day of the Nazi German invasion in 1939 (*14 godzin. Pierwsi w walce* (14 Hours—The First Ones Fighting, 2013, TVP Historia), the following rules were applied: in principle, the few existing documentary records were not used because they were German—and therefore seen as untrustworthy. The post office defenders were played by Polish actors, while the German invaders were acted out by members of the 'Pomeranian Independent Historical Reconstruction Group' (SGO Pomorze). The TV programme oscillates on the border of authenticity, or rather, between different ways of interpreting it. On the one hand, the almost amateurish pyrotechnic work is conspicuous, as is the use of Poles to play Germans in reconstructed scenes. On the other hand, however, one feels a great deal of authenticity in this lack of professionalism, since one is encouraged to identify with the heroes of 70 years ago. The interesting thing was that the film was allocated simultaneously to public TV and to the only existing Polish cinema-theatre for documentary films— (named 'Charlie' after Charlie Chaplin) in Łódź.

The recent case of the German docudrama *Unsere Mütter, unsere Väter* (Generation War, ZDF Germany, 2013) shown on Polish television with the title *Nasze matki, wasi ojcowie*[7] (TVP1, 2013), is very intriguing. It is a story of German's young generation during World War II, and the mini-series demonstrates clearly how fragile and controversial historical interpretation can be even 70 years after the war. The narrative at first sight follows personal stories of family and friendship, and the series did not try to disavow Nazi cruelty nor absolve the regime from its responsibility for the Holocaust. But the main controversies in Poland were based on the problem of scale. German soldiers, for example, were not depicted as being as cruel as some viewers remembered them to have been. But the official protest by the director of public television to German ZDF, as well as the Polish Embassy's protest in Berlin, referred much more to the image of Poles in the German series.

What these protests questioned in particular was the way Polish soldiers of the clandestine Home Army were shown as acting as cruelly as the German occupiers. In some cases they were seen as even more anti-Semitic than the Nazis—this was the main argument of the Polish institutions concerned with protest. Some internauts (internet bloggers) stated that it was unclear at times who was the invader and who was the victim. While it is true that the cruelty of this war is located far away from us in time, and we are only able to see its consequences, for the grandparents' generation, the smell of death, and the prevalence of rapes and inhuman cruelty was—internauts continued—a significant characteristic of the disastrous Hitler years, and this caused the series to be questioned.[8] The docudrama thus played an important social role. It provoked the interpretation and reinterpretation both of experienced history and the myths behind that experience. It teased its audiences with an alternative view, and put them in an uncomfortable position as well as making them more conscious of the ways in which historical facts can be disputed.

TRAGIC HEROISM: DRAMATIZING THE WARSAW UPRISING

I will now examine three popular television and film docudramas from very recent times that represent different methods of dealing with reality. My first example is *Powstanie warszawskie* (Warsaw Uprising, dir: Jan Komasa 2013—shown in cinemas and released on DVD), in which reality was, so to speak, glued together and colourised in order to make it attractive. The history of Poland constitutes a range of great wars, battles, uprisings, and diplomatic initiatives which were often doomed to a tragic failure from the very beginning. In the late eighteenth century, Poland had disappeared from the political map of Europe, seized and divided among its neighbours. Its history meant that, until the end of World War I and the regaining of independence, there was little pragmatic positivism in this part of Europe; instead there was much tragic heroism. The Warsaw Uprising occupies a special place in a sad sequence of national events. When the Red Army reached the Vistula River in August 1944 they effectively divided the city into two parts. Then they waited, standing by while for two months a patriotic youth movement was bled to death trying to liberate its half of the city. During the two-month battle on the streets of Warsaw, a filmed chronicle of the Uprising was also being recorded. According to the DVD booklet that accompanies the new film (based on the original footage), the chronicle is 'the world's first non-fiction war drama [...] the real picture of the uprising'. The film presents a challenge to interpretation because of its stance on 'non-fiction'. It uses a number of rhetorical strategies that reveal the amateur filmmakers' way of dramatizing reality.

Throughout the actual uprising, a team of insurgent filmmakers shot six hours of original footage we can consider as unquestionably documentary. The new film was edited from this footage by a team of consultants and filmmakers who worked on the material for over seven months. The DVD's cover notes the scale of the task: '1,440 hours of colouring, 112,000 selected frames, 648,000 minutes of frame-by-frame film reconstruction.' The result is, they claim, 'an unprecedented realism'. This 'realism' was achieved partly through restaging sequences in order to dramatize the material. The 1944 filmmakers, whose voices are supplied by contemporary actors, are heard, often instructing their filmed subjects as to how they should behave. Sometimes, repetitions of shots are seen, as is often necessary whenever a film is being made. The real concern of the original film crew for the insurgent-actors' safety can be heard, as can their worries about whether the work is expressive enough to show the drama and danger of the situation.

When, years later, this footage was found, it was colourized and strung onto a humble narrative thread. The Ur-film became the basis for a drama about two brothers making a film during the uprising. The 'exceptionally realistic material', then, became a metafilm with a docu-dramatic element. While the brothers/filmmakers never appear in the frame, their conversations with the insurgents can be heard, and they control the film's narrative as its voice-over narrators. In addition, the fictional relationship is developed; the older brother teaches the younger the tricks of the film trade, and they write letters to their mother—the audience learns all this from their voice-over. So 'real' and invented filmmakers interact in a variable dramaturgical structure with the on-screen, actual, insurgents. Thus *Warsaw Uprising* goes beyond documentary, boldly entering the sphere of fictionalization.

One further element of invention must be noted. The images could be, and were, re-processed and coloured, but the Ur-film was silent. The new film reconstructs the insurgents' utterances from their lip movement. So the insurgents addressing the camera in the world of the uprising are saying what they actually were saying, but in the film they have a different voice—that of a contemporary actor. Sometimes this leads to uncertainty about what can be heard. For example, we see a battle group marching (authentic images). The filmmakers are asked 'What are you doing?' This is, of course, authentic in the context of 1944, but it has been lip-read and, strictly speaking it is inauthentic because acted. The latter respond (no less authentically): 'We are filming the uprising.' The group keeps marching ahead until we can no longer see the faces, but the soundtrack offers a jaunty reply that shows both the insurgents' attitude to the filmmakers and their bravery: 'And we are doing an uprising!' This is good dramatically, but this fragment was clearly added by the contemporary crew. It is good because it is in line with the original intent (a film contributing to a brave action). What we are dealing with here is a documentary that is manipulated dramatically in 'good faith', as it were.

The authoritative voice-over (especially towards the end of the 85-minute film) creates yet another plane: viewers repeatedly hear that they will see the truth. But what is 'really true' here forms an interesting question. The black-and-white original film has been reconstructed, and made into a colour film. The sound has been partly reconstructed and partly added to by scriptwriter and director. A kind of 'supertruth', made up after 60 years, has been claimed, and rests upon the belief that this dramatization documentary is capable of coming closer to reality than the bare bones of the Ur-film could. Whether it is or not must depend on whom we ask: Jan Komasa, producer of *Warsaw Uprising*, clearly feels it is.

My second example *Czas honoru* (Days of Honour dirs. Michał Rosa and Michał Kwieciński) is a drama series that looks gestures towards features of docudrama. This television series has been broadcast on the public TVP2 channel since 2008. It tells the story of the underground soldiers in German-occupied Poland who were initially known as the 'Union of Armed Struggle', then as the 'Home Army' (AK). After the war they became the Armed Forces Delegation for Poland, and were commonly referred to as *cichociemni* ('the silent unseen'). These are the very people depicted controversially in the German docudrama *Unsere Mütter, unsere*

Väter, discussed in the previous section. The script for the series was inspired by the stories of British-trained Polish soldiers who went back to Occupied Poland to join the resistance. Sadly, the group they joined was infiltrated by the Nazis.[9] The action of the first six seasons (over 80 episodes) takes place mainly in Warsaw, with some parts set in other areas of the General Government as well as other occupied countries in Europe of that time. The plot incorporates historical events connected with Home Army activity. This includes the assassination of Igo Sym, director of the 'Theater der Stadt Warschau'; combat actions aimed at the liquidation of German intelligence groups; the failed assassination in Kraków of the SS-Obergruppenführer, William Koppe; the 'Hotel Polski affair' (a Gestapo provocation against the Jews); 'Operation Góral' (the capture of a German bank transport carrying money); and many actions aiming to liberate Polish prisoners from the hands of the Germans.

The scripts use historical facts in a characteristic way: the events presented are basically consistent with the facts, with any inconsistency traceable to an approach that regards facts as inspiration for drama. For example, the assassination of Franz Kutschera (SS and Police Commander for the Warsaw district of the General Government) here is presented as an operation against Peter Klaus Schoebbel. This fictional name was used partly to distinguish this work from two feature films about Kutschera (*Zamach*, 1959 and *General Nil*, 2009) and also a 2009 son et lumière performance in Warsaw. The television series makes much more of the characters' human emotions and behaviour. The episode 'Oflag VII-A Murnau' is about the liberation of the so-called German 'Generals' POW camp, located in the Bavarian town and liberated by troops of the US 12th Armored Division. In another episode, 'Bullets over the Pawiak' (episode 22—which includes scenes of tortures in the largest Nazi prison in Warsaw), the scriptwriters use the proper name of the institution possibly because it is so widely known in Poland. The attention to detail is worth a special mention:

> The series features a scene in which the prisoners are forced to exercise on hot gravel. The incident really happened and was the subject of a hearing in the post-war trial of the SS-Standartenführer Ludwig Hahn and the SS-Rottenführer Thomas Wippenbeck, who was a prison guard at the Pawiak.[10]

The *Days of Honour* series is a kind of popular encyclopaedia of World War II for Poles of any age. The series teaches its viewers, in a basic way, about the kidnapping and the Moscow trial of the 16 leaders of the Polish Underground State; about the famous incident in which the Home Army soldiers were arrested and held in a cell with their Nazi torturers; about the numerous battles of the Warsaw Uprising. Actual locations have been used whenever possible, and many scenes are set in historical places in or near Warsaw—thus offering the viewer an aura of reality. Symptomatic of this production style is the internauts' response on the TVP official website.[11] In the tab 'Errors of the series' there are various complaints, both trivial ('improper holding of the gun' being one) and serious (insufficiently developed characters). Still, these are relatively rare and hardly ever aimed at the presentation of historical facts. The docudramatic treatment, with its clear and stable narrative thread, essentially based on historical facts, and provision of a contemporary interpretation, has pleased audiences.

Each episode (with its own title) opens with the credits appearing on a black-and-white background—the only element of colour is the white-and-red Polish flag. There follows a rapid succession of shots (scenes of war, scenes of romance—the public and the private intermingle). This is succeeded by a brief recap of the events from the previous episode. The new episode begins with a caption announcing the time and place of the events that will follow. Each episode includes a set of black-and-white photographs that 'come to life' by transforming into colour images and serve as a colourful context to the world portrayed in the series. The opposite is also the case: the artificial world of the film can suddenly freeze and turn into an original black-and-white photograph. The viewer often learns about a change of location from a voice-over that also comments on the action. This serves two opposing goals: firstly, the series tries to actualize the world it presents, to explain and interpret all that the characters might do in this black-and-white world. The discussions about errors in the series show that the vast majority of the audience believe that the colour segments explain the black-and-white scenes in a reliable way. Secondly, people often feel that the colour footage appears artificial compared to the black-and-white images (a case similar to that of *Man of Marble*). The viewers' empathy is on the side of one world (that of colour), while they are overwhelmed by the logic of the other. Thus there is a persuasive aspect to the series, which attempts to convince the audience that the two approaches do not exclude each other, but cooperate (each in their own way) in order to create belief in the credibility and authenticity of the world presented. Their mutual acknowledgement (emotional faculty) and denial (logical faculty) contribute to an overall conviction that 'The Events You Are About to Witness Are True'.

A journalist from Gazeta Telewizyjna , who was present for the filming of episode 2 singled out Weronika Humaj, who plays Irena, a nurse in the series. Humaj is a young drama school student, well known for her role in the *BarON24* series. She notes the transformation effected in her by costume and make-up—both reflecting the fashion of another era, with hair and make-up in particular taking some time to arrange. Other actors, too, wear the clothes of the 1940s, and the men's shaving must reflect the fact that the insurgents of seventy years ago shaved with pieces of glass, razors being hard to come by. Humaj says: 'Wearing make-up and costume, one [...] finds oneself in a different reality, in different times. One is suddenly not sure what is truth and what is fiction. Especially when we are filming and we hear shots or explosions, or see wounded people.' Maciej Musiał, another young actor in the series who plays Humaj's brother, an insurgent with the pseudonym Apacz, agrees: 'It is easy', he remarks, 'to get lost in all this!' (Wróblewski 2014, p. 3). The phenomenon of actors 'getting lost' in the truthfulness of a partly invented world is evident in another contemporary film, the youth-oriented *Miasto 1944* (Warsaw '44, 2014). The elements of video clip poetics that it uses (slow motion, soft editing, extra-diegetic music) are not, paradoxically, intended for the audience's eyes and ears, but they contribute to the characters' and actors' self-expression.

My final example of docudramatic practice, *Wielkie ucieczki* (Great Escapes, TVN 2005–6), comes from a young and expansive commercial channel. Poland, it should be noted, is several years behind other European countries in terms of the formation of commercial stations. While in Western Europe this took place in the 1980s, this kind of freedom was not possible in Poland under martial law. It was only in the 1990s that the POLSAT and TVN stations emerged and established a serious, challenging alternative to the state-public TVP. In the new dispensation, a game show or a variety show can be created relatively easily to give 'easy pleasures' to an audience. More 'difficult pleasures', like those of classic docudrama, take longer and cost more. *Big Brother*, broadcast from March to June 2001, and, it must be stressed once again, for the first time in the former Communist East, had a big part to play in this shift. The show yielded huge profits for TVN. Public television's response to this was a series of docusoaps that fictionalized, by narrativizing, the stories of unemployed coalminers (*Serce z węgla*/Heart of Coal, 2001), alcoholics (*Ja, alkoholik*/I, the Alcoholic, 2003), young hospital patients (*Szpital Dzieciątka Jezus*/The Infant Jesus Hospital, 1999) or preschoolers (*Przedszkolandia*, 2002). In my view, some of those films far exceeded the limits of intimacy and good taste: however, the public channel could at least claim that they were pursuing a social mission.

It was in this context that the *Wielkie ucieczki* (Great Escapes) series was broadcast, initially on TVN, later on Discovery History (2005–6). The series attracted large audiences and demonstrated an efficient and original use of the language of television. In addition, it made several important contributions to investigative journalism. Basically it consisted of two parts: a real historical event that served as a background—this was fictionalized, its script played out by professional actors—and an interview between a journalist and the actual participants in the events portrayed. One reason for the success of the series was the producers' shrewd selection of period and events. The title referred to escapes from behind the Iron Curtain during the Cold War. These took place in Poland from shortly after the end of World War II until the regaining of sovereignty in the early 1990s. Within those 40 years, many stories were available about Poles who fled to Western Europe. There were people who had escaped with their families and friends (portrayed, for example, in the episodes 'Jarecki', 'Tempelhoff—brama do wolności'/'Tempelhoff—The Gateway to Freedom'). There was also the group of soldiers on board the ORP Żuraw minesweeper, who took the crew hostage over the ship, and rerouted it to Sweden ('Bunt na Żurawiu'/'Rebellion on the Żuraw'). Then there was the escape in 1947, also to Sweden, of two students in the small boat 'Ramar' ('Żaglówką przez Bałtyk'/'Sailing a Boat Across the Baltic'); the glider pilot who built a plane in his flat and flew to Yugoslavia ('Kukułka'/'The Cuckoo'); and the romantic story of Nikolai Artamonov, a Soviet naval officer who fell in love with a Polish woman ('Potrójny agent'/'The Triple Agent'). This couple defected on a naval launch to Sweden, and then went to the United States (where he became the 'triple agent' of the title).

All these stories are real, and the TVN reporters who investigated them did so diligently and independently. They were able to enrich the archives of The Institute of National Remembrance (IPN)—instead of just relying on them. The series is intriguing also because of the way that the plot is constructed to respect human choices and individual freedom. In some cases, the characters are still anxious about their safety today, partly because they remain burdened with serious accusations. The journalist arrives at their current place of residence and asks them to tell their own version of the past events. These are quite often in conflict with the accounts of the others. The series focuses on the protagonists' motivations, the most common of them being the threat posed by the authorities, and a strong desire for freedom, supported by the frail belief that the life on the other side of the Iron Curtain was incomparably better (even if Communist propaganda did its best to tell them otherwise, and despite little or no access to objective information). The genuine value of the series is its lack of a uniform structure. The only invariable rule is the confrontation of real events, as revealed by documents, court files, and witness accounts, plus the memories of the actual people—the heroes of those events.

The first episode was ('Jarecki'), the story of Franciszek Jarecki, the airman who in 1953 hijacked a MiG-15 jet fighter and flew it to the island of Bornholm in Denmark. The complex narrative journey starts with a journalist's conversation with the hero who has come back to Poland after half a century. His arrival and the way he is welcomed at the airport are moving. The male voice-over acts as 'Voice of God', dispensing information like an omniscient nineteenth-century narrator, and fully aware of future events. For quite a while the viewer does not know what Jarecki accomplished in the past—all the more so because straight from the airport we go to Gdów, his home village in the Lesser Poland region. There, he is revealed to be the 1953 plane hijacker. Sepia shots show the scenes of war that shaped this future aviator: Jarecki watches war atrocities, the most powerful of them being the shooting of German prisoners of war by the Red Army. Enrolled at a school for pilots, he is persecuted by the Secret Police (UB), who are trying to recruit him as an informer. Much that follows is dramatic rather than documentary—some scenes turn out to be fantasy or dream sequences. This is followed by two fragments of a newsreel from the past. Hybridization is a feature of this episode—there is material shot in the 1950s side by side with footage from today.

'Rebellion Aboard the Żuraw', representing a 1951 incident, maintains the style of the black-and white films of that time. The episode 'Lot 747'('747 Flight') presents yet another escape that took place nearly during the period of martial law. The captain of the LOT Polish airlines hijacks a plane flying to West Berlin. This time, the journalists interview not only the captain, Czesław Kudłek, but also Jerzy Dziewulski, an anti-terrorist commander at that airport (and a man very popular in the media). 'Sailing a Boat Across the Baltic Sea' begins with a shot of a rough sea and a voice-over that sets the scene saying: 'The Baltic. A sea unfriendly to sailors. Short and steep waves. The weather changing rapidly. Violent storms.' This is followed by a conversation with a young sailor, an actor playing one of the students preparing to cross the Baltic in 1947. Thus the film actor, repeating the activity of the 1947 student, links past with present. The second layer presents a conversation taking place in Australia on board a huge yacht. Its owner is one of the actual fugitives as his older self, telling the journalist a story dating back over half a century. The stories constructed are full of telling contrasts: a rickety boat on the one hand, a luxury yacht on the other. A homemade plane versus combat fighter planes lying in wait.

The rhetorical structure of the 'Great Escapes' narrative is thus very interesting. Its task is generally to bring us close to the characters' emotional attitudes—the sphere of their choices and the responsibility for these choices. To achieve this, the voice-over constantly highlights the dangers faced, compensating for the fact that—as the journalist maintains—the 80-year-olds find it difficult to remember and to communicate. There is in one episode a clash, not of things or situations, but of the participants' memories of the past events. In the episode 'The Cuckoo', we see Mr Pieniążek building a glider which he intends to use for his escape. He wants to 'thumb his nose at the regime'. He talks of a particularly unpleasant security police officer who has been persecuting him. The series researcher/reporter seeks out this man, who denies any bad conduct towards the former fugitive. In that theatrical scene, one might say, the persecutor and the victim must agree to differ. It becomes clear that, actually, neither of them is sure of the accuracy of those events—their memories are cloaked in a 'semantic fog', so they begin to doubt their recollections of what happened. I think of this as 'confrontational docudrama', which has the potential to pose significant questions, many years after the events, and not insist on clear answers—docudrama becomes a serious educational and pop-science genre here.

CONCLUSION: A SILENT GHOST OF REALITY?

As John Corner has written in his account of the postwar changes to British documentary, as a result of the rise of television some of the prewar documentary impulse shifted towards the 'production of an event precisely for the purpose of spectatorship' (1996, p. 32). The challenges to representations of reality that followed have been many, but the advantages of this approach lay in what Corner calls the '*proxemics* of the dramatization' allied to the 'distance' inherent in rational documentary. I want to outline some general issues arising from my analysis of the three Polish docudramas above that typify this clash between drama and documentary. The first issue is the characteristically Polish attitude towards history which they display (though this might also apply to most countries in Central and Eastern Europe). Representation of the past has historically usually been tied to politics, as a result of regimes' control. Filmmakers in post-Communist countries have eagerly undertaken representation of the past in the era of the new dispensation. However, in general I find the approaches taken shallow and overemotional. Here I refer to those cases in which the docudrama framework (being most often a historical event subjected to reconstruction) has been burdened by a tendency towards trivialization, pushing aside serious function and impact.

On independence, Poles did indeed feel the hunger for documentary, and documentary filmmakers rose to the occasion, aided by the establishment of two specialist TV channels—'TVP Historia' (from 2007) and 'TVP Dokument' (2012). The latter, however, was suspended shortly after it started broadcasting, perhaps an effect of the preference already being shown for different docu-genres, which have been widely criticized for lowering the level of the viewers' tastes. These still dominate the schedules of the majority of TV stations. Polish TV viewers are nouveau riche in their dealings with the post-Communist media, and seemingly anxious about missing anything that the so-called Western TV culture can offer. This suits the general strategy of a media business whose aim is always to win and then keep the attention of the audience. Polish docudrama's chances for the future are a slightly different case: in this crazy world of rush and mediocrity, docudrama has begun to play the role of a serious genre, being in its best manifestations an educational, high-end, product. The biographical series format has increasingly shown this to be the case; for example, in the case of the 2013 series *Anna German* (TVP1). It tells the story of a famous Polish singer, a long-time resident in the Soviet Union, offering the viewer strong elements with which to identify. Reconstruction is tackled very diligently, with a great deal of care for material details: Anna German ceases to be a singer/person and becomes a metaphor for Poland and its people. Something similar can be claimed for *The Spies of Warsaw* (TVP1/BBC Worldwide, 2012–13), a mini-series based on the bestselling novel by Alan Furst.

These programmes go beyond the area of the sensational because—while still producing something for a wide audience—they enable us to consider questions about historically relativized notions of ethics. The docudrama *Gra o Nobla* (Nobel Game) is a similar case in point. A commercial television production (TVN, 2008), it depicts events behind the scenes of, and controversies over, the awarding of the Nobel Peace Prize to Lech Wałęsa in 1983. So, seen from the Polish perspective, docudrama has begun to occupy a special place on the map of genres and subgenres with the prefix 'docu', all of which bear some reference, however slight, to the documentary tradition of the twentieth century. Entertainment has been left to other forms, the easier ones, while docudrama is distinguished by its high-end production skills as well as a serious, pro-social, attitude towards the reality presented.

The other general issue is theoretical in nature and refers to situating docudrama as a specific television genre on an axis between the two poles: fact and fiction. I anticipate that the development of docudrama in Poland in the coming years might be marked by its bouncing between these poles. I see the genre going through a documentary + drama + entertainment stage in the future. As one phase ends, something new is born, as is the case in any part of the contemporary media. A British television series *Witold Pilecki: a Volunteer for Auschwitz* features a Polish soldier, a Rittmeister in the Polish Cavalry—Witold Pilecki (in an episode directed by Joshua Whitehead).[12] The documentary presents the profile of a Polish hero who volunteered to be imprisoned in Auschwitz in order to organize a resistance movement on its premises as well as gather information for the Allies. The documentary is accurate in terms of historical data, and many famous people contributed interviews.[13] From time to time the viewer notices a ghost figure flashing by the screen: a man in his thirties, wearing a military uniform. It is the hero, Witold Pilecki, who says nothing and does not take part in the narrative. By his presence he guarantees that the events presented are credible. I am afraid that in a tangle of ignorance and doubt as to whether fiction confirms reality, or whether reality demands an element of fiction so as to be better accepted by the public, the idea of a silent ghost might be the only option for the future of the Polish docudrama: witnessing the world more or less truthfully presented; a world caught between difficult and easy pleasures. A world of viewers who may have abandoned the pastime of 'amusing themselves to death', yet think they are done with their docudrama lesson.

NOTES

1. See Ł. Maciejewski (2005, p. 155).
2. On the *Big Brother* phenomenon in Poland, see Godzic (ed. 2001) and Godzic (2004).
3. http://ninateka.pl/film/rozmowy-istotne-kazimierz-karabasz, accessed 15 October 2014.
4. While documentary films were often screened in cinemas, during the Communist era's period of martial law they were banned from television. In the brief Solidarity period, some were, however, shown on TV.
5. For example, see the comments of Prof. Paweł Wieczorkiewicz on the popular TVP Historia channel.
6. Barbara Blida was a prominent left-wing MP. She was accused of taking bribes and during the process of arrest in her apartment she shot herself.
7. Literally, 'Our Mothers, our Fathers'—but *Generation War* is the title of the international release.
8. See http://www.filmweb.pl/serial/Nasze+matki%2C+nasi+ojcowie-2013-625585, accessed 20 May 2015.
9. http://en.wikipedia.org/wiki/Czas_honoru, accessed 7 January 2015.
10. http://pl.wikipedia.org/wiki/Czas_honoru, accessed 7 January 2015.
11. http://forum.tvp.pl/index.php?topic=677349.0, accessed 7 January 2015.
12. This was a Sky Vision production for the British History Channel, 2013. The documentary has been shown in Polish on TVP1 (with Polish translation). The series was titled *Heroes of War*.
13. Among those interviewed were Dr Halik Kochanski (author of *The Eagle Unbowed*), Professor Władysław Bartoszewski (former prisoner in Auschwitz and also former Polish Minister of Foreign Affairs), and Professor Jan Wysocki (Pilecki's biographer).

Italian Docudrama: From the Experimental Moment to Biography as Text of Identity

Milly Buonanno

A NEGLECTED FORM OF STORYTELLING

'For more than forty years now I've been speaking prose without knowing it.' Paraphrasing Monsieur Jourdain's famous remark in Molière's *Le Bourgeois Gentilhomme*, one could say that Italian television has been producing docudramas for more than half a century without apparently knowing it. Or to be more precise: without this specifically hybrid 'mode of story-telling' (Lipkin 2011, p. 2), which is made up of a variegated combination of documentary and drama, fact and fiction, ever having been acknowledged and categorized even by means of the basic way of identifying things—the choice of 'the word to say it' (Cardinal 1983). In fact the word docudrama—or one or other of the 'Siamese twin terms' (Paget 2011, p. 94) drama-documentary and documentary drama—is almost non-existent in the professional vocabulary of Italian television and hardly ever crops up in scholarly discourse. It is not used in references to Italian TV drama, as if the docudrama form were alien to the tradition of Italian storytelling. The absence of any definition (whether taken directly from English or reformulated in Italian) seems all the more strange in that—as I intend to demonstrate—the docudramatic mode of representation of real-life people, events, and problems is anything but alien to Italian television's narrative practices: it has played a major role from the beginning of public broadcasting (RAI) in the 1950s, helping to mould the form and

© The Editor(s) (if applicable) and The Author(s) 2016
T. Ebbrecht-Hartmann, D. Paget (eds.), *Docudrama on European Television*, Palgrave European Film and Media Studies,
DOI 10.1057/978-1-137-49979-0_4

content of a steady stream of programmes, both drama-documentaries and documentary dramas.[1]

Admittedly, labelling a generic hybrid that can encompass an 'amazing variety' (Rosenthal, 1999a, p. xv) of combinations is objectively a complicated task. As noted by Derek Paget, 'the difficulties peculiar to the docudrama' [are not just] 'a question of definition', which often 'lags behind practice' in the case of the arts (2011, p. 120); the same author however acknowledges that the definition is useful in informing discussion and promoting understanding. But in the Italian case more than five decades of intensive production of biographies, historical reconstructions, dramatization of headline news, crimes, causes célèbres and much else besides do not seem to have stimulated any interest or commitment in professional and academic circles when it comes to defining and debating the form, beyond a few discussions surrounding the very first experiments, to which I will refer later.

One could cite as partial explanation the weak level of formalization and analytical articulation in Italian television jargon, which prefers to use umbrella terms such as *sceneggiato, telefilm, miniserie*, perhaps accompanied by a generic specification: for example, biographical or historical mini-series (in this connection see Lipkin 2002, p. x). This is something essentially different, in terms of information supplied and expectations aroused, from calling a programme a 'documentary drama' (Paget 2011). But it is also likely that, from the beginning, it was the intersection between fact and fiction—the two elements conventionally regarded as hardly compatible, indeed opposed, in relation to generic codes and conventions, ethics and aesthetics, and truth-claims—that complicated and in short discouraged the conceptualization and definition of a mode of representation that was hybrid, mixed, 'impure' and therefore liable to provoke reactions that were equally mixed and ambivalent. On the one hand, this mix did indeed lend itself to being identified and tried out by a group of convinced pioneers as an innovative way of making television, more consistent with both the (claimed) reality-oriented nature of the medium and public service broadcasting's mission to inform and entertain. At the same time the unprecedented typology of programmes generated by the merging of documentary and drama was bound to arouse some anxiety, since it seemed to challenge more legitimized and approved forms of storytelling, taking shape straight away as a potentially critical and controversial field; all this counselled caution in activating the processes of recognition starting from the coinage of a name.

Be that as it may, the lack of a proper name to acknowledge the existence and identity of docudrama did in all likelihood have an impact on the historiography of television. Italian television scholarship in fact largely failed to focus attention on this form of storytelling—especially the intense experimental phase that coincided with the first two decades of public broadcasting. Although it cannot be singled out as the decisive factor, the generic indefiniteness of this unnamed form has served to undermine the perception and evaluation of its relevance. Not by chance, a large number of historiographical reconstructions, exhaustive and well-documented in other respects, devote only brief passages to 'hybrid genres halfway between fiction and documentary' (Bruzzone 1984, p. 112),[2] to forms of 'merging between theatre, television and reality' (Grasso 2000, p. 865), to 'the first examples of hybrid genres in Italian television, a bit of TV drama, a bit of journalistic investigation' (Sorice 2002, p. 68). Other works confine themselves to pointing to 'an assumption of rather suggestive mixtures' (Monteleone 1999, p. 356); indicate that 'literature mingles boldly with journalism and history' (De Fornari 2011, p. 31); develop the definition of 'impure telefilm, that is to say the outcome of a contamination between televisual narrative and journalistic investigation' (Costa 1985, p. 26) or of 'derived forms' (Bellotto 1996, p. 189). In only one case, within a note of a few lines, is the term 'Italian-style docudrama' used (Barlozzetti 1988, p. 32). But this very recomposition of various fragments only restores a dwarfed vision, in terms of magnitude, continuity, and significance, of Italian docudrama at its inception: the picture that emerges from it, in the best cases, is that of a phenomenon not without interest in its considerable and often effective innovatory panache, but essentially residual. I must honestly admit that in my own study of Italian TV drama (Buonanno 2012a), I missed the opportunity to consider this neglected topic.

Neglect or unawareness of one aspect or another of the past or present televisual scenario is by no means unusual in historical studies, or in television studies in general, nor should it cause surprise: we are all aware that '[t]he selectivity of the discipline operates at a number of levels' (Wheatley 2007, p. 6) and that a greater or lesser measure of incompleteness or bias is inevitable when one has to deal with unlimited material. In this specific case, bias and omissions are also and perhaps mainly attributable to the monumental presence, in the same historical phase, of a narrative form that has enjoyed true hegemony in the production, supply, consumption, and not least the historiography of Italian TV drama: the *sceneggiato*.

Sceneggiato was the Italian name for 'literary adaptation', which was the privileged narrative genre of Italian television for two decades from the mid-1950s to the mid-1970s. It enjoyed huge success and remains to this day firmly established in the generational memory of older viewers (Colombo and Aroldi 2003). Italy did not of course have exclusivity in literary adaptation, which was cherished by European public television because it combined two of the three fundamental purposes of the public service: to educate and to entertain. But it was possibly in Italy that literary adaptations achieved a pre-eminent position on the domestic drama scene in terms of production volumes, very high ratings, and reputation for quality. The great patrimony of the nineteenth-century novel provided the sources for hundreds of adaptations that were destined to become immensely popular (Buonanno 2012a). The success of the *sceneggiato* was such that the word soon came into common use: not as the signifier of a specific narrative genre, but an all-embracing synecdoche and epitome of TV drama *tout court*, irrespective of different genres, formats, and styles. Not only literary adaptations in the true sense but also biographies and historical dramas were brought back at that time under the umbrella of the *sceneggiato*, which still has a certain currency today.

That such a widespread and sensational phenomenon should have attracted the attention of television scholars is easy to understand; but this was not without consequences. Although it has been said that 'paying scholarly attention to a genre and a form that is already privileged does not necessarily mean that others will be neglected' (Jacobs 2011, p. 508), the facts tell a different story. The superior standing of the *sceneggiato* has overshadowed the emergence and the burgeoning variety, in the same period of time, of the docudrama form. To attempt to throw a full light on this shady area of the historiography of Italian television would require far-reaching research into TV screenings in the past, which falls outside the objectives of the present work (and what is more this research would partly be thwarted by the difficulty of finding much material from that era in the archives). The overview that I am going to present is largely based on printed sources: TV reviews in newspapers, and especially the often very detailed descriptions to be found in the weekly magazine *Radiocorriere TV*.[3]

The Turn to Reality

'This hybrid of fact and fiction does not exist in a vacuum but is found in a complicated social, political, and economic environment' (Hoffer et al. 1985, p. 182). In order to trace a brief outline of the context in which forms of docudramatic representation began to flourish and multiply, we need to turn to the *sceneggiato*—if for no other purpose than to reassert that this veritable juggernaut of literary adaptation was not the only form of storytelling in the early history of television. We can place alongside the *sceneggiato* what was defined in Italy as the *originale televisivo* (television original), equating to the English term 'teleplay'. The name denoted a work that was created expressly for television and was not derived from other cultural forms like the novel. At that time the label 'original' seemed more like a piece of fanciful pretentiousness than a hallmark of artistic distinction, if for no other reason than because it betrayed the flawed cultural status of a new entrant lacking the legitimization accorded to more established and dignified art forms. And indeed the television original constituted a sort of 'cadet branch' of storytelling—and has continued to be so regarded—that needed to try out new paths to build up its own success and reputation. This made it an experimental ground, in which docudrama put down roots.

Interestingly enough, by taking the docudrama route the *originale televisivo* ended up following in the footsteps of the *sceneggiato*. While the *sceneggiato* drew its inspiration and narrative material from literary fiction, the docudrama established a privileged relationship with real-life people, events, and concerns. In fact both branches of televisual storytelling found conditions of existence and forms of nourishment, as it were, in external references; these also served as necessary and opportune sources of legitimization. As Charlotte Brunsdon observes, the image of good television was traditionally constructed in two main ways: [t]he first draws its legitimization from other already validated art forms: theatre, literature, music, [...] The other [...] poses a privileged relation to the "real" (Brunsdon 1997, pp. 112 and 113).

In cultivating special alliances with, respectively, literature and reality, *sceneggiato* and *originale televisivo* brought about diverse and complementary logics of distinction. These special alliances were guided by the same purpose, namely to earn the credentials of a 'good' form of storytelling, as expected of programming in public broadcasting. One of the major principles of the functioning of television as a cultural form, and more generally of popular culture, was thus acknowledged and applied from the beginnings of Italian TV drama. I am referring to the ingenious device of repetition (Eco 1984; Buonanno 2007), which draws on the vast reservoir of inspiration of 'the previously known'—whether it be a novel, a famous trial, top headline news, a celebrity, or an historic event—in order to capitalize on the proven appeal that already familiar texts or events can have to viewers. I shall return to this topic later, in connection with more recent shifts in docudrama.

While the *sceneggiato* had immediately assumed the distinctive features of a cultural vehicle, aimed at spreading awareness and appreciation of literary heritage among the (at that time) still largely illiterate Italian population, the turn of the *originale* to the docudrama needed a phase of trial and error before it took off in the 1960s, with the help of two driving factors. The first of these had matured into the context of a fairly intense discussion, involving scholars and theatre critics, on the possible course of the development of the *teledramma*.[4] The second factor by contrast originated from the process of redefining television's role, maintaining its non-renounceable principles of public service, in a phase of rapid transformation of Italian society as well as the evolution of televisual technology.

On the first point, even though in the beginning innovation and distinctiveness were not exactly the major concerns of Italian television, the RAI was urged by critics and theatrical personnel to develop a distinctive dramaturgical production for television. The live broadcasting of theatre performances or, more often, the transposition of theatrical settings and performances to a television studio—these being the ways in which television plundered traditional repertories—was deplored by many critics; they saw in such forms of filmed theatre an unresolved hybrid, chargeable with a double betrayal of both the stage tradition and the unexplored aesthetic potential of the small screen (D'Alessandro 1957; Doglio 1963). Precisely in this connection, experiments carried out abroad, especially in Anglo-American TV contexts, were considered with interest. For instance the US school of television dramaturgy, which during the 1950s had created a number of daring and socially progressive teleplays, was renowned and highly regarded in Italy. Innovative work by significant American creatives was well known; and the features of such work, including realistic dialogue, treatment of controversial political and social issues that drew inspiration from real-life situations, and the commitment to support 'risky confrontation with themes and reality' (Doglio 1963, p. 25), were particularly appreciated. Thus the nascent Italian television dramaturgy was offered, as an example and a model, the 'evolutionary parabola' that had brought American TV to experiment successfully with close encounters with reality, culminating in 'the form of a direct dialogue with the viewers, a dialogue about headlines stories and very topical issues' (Doglio 1963, p. 26).

There was an initial attempt to emulate international models towards the late 1950s with the teledrama *I figli di Medea* (Medea's Children, Programma Nazionale, 1959, dir. Anton Giulio Majano), which won a competition for best TV original. This Italian teleplay combined the codes and conventions of classical theatre with those of live television coverage of breaking news to tell the (purely invented) story of a child kidnapping (Buonanno 2016).[5] 'Medea's Children' was certainly not a docudrama, since it was not based on a true story (although the staging was orchestrated in such a way as to let viewers believe it); but it was more than just an experiment of stylistic innovation in the service of a hoax.[6] In fact it functioned as a sort of preliminary test of what would soon become a surge of docudramas in a broad spectrum of variants. It assessed, for instance, the appetite of Italian viewers for true stories and the possibility of making the conventionalized features of different genres coexist in the same piece of storytelling, so as to enhance the sense of truthfulness and the cognitive and emotional impact of the story. Critics' negative comments and the outraged reactions of viewers, once they had discovered the trick, probably served as a timely warning for the future. But from at least one point of view 'Medea's Children' could have been considered a forerunner of the docudrama, in its intent to stir up a debate on the incipient crisis of the traditional family structure: a crisis that in the experience and above all the perception and collective anxiety of Italians at that time showed all the evidence of a real fact and was without any doubt 'a issue of concern' to the national community (Lipkin et al. 2006, p. 14).

The shift to reality that had just been taken up by the teleplay received a strong boost in the 1960s, after the RAI had readjusted its own strategies, redefined its role in the country and—importantly—changed its top management. The RAI's new leadership chose to focus on the information component of the Reithian triad (to educate, inform, and entertain), wishing to make public television the central information system and opinion leader in a society that was in the grip of major sociopolitical and cultural changes. Italy was then in the midst of the so-called 'economic miracle' and was witnessing a massive phenomenon of migration from the south to the north of the country and the spread of new and modern customs and lifestyles. Television, having from its earliest years been used mainly for the transmission of humanist culture, now found itself given the priority task of helping to spread the knowledge of reality; for example, when the magazine *Radiocorriere TV* asked the most authoritative television critics what was to be expected of television in the future, nearly all of them put the emphasis on 'the need to widen contact with life's realities in all their aspects' (Colonna 1961, p. 8). Thus journalism departments were considerably strengthened and new fact-based programmes were created that introduced 'models of social investigation, historical reconstruction, current affairs discussion and popularization of science' (Monteleone 1999, p. 349). The docudrama was born in this context.

A Period of Intense Experimentation

In keeping with the new turn to reality, the inauguration of RAI's second channel in November 1961 also signalled the launch of the docudrama in its proper sense.[7] The teleplay *La trincea* (The Trench, Secondo Programma, 1961, dir. Vittorio Cottafavi) was the work of the novelist and playwright Giuseppe Dessì; he used family archives to reconstruct an episode from World War I in which his father had played a leading role. At the start of the broadcast, the author himself informed viewers that this was a true story; the dramatization in dry journalistic style was accompanied by comments in voice-over and displayed signs of authenticity such as the use of real military uniforms, arms, and World War I equipment. The critics acknowledged that the work 'was comparable to the most recent American "mixed originals"' (Doglio 1963, p. 363).

The spate of docudramas that followed in the course of that decade and the next encompassed the form's main functions or intentions—retelling historical events, representing the lives of significant figures, and provoking debates about relevant issues—as indicated by Lipkin et al. (2006) and further elaborated by Paget (2011). In its contrived and ineffective fashion, 'Medea's Children' had already indicated how crisis in the family was an issue of serious concern to traditional family-orientated Italian society, or was widely perceived as such: that is to say, this crisis took the form of the transformation of the patriarchal model under the impact of modernization processes. Therefore the extensive production of teleplays was intended to investigate and analyse the causes and consequences of the changes taking place in family life. Worth mentioning in this connection is the successful anthology series *Vivere insieme* (Living Together, Programma Nazionale, 1962–1970), which unfolded over almost the entire decade in 80 monthly episodes, each of them portraying a typical case of 'breakdown of family life' (Sciascia 1965, p. 10). The original idea of basing each episode on a recent headline story was abandoned for reasons of prudence, so the teleplays did not relate real events; but their explicit claim to be portraying reality rested on an in-depth style of documentation that made them 'well-documented dramas' (if not documentary dramas), to cite the definition suggested by Woodhead (1999 p. 105) for *Cathy Come Home* (see also Corner 1996). In fact the cases that were dramatized in each episode, although not true, had been based on a range of situations and events taken from newspaper reports, social research, and advice from experts and scholars. Furthermore the stories, though invented, did not adopt the narrative structure of a fictional tale as they did not come to an end; the conclusions were left to be discussed by a panel of experts, tasked to provide tools of interpretation and suggestions on how to resolve the issues in question. Critics were probably right to deplore the failure of Italian scriptwriters to emulate the vibrant realism of English and American dramatized documentaries. Nevertheless the series managed to enter the public sphere thanks to a range of 'extra-textual elements' (Paget 2011, p. 117): these included the panel discussion already mentioned, letters from viewers, radio phone-ins, and numerous conferences and debates on the crisis of the family that were fostered by the programme's popularity.

Family matters would continue to inspire docudramas up to the early 1980s; their acute sociological sensitivity compensated for the fact that they were not based on true stories. They were inspired by what Corner defines as 'a documentarist ambition' (Corner 1996, p. 38) to portray the most problematic and even harsh sides of the changing social reality. Sometimes, as in the case of the teleplay *Dedicato a un bambino* (Dedicated to a Child, 1971, Programma Nazionale, dir. Gianni Bongioanni) on the theme of an unhappy childhood (a production much appreciated by both public and critics) the dramatization assumed the structure of a press investigation and introduced interventions from experts and witnesses into the extra-diegetic space. The formal variations in the works did not however form part of a process of codification of the docudramatic mode, but were an expression of the author's personal style. Gianni Bongioanni, the director, was renowned for his neo-realist approach and documentary filming style, which had matured through his earlier experience as a war documentary filmmaker.

Vittorio De Seta's *Diario di un maestro* (Teacher's Diary, Programma Nazionale, 1973, dir. Vittorio De Seta) is another work that can be traced back to the author's original artistic profile. De Seta, one of the greatest Italian directors of the age (though for a long time neglected), was the creator of unique works that combined the filming styles and expressive resources of both *cinéma-vérité* and realistic narrative in order to create a truthful and at the same time poetic rendering of reality. 'Teacher's Diary' was inspired by the experience of a schoolteacher and set in the elementary school of a poor suburb in Rome. In accordance with neo-realist practice, the young actors appearing in the roles of the classmates were taken from the street and were left free to express themselves in a spontaneous *extempore* fashion, while the teachers and school staff were played by professional actors following a script (which nevertheless remained open to improvisation). Thus De Seta constructed a story with strong connotations of naturalness and veracity, which in its well-calibrated amalgam of documentarist approach, narrative fiction, and social criticism succeeded in portraying in the most convincing and involving manner the social marginalization and cultural deprivation—but also the possibility of deliverance—of the inhabitants of the urban suburbs in an Italy that was on course to become an affluent society. The programme was enormously successful—15 million viewers watched the final episode—and received critical acclaim for its 'high artistic and civic standard' (Buzzolan 1973, p. 7). 'Teacher's Diary' was later to be defined as 'the most influential example of the possibilities offered by a combination of TV fiction and documentarism' (Aprà 1995, p. 290).[8]

By the beginning of the 1960s, public TV had reached half of Italy's population and the launch by RAI of a second channel created the conditions for a growing differentiation between the demand and supply of programmes. Research on viewers' tastes demonstrated that although light entertainment, music shows, and *sceneggiati* remained at the head of preferences, the interests of a significant number of viewers were shifting towards 'more serious genres, in particular informative programmes, documentaries and above all *those of a historical character*' (Lugato 1963, p. 7, italics mine). Thus numerous documentary and popular history programmes came into existence, especially on the second channel, and a great many dramatized reconstructions of historical events were produced. Docudrama using historical reconstruction grew in a fairly blurred area at the intersection between *sceneggiato*, teleplay, and theatrical prose (thus boasting real potential for spectacular staging).

A number of *sceneggiati* on the Italian Risorgimento—the sociopolitical process of nation-building in the nineteenth century—had already been attempted, but were mediated through novelistic fiction. The programmes of the 1960s established a direct relationship to historical reality and also drew on the international scene. Thus the big season for historical docudrama was inaugurated by *I giacobini* (The Jacobins, Programma Nazionale, 1962, dir. Edmo Fenoglio), an 'original' (of theatrical origin, if the truth be told) in instalments that portrayed the French Revolution through the towering figures of Robespierre and Saint Just. The potential for controversy inherent in docudrama emerged immediately with *The Jacobins*. Its re-enactment of the French Revolution was clearly biased in favour of Robespierre as the positive hero, the most authentic incarnation of the revolutionary spirit. This interpretation was 'corroborated and in part authorized by studies of recent historiography' (Calcagno 1962, p. 15), as RAI's house magazine reassured its readers, insisting on the author Federico Zardi's 'objective, continuous and almost meticulous verification of facts' (ibid). The general appreciation of the excellent direction and acting did not spare the programme from political controversy, destined to generate quantities of extra-textual material—especially after the then secretary of the Italian Communist Party, Palmiro Togliatti, normally a harsh critic of state television, defined the transmission of *The Jacobins* as 'an important event of national culture'(see Ferretti et al. 1997, p. 241).

The *Grandi processi della storia* (The Great Trials of History, Programma Nazionale, 1962, dir. Carlo Lodovici), again devoted to key personalities of the French Revolution (Louis XVI, Marie-Antoinette, and Danton), was in turn broadcast in 1962. Viewers were assured of the 'substantial' fidelity of the text to the selected subject and were shown a dramatization of the trials accompanied by a voice-over that served as a commentary, link, and contextualization of the scenes. The courtroom formula proved very successful and went beyond reconstruction in the historical and political sense. It gave rise to a flood of anthology series and single plays in the 1980s, inspired by *causes célèbres* and crime news (Buonanno 2012a). Between 1967 and 1974, for example, the series *Di fronte alla legge* (In the Face of the Law, Programma Nazionale, 1967–74) broadcast events in court that had troubled public opinion, creating a conflict between legal order and moral consciousness. *Processi a porte aperte* (Trials with Open Doors, Programma Nazionale, 1968–71) for its part chose to recall major judicial events of the present and past, national and international, which had caused a scandal because of the nature of the crimes or the people involved, and had over a long period fired and divided public opinion on the guilt and innocence of those accused, and the justice or arbitrariness of the final verdict. The claim that the programme was a documentary was expressed in the assertion that 'the screenplay is based on the transcripts of the discussions and every particular is strictly authentic' (Kezich 1968, p. 57) and corroborated by the use of various types of documentary material. The voice-over was replaced by the visible presence of a narrator, whose task was to guide viewers through the meanderings of legal debate.

The *causes célèbres* genre, whose origins go back to the first half of the nineteenth century, may be regarded as a literary forerunner of the TV docudrama. A hybrid composed variously of elements from the popular novel, courtroom reports, literature, and law, the genre drew its narrative material from the vast reservoir of legal archives of famous lawsuits. Published collections of *causes célèbres* enjoyed massive national and international popularity, until the dramaturgical potential of the genre and its capacity for involving viewers turned it into a suitable resource for television. Or at any rate, for Italian television.

It is worth mentioning in conclusion the series *Teatro-inchiesta* (Theatre Inquiry, Secondo Programma, 1966–71) devised by Leandro Castellani, an experienced and award-winning director of *sceneggiati*, historical documentaries, and journalistic investigations. Keeping its distance from both banal documentarism, essentially limited to iconographic materials, and fictional reconstructions, the scheme of 'Theatre-Inquiry' was based on the alternation and fusion of two basic elements: 'dramaturgical documentation' (Castellani 1995, p.175) or rather the dramatization of official documents, letters, and trial records, brought to life by professional actors; and a true investigation based on witness statements, interviews, documentary shots, analyses, and debates on spoken and visual materials. Of the various forms of docudrama that were being tried out on Italian TV in the years of the 'turn to reality', 'Theatre-Inquiry' was probably the one that came closest to the idea of a drama-documentary. In subsequent decades public TV has produced a continuous sequence of docudramas; commercial TV, born in the 1980s, has gone in the same direction, although to a lesser extent. But there is no doubt that the 1960s were for Italian docudrama a unique period of pioneering experimentation in new expressive modalities and new forms of storytelling; it is worth recalling that in keeping with the educational intentions of the public service, the aim of these experimentations was not 'ever purely escapist but inclined towards knowing, acknowledging and possibly interpreting the social and cultural reality of Italy and the world' (Monteleone 1999, p. 355).

THE RISE OF BIOGRAPHICAL DOCUDRAMA

These same years also saw the birth of the biographical docudrama in Italy.[9] This came into being half a century ago, in 1964. In the first half of this timespan 50 biopics were produced and broadcast; the second half, from the early 1990s to the present day, has seen as many as 135 television biographies, most of them broadcast in the 2000s. These figures show how the dramatization of the lives of real personalities has grown over a quarter century. It is now a staple of Italian prime-time drama under the 'biographical miniseries' label and a key storytelling resource for popular successes. Historical and topical docudramas have also flourished, but biography has often come to encompass history and topicality, further enhancing the inherent hybrid nature of the docudrama form; my selected case study *Perlasca. Un eroe italiano* (Perlasca. An Italian Hero, RAI 1, 2002, dir. Alberto Negrin) is a case in point, as I shall show. In talking about the rise to prominence of the biography genre, it is worth stressing that the latter and more generally any kind of reality-based television drama in Italy are no longer what they used to be in the experimental phase: the major change is that documentary codes, conventions, and styles have progressively disappeared on the way to a canonized mode of fictional storytelling that hardly if ever makes explicit claims to a documentary status and authenticity, but nonetheless asserts and displays the essential docudramatic requisite of being 'based on' real-life documented stories.

A number of 'great Italians'—an artist (*La vita di Michelangelo*/The Life of Michelangelo, Programma Nazionale, 1964, dir. Silverio Blasi), a poet (*La vita di Dante*/The Life of Dante, Programma Nazionale, 1965, dir. Vittorio Cottafavi), an architect of Italian unification (*La vita di Cavour*/The Life of Cavour, Programma Nazionale,1967, dir. Piero Schivazappa), and a genius of the Renaissance (*La vita di Leonardo da Vinci*/The Life of Leonardo da Vinci, Programma Nazionale, 1971, dir. Renato Castellani)—provided the inspiration for the first biographical dramas. In an attempt to classify something that was neither a documentary nor a dramatized novel, the definition 'cultural performance' was put forward to epitomize the alternation of documentarist sequences, historical reconstructions, and dramatization of episodes in the life of the subject.

The advance publicity for the programmes in the pages of RAI's official magazine was at pains to make impassioned claims for, and guarantees of, rigorous historical reconstruction: '*La vita di Dante* is drawn entirely from the documents [...] it has the riveting accuracy and urgent force of a historical document' (Castellani 1965, p. 21). In introducing 'The Life of Cavour', which used extracts from the statesman's letters and speeches and even transcripts of parliamentary sessions to construct a large amount of the conversations, RAI's press office promised that 'nothing was left to unfettered imagination' (quoted in Grasso 2000, p. 177).

Never before had there been such insistence on the sacredness of historical sources and documentary materials; this was a rhetorical strategy (though adhering to authors' accepted practice). They were intent on legitimizing the nascent form of biographical docudrama through the appeal to authoritativeness and trustworthiness of a scrupulously explored documental corpus. This 'strategic ritual' was aimed in part at anticipating and forestalling criticism or controversy—all vital when dealing with monumental figures in Italy's history. The ritual was also informed by the ethical standards of accuracy and truthfulness required by public service broadcasting. But from the repeated denials that the biographies had been 'fictionalized', and in particular the irrefutable and almost indignant tone of affirmations such as 'nothing is left to the imagination', a certain suspicion emerged as to the intrinsic inadequacy of fictional storytelling to portray real-life subjects, except with the decisive support of a documentary mode of engagement. Paradoxically, for a televisual culture that has never acknowledged the docudrama, this was an endorsement of the docudramatic form.

An unusual confrontation between fact and fiction was staged in *The Life of Leonardo da Vinci*. This biographical docudrama, awarded the Golden Globe in 1972 for the best television special, for the first time in Italy allowed the figure of a narrator in modern dress to feature in the same stage space as the dramatic action, assuming the role of guarantor of factual accuracy as against the imaginary versions to be found sometimes in the same historical sources. The scene of Leonardo's death, for example, was initially re-enacted on the basis of a widespread popular belief about its circumstances, borne out by one of his biographers, only to be immediately denied by the verdict of the narrator on the stage: 'It's all fiction'.

Famous film directors were judged against the standards of televisual biography. Roberto Rossellini, the world-famous master of neo-realism, was the director of the philosophers' tetralogy in the 1970s: *Socrate*

(Socrates, Programma Nazionale, 1971), *Blaise Pascal* (Programma Nazionale, 1972), *Agostino di Ippona* (Augustine of Hippo, Programma Nazionale, 1972) and *Cartesius* (Descartes, Programma Nazionale, 1974). *Gesù di Nazareth* (Jesus of Nazareth, Rete Uno, 1977) was directed by Franco Zeffirelli, a former pupil of Luchino Visconti. It remains 'the biblical drama in television against which all others are judged' (Marill 2007, p. 107). Cesare Zavattini, himself an exponent and a theorist of neo-realism, provided the screenplay for *Ligabue* (Rete Uno, 1977, dir. Salvatore Nocita), depicting a human and artistic rise and fall of one of the most important naive painters of the twentieth century.[10]

A run of international awards and a high reputation, and the touch of the maestros of cinema—even if, truth to tell, the biographies directed by Rossellini turned out to be rather disappointing in their mix of intellectualism and didacticism—did not prevent the biographical docudrama from acquiring a rather unflattering 'narrative image' (Ellis 1992) as a genre weighed down by its didactic armour, resorting too easily to pedantic tones and deploying the conventional and hypocritical modes of the hagiography. In fact the biography genre suffers from a sort of 'imbalance of status' between, on the one hand, a high position in the scale of viewers' preferences and, on the other hand, a seemingly widespread neglect on the part of scholars and critics, as confirmed by a number of authors. In the opening of his famous study on biographies in the popular American press in the first half of the twentieth century, Leo Lowenthal observed that 'surprisingly enough, not very much attention has been paid to this phenomenon' (Lowenthal 1944, p. 109). For his part Steve Neale, in placing the biography among the 'major genres' of Hollywood films, noted the lack of 'critical esteem' (Neale 2000, p. 60) that has been a constant feature of the genre's history—George Custen's study (1992) being among the few exceptions. Finally Dennis Bingham makes a point of emphasizing the 'low repute' of this 'respectable genre' (Bingham 2010, p. 3). Italy is no exception to this. Yet low repute does not seem to have prevented the rebirth of the biographical docudrama, after a partial eclipse between the late 1970s and the early 1990s. There is no doubt that 'an active interest in life-stories continues' (Anderson and Lupo 2008, p. 50), in Italy as elsewhere.[11]

What has changed over time, however, are the conventions and styles of narration, as I have already noted at the beginning of this section, and the choice of whose lives are considered to be worthy of biographical treatment. The earlier mentions of some of the biographies of the 1960s and 1970s provide clear indications of the categories of subjects whose lives 'should be told' (Lipkin 2002, p. 1). Creative artists, scientists and inventors, thinkers and philosophers enjoyed pride of place and were the protagonists of half (25 out of 50) of the biopics produced in that period, consistent with the ideals of humanistic and literary culture, as well as with the educational mission of public television—progressively watered down and left behind though the latter may have been in the competitive climate brought about by the advent of commercial television in the 1980s.

By contrast, artists and thinkers are in short supply in the substantial corpus of biographical docudramas produced in more recent years, where the most frequently portrayed personalities are unquestionably religious figures; biographies of saints, popes, holy men, and figures from the Old and New Testaments make up more than half of the entire corpus and, still more importantly, have dominated the ratings and thus ensured a long series of popular successes. In Buonanno 2012, I analysed the surge of interest in religious personalities that began to surface in Italy in the early 1990s. Here I shall address the cluster of biographical docudramas that have their origin in, and are constitutive of, a significant and enduring trend of the 'return to the past' that has been a feature of televisual storytelling in the 2000s, in Italy and elsewhere.

In the last twenty years or so the biography genre, and Italian docudrama in general, has drawn more than ever before on religion and the historic past, as well as headline news (the docudramas produced by the commercial networks rely for preference on the latter). These sources have supplied a host of people and events for dramatization. Indeed Italian television drama has a growing appetite for reality-based stories, which play an essential role in providing 'previously known' subject matter for a storytelling system that has only recently been oriented towards seriality. This peculiar feature is testified to by the predominance of the quasi-cinematographic two-part mini-series in prime-time drama production, supply and consumption. The mini-series is deprived of the serial device of repetition, which in drama series and serials is an integral part of narrative structures—think of the lengthy portrayal of the same situation or issue, the equally protracted representation of the same community of characters (Buonanno 1993). It is inclined therefore to rely on external reference systems in order to exert an effective 'convocative power' on viewers. And there is no doubt that religion, history, and the news constitute an immense reservoir of reality-based subjects from which a wealth of narrative inspiration can be drawn. These subjects have considerable dramaturgical and emotional potential; they allow the creation of docu-dramatic works that benefit from the promotional value inherent in the notoriety and popularity earned by the people and facts chosen (saints, popes, historical events and personalities, news items). Or at any rate they benefit from the curiosity aroused by names and stories that re-echo and resound in the common memory, even if only by hearsay. Real-life stories, whether biographical or of another type, assure the viewer of a 'return of the previously known', which has made them a source of special inspira-tion for the Italian mini-series and, together with other factors, contrib-uted to the growth of docudrama at a time when the mini-series was the unquestioned queen of Italian prime-time drama.

THE RETURN TO THE PAST

At the beginning of the third millennium an extensive trend of 'return to the past' affected Italian televisual storytelling, providing the breeding ground for a flurry of costume dramas, and in particular docudramas, that only in very recent years have started to decline in number. Admittedly, the temporal switch of television drama from the present to the past is a phenomenon that has impacted on many other countries in Europe. This is attested by the chapters in this book; but perhaps we can find no more compelling evidence of the temporal turn than in the profusion of biographical and historical docudramas that have been aired on Italian television in the 2000s. As previously mentioned, biographies have had the lion's share, followed by historical reconstructions—although in real-ity it is difficult and perhaps unproductive to trace dividing lines between the two narrative typologies, since most of the biographies are insepa-rable from, and indeed constitute a primary vehicle for, the recreation of events and processes in a true historical sense. Life stories are often complex narrative constructs, where the portrait of the protagonist stands against the background, or is placed in the midst, of the historical events and circumstances that characterized his/her times. Fascism, Nazism, World War II and the genocide of Jewish people, for instance, have much more than a marginal place in the biographies of Pope John XXIII (*Papa Giovanni/Joannes XXIII*, RAI 1, 2002, dir. Giorgio Capitani) and John Paul II (*Karol: un uomo che divenne papa*/Karol: A Man Who Became Pope, Canale 5, 2005, dir. Giacomo Battiato), in addition to being the basic narrative material of the biopic of Giorgio Perlasca.

A particularly distinguishing feature of the turn to the past in contemporary storytelling is the focus on twentieth-century history. More precisely, the great majority of docudramatic works created in the 2000s were set in the restricted timespan of the early 1940s, in the final phases of World War II and its immediate aftermath. Television drama, in assuming the role of narrator of this history, followed in the footsteps, and considerably increased the number of viewers, of popular historical programmes that from the late 1990s onwards began to be aired in prime time on the third RAI channel (Anania 2003). These documentary series gave preference to topics related to Fascism, Nazism, and World War II and adopted a presentational style that, in taking advantage of the rich film documentation to be found in national and international archives, heavily relied upon the appeal of images to represent the people and events of a still recent and controversial period of history. While not yet 'a big business', to quote Edgerton (2001, p. 2), history had given significant proof of its potential as a driving force for success.

The displacement from documentary to fiction achieved the objective of reaching a broader generalist audience, who in most cases responded favourably, at times en masse, to the appeal of dramatized historical facts and life stories that were more or less shaped by imagination. Although the range and intensity of the successes earned by historical biopics remain below the extremely high level of religious dramas, the re-enactment of the twentieth century managed to corroborate—in both supply and demand—the role of 'television [docudrama] as historian' (Edgerton 2001). In fact phenomenological observation and an ever-growing corpus of studies bear out convincingly the assumption that 'television is the principal means by which most people learn about history today' (Edgerton 2001, p. 1). 'Television', confirms Lynn Spigel, 'serves as one of our culture's primary sources for historical consciousness' (Spigel 2001, p. 368). Pickering and Keightley, for their part, state that 'uses of the past in contemporary media contribute to a historical imagination' (2006, p. 930). More critically, Silverstone has observed that the media 'claim historical authority in drama and documentary' (1999, p. 127).

To recognize television as a primary source of historical awareness for the majority of individuals today is not of course the equivalent of according television the status of a source that is appropriate, reliable, and truthful. 'Television as historian' is a contestable and contested subject, still more so when it comes to dramatized reconstructions: not only when the relationship of the story with an external reference is declaredly ephemeral or elusive (television dramas vaguely or remotely inspired by....) but also when the strategic ritual of scrupulously followed documentary evidence and expert advice is deployed. The truth is that television drama is set in the field of popular historiography and popular memory; hence it is more committed to creating the conditions for emotional involvement and persuasion (Lipkin 2002) than to pursuing the objective of accurate historiographical knowledge. Popular historiography, in particular, revisits the past and offers versions reworked in the light of contemporary sensibilities and interests. As John Caughie succinctly remarks: 'History becomes the present in costume' (2000b, p. 211); and the past proves useful, lending itself to be re-enacted and even rewritten from a perspective that is more consonant with the concerns and designs of the present. This is what has happened with the docudramas of the 2000s; they appear to have been largely informed by a specific politics of memory and identity pursued by Italian television, at a time when the sense of community and national identity seemed to be wavering under the impact of political and ideological tensions and a pervasive 'syndrome of decline' (Diamanti 2009) in Italy.

Historical memory is often marked by conflict. For reasons pertaining to the civil wars and deep politico-ideological fractures that have characterized Italian history and life since national unification, 'Italian memories have often been divided' (Foot 2009, p. 1); and 'markedly different and often conflicting strands of memory' (Perra 2010, p. 4) have clashed and still clash concerning the 'legitimate version' of historical facts. Thus the intention to create a common memory about Italian history in the twentieth century, a crucial and controversial period, has informed the docudramatic narratives prompted by the temporal turn of the early 2000s; this intention was closely intertwined with a project of national reconciliation that hinged upon the recognition of a common matrix of Italian identity.

The Perlasca Case and the Memory of the Shoah

The 2002 biographical docudrama *Perlasca. Un eroe italiano* (Perlasca. An Italian Hero) is the most successful exemplar of that politics of memory and identity. The word 'successful' encompasses in this instance a double meaning: accomplishing an aim and gaining popularity. As for popularity, the two-part event mini-series, which premiered on the flagship public channel 28 and 29 January 2002, attracted over 12 million viewers and still holds the fourth position among the ten most watched TV dramas of the 2000s see Buonanno 2012a, pp. 191 and 211.(preceded in the ranking by three religious biopics). However I have chosen *Perlasca* as a case study not simply as an example of a success but for other reasons: in particular, the long period of time that was to elapse before the shifting 'politics of memory' relating to Italy's changing political climate rescued Giorgio Perlasca from oblivion and made him an appropriate figure for a docudramatic re-enactment as an emblem of Italian identity.

For decades hardly anyone in Italy had heard of Giorgio Perlasca and his efforts to rescue thousands of Hungarian Jews from extermination by the Nazis; but when his biopic was broadcast in the early 2000s, his story had already entered the public sphere thanks to a popular television current affairs programme (*Mixer*, RAI 2, 1990) and a biography *La banalità del bene* (The Banality of Goodness: The Story of Giorgio Perlasca, Deaglio, 1991). These had 'discovered' and revealed the story of the man who was soon—after the release of Spielberg's film *Schindler's List* in 1993— to be described as 'the Italian Schindler'. However the story of Perlasca entered the public consciousness not so much as a glorious page of hero-ism but as an 'incredible' case of an unsung hero whose noble deeds had remained buried in oblivion for nearly half a century. Thus the production of a docudrama fulfilled a double obligation: to confirm that those events actually happened and make overdue amends for the injury inflicted by a prolonged denial. As Millicent Marcus noted: '[t]his is a story about res-cue, but it is also about the rescue of a story' (2007, p. 126). Therefore the interest and pleasure derived by viewers from the re-enactment of an extraordinary story about rescue was presumably accompanied and inten-sified by their awareness of participating in the rescue of a story, thus making the docudrama something of a ritual of reparation. Wanting to do justice to a previously unsung hero would perhaps not have been a suf-ficient reason on its own; indeed a more compelling reason why the life of Perlasca 'should be told' (Lipkin 2002, p. 1) must be identified in the 'process of major change in the co-ordinates of public memory' (Focardi 2012, p. 242) that Italy witnessed at the end of the twentieth century. This change involved, among other things, criticism of and dissociation from the anti-Fascist paradigm that prevailed in postwar Italy.

Perlasca, of course, was an unconventional heroic figure, an 'unsuitable' person who did not seem to fit in with the heroic panoply of the post-Fascist Italy that emerged from World War II. Giorgio Perlasca's story is today sufficiently well known internationally to allow me to give only a brief outline. As a young man he participated as a volunteer in Mussolini's military campaigns in Ethiopia and Spain, but distanced himself from Fascism—though without becoming anti-Fascist—after Italy's alliance with Nazi Germany and the promulgation of the racial laws against Jews. As a dealer in livestock he found himself in Budapest in 1944 when the pro-Nazi party that had taken over after the German invasion of Hungary began to persecute and deport Jewish people. Initially trying to leave Budapest, Perlasca took shelter in the Spanish embassy; here he collaborated with a programme to save the Jews, put into effect by Spain in its position as a neutral country. When all the diplomatic staff of the embassy were transferred to Switzerland Perlasca elected, at the risk of his life, to stay behind. In his bogus post as Spanish Consul he managed in a few months to save over 5000 Jews by supplying them with false certificates of Spanish citizenship and giving them shelter and sustenance in 'safe houses' under the protection of the neutral countries. When he came back to Italy in 1945, Perlasca's attempts to obtain recognition for his deeds repeatedly came to nothing. It was not until the late 1980s that his 'heroic imposture' was revealed by a number of Hungarian survivors. In 1988 Perlasca was recognized by Yad Vashem, the Holocaust Martyrs' and Heroes' Remembrance Authority in Jerusalem, as one of the 'Righteous among the Nations'. His 'reputational trajectory' (Jansen 2007) in Italy began in the 1990s and reached its height in 2002, thanks to the eponymous docudrama.

A former Fascist who became a saviour of Jews: Perlasca, as a living oxymoron, was to prove a particularly inappropriate figure in the political climate of postwar Italy. By demonstrating the possible compatibility between being a (supposedly) wrong man (ex-Fascist) doing the right thing (saving Jews), Perlasca was casting doubts on the trend that then prevailed towards polarized political positions and opinions: the right or wrong side of the war, winners versus losers, Fascists against anti-Fascists. This biased stance effectively marginalized anyone who, like Perlasca, could not easily be identified with any of the opposed polarities. In any case, the continuing construction of a received truth concerning the anti-Fascist Resistance, which was to constitute the dominant narrative of memorialization for a long time to come, meant that nearly all the acts of heroism that were acknowledged and commemorated were those done by armed Resistance fighters. As Perlasca's story 'didn't fit' (Foot 2009), it was ignored.[12]

Furthermore, for some time after the war the subject of the Shoah was hardly a prominent issue of public debate. Perhaps also because they risked opening up embarrassing revelations about Italy's responsibility for the persecution of the Jews, stories circulating at the time about deportations and death camps were primarily about political deportees (Perra 2010; Gordon 2012). The extermination of Jews did not rank high among the things that 'should be' remembered.

It is therefore not surprising that the end of the *damnatio memoriae* that had silenced Perlasca's story (though his was not the only case) should have coincided with the rise to prominence in the Italian public sphere of the commemoration of the Shoah. The promotion of the memory of the Shoah, acknowledged in 2000 by a law instituting the solemn occasion of a national Remembrance Day, had taken shape in the 1990s during the dramatic political transition to the so-called Second Republic, following the Tangentopoli/Bribesville corruption scandal.[13] Owing to a range of both national and international factors—including the reinterpretation of Fascism advanced by an influential school of historiography, the turn already taken by the main Left political party after the fall of the Berlin wall, the rebuilding of identity put in train by the formerly Fascist-inspired right-wing party—the will to 'promote a new public memory that was disengaged from the conflict between Fascism and anti-Fascism' made strides in the 1990s political scene (Focardi 2012, p. 246).

The efforts to create a 'shared memory' found in the Shoah a special area of consensus, since anti-Semitism was by then being explicitly condemned by all political parties. The law that instituted the Remembrance Day, to be celebrated on 27 January (the date when the gates of Auschwitz were broken down) was unanimously approved by the Italian parliament; the wording of the law bore the traces of inevitable compromises (Fascism and Nazism were never mentioned) but included among the people who must be remembered 'those who even in camps and various groupings and at risk of their own lives saved other lives and protected the persecuted' (Art. 1, Law 211, 2000).

The valorization of the memory of the Shoah that gained ground in the new political and cultural scenario was a significant factor in making Perlasca's story 'fit in'. Meanwhile Perlasca had attracted international acclaim; the television programme and the biography already mentioned had made him known to a fair number of Italians; an important publishing house had issued his diaries posthumously *L'impostore*/The Impostor (Perlasca 1997); and in the wake of the huge resonance of Spielberg's film he had been dubbed 'the Italian Schindler'. Thus at the start of the twenty-first century (but not before), things had reached the stage when Perlasca's story 'should be told'—and there was also a way in which it 'should be told'.

In its fundamental definition, the docudrama is a reality-based form of storytelling where 'reality' refers to lives that have truly been lived, to events that really happened, recreated and re-enacted by the docudrama and often (but not always) pertaining to an era of the near or distant past. The Perlasca case—and in all probability it is not the only one—suggests an ulterior nuance of the reality with which the production of the docudrama is concerned: the reality of the present moment, the specific culture and political climate of the time that works as a 'gatekeeper', either favouring or obstructing the access of noteworthy lives, events, and deeds to the public storytelling scene. In some cases, noteworthiness has to pass the test of the *air du temps*.

BIOGRAPHICAL DOCUDRAMA AS A 'TEXT OF IDENTITY': *PERLASCA. AN ITALIAN HERO*

Perlasca's televisual biography (the customary Italian two-part mini-series) was made by RAI in 2001 in partnership with Hungary, Switzerland, and France. A big-budget international co-production it cost €12 million: a very high figure by contemporary Italian standards. A renowned director (Alberto Negrin), a successful producer (Palomar), a pair of well-known cinema scriptwriters (Stefano Rulli and Sandro Petraglia), an Oscar-awarded musician (Ennio Morricone),[14] and the most popular Italian TV drama actor (Luca Zingaretti) were mobilized in the production (filmed entirely on location). An impressive advertising campaign announced it as an event-mini-series. Italian historical docudramas, biopics, or even stories based on headline news are seldom conceived as 'low-concept low-budget' productions, like the movies of the week that were a feature of American television a few decades ago (Rapping 1992), since as a rule two-part mini-series are associated with higher production values and above-the-line expenditure. But in the Perlasca case public television's efforts in the production and advertising were almost without precedent, obviously in keeping with the ambitious objectives and the expectations linked to a story that was loaded with deep symbolic meanings and undeniable political implications. Not by chance, and replicating a ritual used for religious biographies (which are sometimes submitted in preview for the approval of high-ranking personalities in the Vatican), *Perlasca* was screened in Parliament a few days before it was aired on television. Even if unintentionally, the preview in Parliament—which the newspapers reported as having taken place 'in an emotional atmosphere'—seemed to bear witness to the accord between the docudramatic reconstruction and the conciliatory 'spirit of the law' that instituted Remembrance Day.

Perlasca. Un eroe italiano was premiered on the first public channel on 28 and 29 January 2002. It was the first and the most successful of the series of docudramas commemorating the Shoah that RAI was to produce in subsequent years and broadcast on each anniversary. As Derek Paget notes, 'Historical docudrama has always been ready to employ the rubric of the anniversary to justify itself and to attract audiences' (2011, p. 274). The introduction of Remembrance Day alongside the secular commemorations provided an institutional legitimization to this practice and has favoured the development of a specific strand of works commemorating the Shoah among the wide range of historical and biographical docudramas produced in the wake of the 'turn to the past'. In this connection, it may be appropriate to borrow from the analytical tools of memory studies the comprehensive notion of 'commemorative genres' (Tota 2001), which applies to the wide range of cultural artifacts—be they a monument, a diary, a museum, a novel, a poem, a plaque, or anything else besides—in which the remembrance of people and events is embodied and expressed in a concrete form. The notion would also prove suitable for biographical and historical TV docudramas, as narrative forms of the embodiment and institutionalization of collective memories as well as channels of historical consciousness and imagination.

Perlasca proved a huge success and generated an impressive surge of journalistic coverage that was almost unprecedented, not so much because of the abundance of extra-textual material as because of the unusually unanimous views of the numerous critics and other commentators (intellectuals, opinion leaders, columnists) who joined the debate. There were obviously gradations of approval, but even the few moderate reservations were expressed in the framework of a largely positive appraisal of the revival and broadcast of a remarkable story of heroism.[15] Many people commended RAI for having revived the lost mission of public service broadcasting and Italian viewers for having been able to distinguish and appreciate a piece of quality television, thus a story about rescue had helped to rescue, if only for a short time, the reputations of television and those who watched it (see Bechelloni 2003 and Marcus 2007 for excellent scholarly reviews).

By docudramatic convention, the mini-series displayed guarantees of truthfulness in its opening credits, in this instance the biography of Perlasca as a documental source and the guidance given to the scriptwriters by his biographer as well as his son and his widow. World

War II film clips were used in the dramatized scenes, tending to resemble documentary (for example, leaden colours in the photography effectively conveying an atmosphere of oppression and fear). At the end Perlasca himself appeared in a brief fragment taken from a television interview; his direct, if posthumous, testimony set a definitive seal on the authenticity of the story, while at the same time the striking lack of physical resemblance between Perlasca and the actor playing the part brought the story that had just been screened back to its status as a fictional narrative. A synthesis of the concept of docudrama was enclosed in a little documentary fragment.

According to Steven N. Lipkin, there are three 'arenas within which docudrama performs the past' (2011, p. 6); these all coexisted in *Perlasca*. It performed the life of a noteworthy *individual*, who witnessed noteworthy *events*, in the context of a *war*; the mini-series used and put together the various settings of the docudramatic representation in order to intensify the potential of the narrative to shape memory and make identity emerge from compelling constraints and confrontations. The miniseries' two-part title, *Perlasca. An Italian Hero*, is not the norm for biopics; the person depicted is normally famous enough to allow the viewer to place him or her in the appropriate agenda of the fame. The second phrase was deemed necessary, not only to attract viewers possibly still in the dark as regards Perlasca, but also to emphasize that the primary purpose of the docudrama was to tell the story of an *Italian* hero. Emphasis clearly needed to be put on his 'Italianness'. The narrative thus gives an account of the heroic deeds of a noteworthy man in whom viewers would be able to recognize (and enable them to see in themselves) the unequivocal features of a common identity and national sense of belonging. To this end it was necessary above all to remove the figure of Perlasca from the politico-ideological interpretation that had helped to keep him for decades under the blanket of a forgetful silence, in order to trace back the reasons for his actions to the sphere of a universalized humanitarian ethics, while demonstrating at the same time that such an ethical stance 'fits in' with the national character of Italians. It must be said that the ethical and non-political nature of Perlasca's heroism emerges from his memoirs, the written biography and numerous testimonies; thus the docudrama's claim to have kept to the truth was well founded. But it is also true that this ethical approach helped with the objective of constructing an heroic figure in whom most people could see themselves mirrored beyond political differences, in accordance with the conciliatory spirit of a shared memory.

The docudrama incorporated explicit verbal (as well as factual) emphasis in the words of the protagonist himself, or his interlocutors, indicating Perlasca's humanitarianism and status as a moral individual. This can be seen, for example, in his recollection of a boyhood dream of helping to 'make the world more humane'; or in his affirmation 'I thought it was a just war', to explain his participation as a volunteer in the Spanish Civil War. In exchanges taken almost word for word from Deaglio's biography: 'Why do you do all that?', one of his collaborators asks. 'What would you do in my place?' Perlasca replies. This question—'What would you do in my place?'—was the foundation of Perlasca's concept of the right thing to do, premised on the conviction that the circumstances of life and history speak to us and that each of us responds to the cogent call to action in accordance with our own system of values and our own inclinations, the inherent qualities of conscience, mind, and character. As Lipkin observes, '[the] extraordinary performance arises because it must' (2011, p. 140); this is without doubt the case with *Perlasca* (man and film). The compelling pressure of circumstances challenged the protagonist to carry out extraordinary and heroic deeds as a matter of moral *duty*—what the Ancient Greeks called *kairos*, the propitious moment for the unhesitant and resolute accomplishment of a crucial action.

The dramatization often recreated the conditions of a direct confrontation between Perlasca's sense of humanity and the evil brutality of Nazism, whether by making the protagonist the pained witness of atrocities against the Jews or through the construction of an antagonist in the ominous persona of an SS official. Admittedly the figure of the 'evil Nazi' is an almost universal cliché in films and television programmes about the Shoah. But we have to recognize the reasons for this melodramatic mode of storytelling—and *Perlasca* was informed by melodramatic imagination and aesthetics, like most Italian television drama—which presupposes a dichotomous moral universe where the personalized forces of good and evil clash, in order to magnify the emotional intensity of the ethical conflict (Brooks 1976). As Marcia Landy said in her analysis of the melodramatic structures of *Schindler's List*: '[Melodrama] strikes an affective chord in the viewers to appeal to the necessity of a moral response' (Landy 2000, p. 387).

'To an extent, every famous figure [...] is filtered through the persona of the star image', George Custen observes (1992, p. 45), and Perlasca certainly enjoyed the reflected light from actor Luca Zingaretti's halo. Zingaretti is universally identified in Italy with the virtuous, upright, and independent-minded Inspector Montalbano, protagonist of the most acclaimed Italian police series (*Montalbano*, RAI 1, 1999–present: an adaptation from the bestsellers of Andrea Camilleri). Although Zingaretti (short, sturdy, and bald) is the physical opposite of Giorgio Perlasca (tall, thin, and blond), he provided a compelling demonstration that 'acting does have meanings and produces effects' (Skirrow 1987, p. 165: quoted in Nelson 2000, p. 69); his outstanding performance proved instrumental in confirming the 'Italianness' of the rescue hero. To achieve this aim, Perlasca's fictional persona presented mannerisms, style features and emotions that are generally associated with the Italian national character: a certain elegance in his dress, for example, and gallantry towards women— whether countesses or waitresses—, and a taste for ironic quips and the quality of cleverness 'on which Italians place high value' (Gannon 1994, p. 57). He is a fearless and daring man, but at the same time sensitive and caring. Perlasca appears in numerous scenes with his face streaked with tears, the emotional response of a compassionate person faced with man's merciless cruelty to man. This happens in particular when the victims are children. The docudrama's insistence on portraying violence inflicted on children, an incarnation of innocence and vulnerability, clearly serves to intensify the moral horror of the evil Nazi machine; but it also allows the protagonist to display the special concerns and caring attitudes towards children of a father figure who was the expression of Italy's child-orientated culture.

In his groundbreaking work on metaphors as a tool to understand cultures, Martin Gannon singles out the opera as a suitable metaphor for Italy. He identifies some distinctive operatic characteristics that cast light on Italian life: namely spectacle, exteriority, and the relationship between the soloist and the chorus. I have already referred earlier to 'exteriority', to be understood as the uncontained expression of feelings and emotions; and I will confine myself to pointing out that the dramatization provided a fine rendering of Perlasca's responsible individualism. Although relying on the information and opinions of a few counsellors and collaborators (the chorus) he is in the end the only one (the soloist) who 'decides how to handle the peril' (1994, p. 61).

But what probably best identifies the connection between Perlasca and Italian culture is the concept of the spectacle. Far from denoting a superficial and even fatuous and ostentatious attitude, the spectacle in its deepest meaning captures the importance in Italian culture of the art of appearing, of performing a façade role on the scene of life: not with the principal aim of deceiving but more often to resolve problems, to seek to thwart fate and 'to face life's injustices with one of the few weapons available to a brave people: their imagination' (Gannon 1994, p. 44). That is exactly what Giorgio Perlasca did in reality, inventing and convincingly performing the role of a Spanish diplomat; the docudrama plausibly rendered 'the marvellous imposture' (Deaglio 1991) of an individual, on his own and powerless, who when challenged by *kairos* to 'fight the devil with bare hands' (quoted from the script) had recourse to the weapons of his imagination—in the colloquial style of the script: 'I talked a load of rubbish and as far as I can judge I did it well'—and to the art of maintaining appearances, in which Italians are unsurpassed. All this could of course have been resolved by a mere combination of stereotypes, even if likeable ones, had it not been put at the service of a high ethical choice. In its engaging endeavour to create a shared memory by re-enacting the Perlasca case as an extraordinary exemplar, a paradigm indeed of the Italian way to heroism, *Perlasca. An Italian Hero* turned into a 'text of identity', to be regarded as one the most significant and influential in the long history of Italian docudrama.

Seen from today's perspective, however, the case of *Perlasca. Un eroe italiano* speaks to us of a lost television world. For many reasons. Successes of such magnitude are hard to come by in the contemporary landscape of channel proliferation and audience fragmentation. Moreover, and more importantly, the standing and popularity of the television docudrama in general, and the docudramatic biopic in particular, seem to be following a trajectory of decline in Italy, even though (not only but especially) public television remains committed to producing several fact-based fictions every year. Sky, the satellite pay-TV service which has recently entered the field of original production, likewise relies on (mainly crime) docudramas to attract niche audiences. But, as a matter of fact, the turn to the past (that in Italy manifested itself earlier than anywhere else in Europe) has now exhausted momentum, and the pool of national heroes whose deeds can be sung, as they were for Perlasca, has largely been drained.

It is perhaps worth noting that some attempts to draw narrative inspiration from personalities and events in not long past Italian history have been made: the tragic experience of terrorism during the 1970s (*Gli anni spezzati*/The Broken Years, RAI 1, 2014, dir. Graziano Diana), the 'Bribesville' scandal of the early 1990s (*1992*, Sky Atlantic, 2015, dir. Giuseppe Gagliardi), and the life of the world-famous yet controversial journalist Oriana Fallaci (*L'Oriana*/Oriana, RAI 1, 2015, dir. Marco Turco) have most recently been re-enacted in historical and biographical docudramas that received a lukewarm response from audience and critics alike. These and similar works seem to indicate that docudrama has now entered a phase in which its potential for event television and compelling treatment of Italian history has given way, to a greater or lesser extent, to the routinization of the genre: a further reason to celebrate a piece such as *Perlasca* as a high point in the development of the Italian docudrama.

NOTES

1. I shall use the term 'docudrama' for simplicity's sake, even though I am aware that it 'often hides important differences in the conception and execution of works' (Corner 1996, p. 91).
2. All translations from Italian are mine.
3. All issues of this magazine are currently available on the online platform of Teche RAI (Italian public television's archive).
4. The *originale* was also called *teledramma*, a somewhat more specific term which made direct reference to the English and American teleplay.
5. 'Medea's Children' started in the guise of a stage play set in ancient Greece, to be interrupted after a few scenes by the official announcement—in breaking-news style—that the child of the renowned actress who performed the lead role of Medea had been abducted by his father; the man refused to disclose where the child, who was in need of medical care, was hidden and threatened to commit suicide unless his reasons were explained on television. Police officers and psychologists repeatedly appeared on the screen to invite people at home to actively cooperate in searching for the child, so that most of the viewers believed that they were witnessing a family tragedy that was unfolding live.
6. It was probably more influenced by the 1938 'panic broadcast' *The War of the Worlds* by Orson Welles than by the contemporary works of Reginald Rose or Rod Sterling.
7. It is worth recalling that six years earlier TV broadcasts had been inaugurated with a live broadcast of a theatre performance.
8. The cinema version, produced some years after the television screening, was included recently in the list of '100 Italian Films to be Saved'. (https://en.wikipedia.org/wiki/100_film_italiani_da_salvare)
9. It is to this subgenre that my case study in the following section, *Perlasca. Un eroe italiano*/Perlasca. An Italian Hero (2002), belongs.
10. The cinema version of the biopic won a prize at the Montreal Film Festival.
11. See also Tobias Ebbrecht-Hartmann's chapter on biographical d/d on German television in Bell and Gray eds (2010).

12. There are similarities here with the difficulties the French—indeed any formerly occupied nation – experienced in naming their Resistance heroes/heroines in the postwar period.

13. In early 1990 a wide-ranging judicial investigation on political and financial corruption subverted the Italian political system; this case is referred to in Italy as Tangentopoli, i.e. Bribesville, 'tangente' being a word for 'bribe'.

14. Ennio Morricone had been nominated for five Oscars from 1979 to 2001. In 2007 he received the Academy Honorary Award.

15. However the scholarly literature that flourished in subsequent years in the context of memory studies did not seem so unanimous (see for instance Marcus 2007; Jansen 2008; Perra 2010; Gordon 2012; Clifford 2013 to name just a few).

CHAPTER 5

French Docudrama: 'Patrimony Television' and 'Embedded Biopic'

Georges Fournier

INTRODUCTION: THE FRENCH TELEVISION ECOLOGY AND DOCUDRAMA

As a popular television genre, docudrama must be analysed within the wider context of television broadcasting in France.[1] The current five main operators can be divided into two main state-owned channels (France 2, France 3), two privately owned TV operator (TF1 and M6), one Franco-German channel (Arte) and one PAY-TV channel that offers un-encrypted programmes during off-peak hours: Canal+.[2] These channels are the most widely available and the programmes that they broadcast are representative of what is viewed and expected by French viewers. TF1 and M6 are popular channels, France 2, and France 3 are informative and educational channels, while Canal+ is a PAY-TV network offering unencypted dedicated to the promotion of sport and cinema. Finally Arte, a Franco-German TV network, describes itself as the European cultural channel.

Digital terrestrial television channels have always been very loyal to the documentary genre, and very early on in French television history they resorted to docudrama as the televised version of the documentary for several reasons: firstly, they sought to bypass the supposed lack of appeal of the documentary genre; secondly, they wanted to draw the audience towards topics otherwise insufficiently explored by current affairs programmes; and finally, they wanted to investigate tabooed subjects that

© The Editor(s) (if applicable) and The Author(s) 2016
T. Ebbrecht-Hartmann, D. Paget (eds.), *Docudrama on European Television*, Palgrave European Film and Media Studies,
DOI 10.1057/978-1-137-49979-0_5

needed to be re-examined from a different angle. Faction and biopics were the genres most commonly used for this latter kind of subject-matter. TF1 was the channel that could be said to have started it all with *L'Affaire Dominici* (The Dominici Case, 2003).[3] *L'Affaire Dominici* can be summarized as the story of the triple murder of the Drummonds: the father, a famous British scientist, Sir Jack Drummond, his wife and their daughter, in the early 1950s. They were on holiday in the South of France when they were found dead. The patriarch of the nearest farmstead was accused and convicted. The death penalty was commuted to life imprisonment and he was finally released. This triple murder case has actually never been solved, but experts soon came to the conclusion that all of the involved parties—the Drummonds and the Dominicis—were actually the victims of intelligence services settling scores at the height of the Cold War.[4]

With the revisiting of past murder cases such as this, a privately owned channel like TF1 was sure to draw an audience spanning from 7 to 10 million viewers—that is to say a 45–55 % share of the ratings. This is a reasonably good figure, though not so astonishingly high as the 22 million viewers (that is to say over 75 %) on average for a soccer final match. The figure is, however, very high if it is compared to the TV ratings recorded by programmes on publicly owned channels. Good viewing figures allow privately owned companies to claim that they can compete with state-owned channels in the field of quality programmes; they also legitimize the criticisms levelled at them. The main criticism is that, though they are tax-funded, they do not fulfil their public remits and tend to toe establishment lines rather than commit to a critique of vested interests. More political and challenging programmes are likely to be commissioned and broadcast by Canal+. This operator has helped to expose several serious cases of political mismanagement by governmental authorities, as in the case of the injecting of patients with contaminated blood, or the killing of political opponents. Along with Arte, Canal+ is also the channel that has questioned French foreign policy during the decades following decolonization, especially where this concerns Africa. Colonization is a politically sensitive subject matter that only privately owned TV channels deal with through fiction. The same is true of the riots in the suburban areas of big cities; these are reminders of colonization since they reflect the alienation of ghettoized populations from the former colonies, who are still struggling for social emancipation.

Conversely, TF1 has, for its part, opted for the revisiting of past and high-profile cases, perfectly in keeping with the expectations of its targeted audience of viewers on the lookout for entertainment. Its films belong to the crime-case category and consist in the re-examination of much-advertised events: all the ingredients are gathered to provide entertainment, information, excitement and indignation at a possible miscarriage of justice or at an unsolved mystery. It is part of what, later in this chapter, I term 'patrimony television'. This is something that allows the television broadcaster to cash in on historical or even historic events.[5] France 2 and France 3, meanwhile, provide potentially challenging political programmes which often lose their edge by being slavish in their attitude to history. Compared to the political impact of the thought-provoking productions offered by Canal+, the political import of productions by France 2 and France 3 is considerably blunted and the result bland. At this stage it is necessary to make a distinction between a state-owned TV channel and a government TV channel, the task of the former being to acquaint the population with what it means to be a citizen and the one of the latter being to assist the government in getting its messages across, especially regarding unpopular measures. This point needs to be underlined since in France, television, and more particularly state-owned channels, has often been accused of being at the government's beck and call.

Docudrama adequately fulfils the public remit of state-owned channels, which consists of supplying the population with information and some form of complementary education, even though many of these productions come from privately owned channels. French filmic productions have rarely favoured the upfront treatment of political issues, and docudramas on history very often correspond ideologically to the standard biopic. The main thrust consists in eulogizing the heroic moments of the nation's past through the lives of prominent historic figures. Yet, films treating topics from the past, whether recent or more ancient, hardly ever resemble exact and complete biopics, but more often describe a historically significant episode in the life of a public figure which is also emblematic of a period in the History of the Nation. By and large, they convey the general mood of the time and mark a turning point in ways of thinking. Yet, historic events are never resurrected for the sake of history but rather because they are connected with topical issues which they treat in a tangential way. Their productions can be seen as indirect approaches to topical issues.

An example of this tendency is *La Séparation* (The Separation, FR3, 2005), where a film ostensibly about the 1905 law which separated church and state in France calls to mind the present time, in which French society is being confronted with the issue of religious fundamentalism. The plot hinges on the men whose names have gone down in French history as the pioneers and founders of *laïcité*, or state secularization. The film was produced and broadcast at a time when the country was torn by the umpteenth controversy about ostentatious signs of religious belief. The present case concerns the wearing of the hijab and the niqab, and the question as to whether this should be tolerated in a secular society or whether there should be a new law forbidding something seen as a potentially provocative religious sign offensive to state secular rules. Thus, the purpose of this TV movie was not only historical; the broadcasting of the docudrama was also clearly targeting the average French person in a popular mode. A subtle reminder of the secular foundations of the French republic, it was additionally aimed at potential opponents of the secular system through its revelation of the origin, current import and significance of an historic moment that spawned the very foundation of the Republic. No surprise, then, that this programme was commissioned and broadcast by the third channel, that is to say state-owned television, aiming to fulfil one of its classic remits: to educate the population. This type of television could also be said to compensate for a deficiency in the secondary education system, certainly in catering for parts of the population; in particular, those parts of the postcolonial nation in which many newcomers have yet to benefit from the compulsory school system, or from regular exposure to mainstream French culture. Designed to oppose ethnic withdrawal and promote integration, this type of presentation is subtler than a regular journalistic programme which may be associated with downright propaganda. Moreover, it is more relevant than a regular fiction film which, for many uninformed people, may not relate meaningfully to the current situation.

With the exception of Canal+, it must be emphasized that French TV channels mainly tend to shy away from politically sensitive issues. They favour consensual topics, or the tangential treatment of burning issues when trying to attract large audiences. This is certainly true of state-owned channels, where highly publicized current issues are approached from a consensual perspective. This is because these channels want to avoid provoking anger among politicians who could scrap their funding. This conservative tendency has the incidental effect of making their output sometimes seem propagandist. In the case of France 2 and France 3, politically challenging programmes are presented from an historical perspective, which allows these channels to pride themselves on being heritage television. There are undoubtedly vested interests in France that miss no opportunity to disparage filmic practices that do not respect cinematic standards and labelling, and that do not fit nicely into manageable genres of fiction or documentary. With its hybrid nature, docudrama is less manageable, and thus often the target of attacks.

Originally, the distinction between fiction films and documentaries about history was clear cut in France, and the programmes that viewers were offered would clearly discriminate between the two even though there would be value judgment about either. In earlier times, factual programmes like documentaries did not necessarily attract more praise from journalists or television critics, and some fiction films have gone down in history as remarkable programmes that have served to increase the audience's knowledge of the past. 'For example, *Si Versailles m'etait conte* (Royal Affairs in Versailles–telling the history of the palace through its famous residents) gathered 7 million viewers on its cinema release in 1954. It then reached more viewers when transmitted by sole broadcaster ORTFF the following year (when there were about 3 million television sets in France). Another example from this period, in which regular weekly fictional programmes were devoted to remarkable historic moments, is the series *La Camera explore le temps* (The Camera Explores Time (ORTF, 1957–66).

A NEW DISPENSATION

Things have changed a lot since that time, and on 7 February 2000 the Paris High Court of Justice upheld the right of artists to draw inspiration from reality, past facts and events. Writer Thierry Jonquet had been sued for infringement of the presumption of innocence and for outrage to the memory of a dead person, following the publication of his book *Moloch*, but was acquitted.[6] The plaintiffs, the relatives of the young woman from whom the writer drew inspiration, lost the case because the magistrates ruled that the writer's added elements (*flagrante delicto*, incest, suicide) 'had not been chosen to strike a blow at the presumption of innocence of Madame Preud'homme nor to persuade the reader of the guilt of the latter but to intensify the narrative.' With this decision, the court made the important decision to assert the power of the artist to be inspired by reality—and even to twist it to fit the narrative. This legislative decision also gave legitimacy to the subtle combination of fiction and reality which had previously existed under something of a taboo.

Docudrama profited from this, and was to change the French audiovisual landscape radically. Its inception dates back relatively recently in comparison to US/UK media history to the 1980s. There were two major causes for its development, the first one being that gradually documentaries about history became branded as aesthetically anachronistic. Up until then the audience, though less media-savvy perhaps, had been brought up with intellectually demanding media like radio and printed journalism and was consequently more likely to be accepting of less entertaining and more informative programmes. Such was no longer the case in the 1980s. Docudrama proved particularly suited for a television audience that was not as captive as a cinema audience and whose attention to serious matters needed to be regularly rekindled with filmic devices, what Dai Vaughan calls 'constantly shifting stylistic practices'(1999, p. 58). Secondly, although the audience for documentaries was loyal and regular, it gradually became too low for financially ambitious TV channels whose standards were established through the 'bottom line'—the profits made on the broadcasting of sport, pure entertainment or fiction films. As a consequence, the dramatic fall in the amount of money allotted to regular documentaries and in particular to documentaries on history testified to the disaffection with the documentary genre and, at the turn of the twenty-first century, the money invested in documentaries had dropped by 40 %, while conversely the amount invested in fiction had risen by 15 %. This trend meant that 'purely' informative programmes about history disappeared from the prime-time segments of terrestrial TV channels. A new recipe had to be found and docudrama provided it at a suitable time.

The main reason for the recent promotion of docudramas on French television is the popularity of such programmes bought in from abroad. These were mainly relayed by ARTE, the first channel to broadcast docudramas made by the BBC and Channel 4.[7] Indeed, the beginning of the twenty-first century witnessed something of a craze for docudramas fashioned after those broadcast by the British channels. Among them was one, home-devised, about the origins of man. Produced and broadcast by France 3, *L'Odyssée de l'espèce* (The Odyssey of the Human Species, 2003) was a fiction film, both historical and anthropological, about the origins of mankind and was broadcast over two consecutive evenings. With almost 9 million viewers, it achieved the best figures for a prime-time programme the channel had recorded since 1998, and was especially popular among viewers aged 15 and over.[8] This programme was the starting point for a mass exodus of producers from regular documentaries to docudramas, whatever the topic. In June 2004, following research conducted into the audience figures for docudramas, Arte announced that they would produce three full-length docudramas every year with a package of €900,000 for each. This policy was in fact based on the one introduced by Channel 4 in the 1990s following their appreciation of the high ratings gained by political docudramas. Other channels followed in these footsteps, opting for controversial topics which they have since tackled in an unprecedented way. The range of prospective issues was wide.

In 2006, a docudrama by Pierre Boutron resurrected the 1985 scandal of the sinking of the Greenpeace ship in the Bay of Auckland, which had been carried out on the instructions of the then Defence Secretary, Charles Hernu. This new approach of political affairs was also adopted by Alain Tasma who produced *Opération Turquoise* in 2007, about the genocide in Rwanda and French involvement in the military training of the Rwandan national army (France supplied weapons and provided assistance to people who later became the perpetrators of genocide). Africa is Alain Tasma's favourite field of investigation. *Opération Turquoise* was broadcast by Canal+ in November 2007, 14 years after the 1990–93/4 Rwandan civil war (April 1994). As for Philippe Triboit, he has specialized in domestic issues and in particular in the shortcomings of institutions, whether the police, the education or the legal system. His most famous docudrama, *L'Embrasement* (Flashover, Arte, 2007) examines the conditions that led a group of four second-generation French teenagers to die after hiding in a power station to escape police patrols (see later section for more on this docudrama).

The other important factor that boosted docudrama was the professionalism of the journalistic approach that infused these programmes. The adjustments to the expectations of the new TV audience through docudrama meant the professionalization of scriptwriting which up until then had been neglected. Among the most successful docudramas have been scripted versions of books and articles by prominent writers. Many criminal cases have inspired famous novelists or playwrights, as illustrated by Marguerite Duras and 'L'Affaire Villemin'. In 1985 she wrote an article in the newspaper *Libération* about this presumed case of infanticide (which is further discussed below). Top-notch writers, and not just in France, have often been interested in the fictional treatment of current affairs, in particular criminal cases. With the noticeable exception of biopics, few relevant writings on politically sensitive affairs have been produced by novelists. It is more often than not journalists who supply the scripts of such productions, partly because they rely heavily on information provided by the press and the media.

Likewise, some channels have lately been seized by a craze for factuality which has led to the production of many docudramas revolving around crimes. A symptomatic sign of this phenomenon is the fact that former police officers have taken to writing for television, which incidentally has afforded drama a higher degree of realism.[9] The famous actor Gérard Depardieu was convinced to act in *36, Quai des Orfèvres* (TF1, 2004) a film about violent gangsters, after he learnt that the script had been written by a former policeman.[10] Even though crime stories are the tip of this iceberg, this phenomenon affects most of the fields of representation from crime to politics.

As far as politics is concerned, whenever a prominent person, a historic figure, is still alive, the commissioning of a docudrama requires extreme caution in France. The case of *Nuit noire* (A Pitch-Dark Night, Canal+, 2005) illustrates this. It deals with the killing of Algerian-born Frenchmen in 1961, a tragic episode in modern French history that this docudrama revealed to TV viewers for the first time. Maurice Papon, who was a zealous collaborator during World War II and who was the Prefect of Police for Paris at the beginning of the 1960s when the killings occurred, was still alive when the shooting of the film began and when the film was broadcast. Consequently, the scriptwriters and filmmakers paid careful attention to details, which they had examined closely by legal advisors in order to avoid having the production halted or its release censored. Under French law, there is no way the fictional treatment of an affair can be prevented, although the reverse was formerly true, and was one of the reasons for the absence of docudrama until relatively recently. The only recourse open to those who feel offended by a script is to invoke the right to privacy or to claim that they have been the victims of defamation.

Professionalization means more accuracy and consequently probable indictments from those who feel that their lives and themselves as individuals have been abused in a fiction film. Docudrama often gains credibility at the expense of the victims and of their relatives who have their names mentioned and who go through the process of reliving difficult times and circumstances. The revisiting of highly emotional and much publicized criminal cases can raise objections from those involved. In *L'Affaire Villemin* (The Villemin Case, France 3, 2008), about the case already mentioned above, a lawyer took action against the production company because he considered that the film smeared the memory of his client (an uncle of the murder victim) who was suspected of the murder and who was killed by the murdered four-year-old child's father. Unfortunately, when high-profile public figures happen to take an interest in such matters, it can make the whole things worse. That is what happened with *L'Affaire Villemin* since Marguerite Duras had written in praise of Christine Villemin, the mother/another suspect, which fuelled resentment. The interest she took in this case contributed to its extensive media coverage, which led the whole affair to spiral out of control.

Criminal cases are difficult to deal with because they are highly sensitive; they involve people and relatives whose grief, ethically, requires protection. Fiction arguably allows filmmakers to adjust their representations of reality to what can be endured by the victims. In the case of recent cases concerning high-profile people, the choice of faction (see paget 2011, 121) is made so as to cash in on the interest lately aroused by much-discussed events, even though this means higher exposure to potential retaliation since people and circumstances can easily be identified. Such is the case with *Notable donc coupable* (Famous Then Guilty, France 2, 2007) about a prominent political figure in the city of Toulouse who was also in charge of the Conseil Supérieur de l'Audiovisuel (The High Authority on Media) in France at the time and who got involved in a case involving multiple murders and sex trafficking. Though the politician had his name cleared, he has ever since been associated with murderers that have been the object of police investigations for years on end, a tragic consequence to which the docudrama on this affair also contributed.

One of the effects of all this is that TF1 has more than 40 lawyers working for the channel on a permanent basis, while France's public television consortium have 23 on their payroll. This is mainly accounted for by the choice made by privately owned TV channels to opt for controversial, personal and criminal cases while state-owned channels opt for topical and societal issues. Another explanation is the fact that state-owned TV channels benefit from the state's heavy artillery, which is both daunting and harder to defeat.

PATRIMONY TELEVISION: THE HISTORY OF CRIMES/THE CRIMES OF HISTORY

Revisiting history is a good way of bolstering national cohesion and achieving good ratings. This is especially true when history is associated with crime and the case belongs to the collective memory, when it is transgenerational and when some recollection of the events is passed on from one generation to another (as in the previously mentioned case of the Dominici murders). Such events not only encapsulate the spirit of a previous time, reminding older generations of the old days, they can also function for younger generations as examples of modern anthropology, recapturing what life was like in the period from the 1950s to the 1970s. This is the kind of drama that unites families, providing family cohesion, at least during the time of the viewing. National cohesion bearing resemblance to family cohesion and vice versa, this kind of programme is promoted by all the mainstream national channels. While the revisiting of cases may appeal to older generations eager to learn more about the unsolved crimes, the elements pertaining to the detective story may also attract a younger audience. Again, with *L'Affaire Dominici*, for some viewers, modern urbanized France could be said to have been reconnected with some mythical rural France everybody was able to identify with and believed they still belonged to.

The revisiting of famous murder cases often touches upon the romantic and very popular notion of miscarriage of justice. This type of docudrama accounts for a large number of recent and current productions of docudramas on French television. The most famous crime cases—*L'Affaire Vuillemin, Marie Besnard* (TF1, 2006), *L'Affaire Dominici, L'Affaire Seznec* (The Seznec Affair, TF1, 1995)[11]—all involve unsolved crimes, controversial verdicts or barbaric murders. Murder cases are hyperbolic, elliptic and fascinating and so they easily capture the attention both of the media and of the population. As far as the film about the Dominici case is concerned, the tension was heightened by the creation of a fictional character in the docudrama, a journalist who throws into relief the innocence of the Dominicis and in particular that of the family patriarch. The same dramatic device was used in *Marie Besnard* In the 1947 Besnard case, a female serial killer became famous when accused of many unsolved murders. Again, a fictional journalist was created for the mini-series docudrama who, because she was born in the same village, could function as provider of legal and expert information. While, in the first part, she sides with Marie Besnard when everyone is against her, she then becomes convinced of her guilt at a time in the story when everyone else believes Besnard innocent. By the time of Besnard's release from prison, the journalist has become entirely persuaded of her guilt. The constant changes in point of view are a striking dramatic feature. It unsettles the viewer and acts as a reminder of the need to be cautious when passing judgement in complex cases.

TF1 has specialized in famous controversial court cases. *L'Affaire Seznec* is another example of the channel's use of this kind of crime docudrama, a series of dramatizations of historical murder cases that paved the way for the recent treatments of controversial and much publicized court cases. The 1995 film is about a man who was wrongly convicted and sentenced to transportation and hard labour for life in 1923. His family fought throughout the twentieth century to clear his name, and in 2006 the Court of Cassation confirmed Seznec's conviction. The reaction of the Seznec's family was that they wanted to take the case to the European Court of Human Rights in Strasbourg. Finally, however, they came round to their lawyers' point of view and decided against it. A 2014 law on procedures, which allows grand-children and great-grandchildren to demand a retrial, prompted the family to make yet another application—their fifteenth. TF1's policy favours such cases because of the general interest they generate in the population. But it equally tends to shy away from political issues, preferring to avoid contentious material.

When broadcast by a state-owned channel, docudramas on famous criminal cases can represent some form of atonement, an ultimate acknowledgement that something in the official version or about the prevailing silence was at odds with what actually happened, especially when murders and politics are inextricably intertwined. Such was the case with the high-profile affairs mentioned above. But it was also the case with the politically sensitive Yann Piat affair. *Yann Piat, chronique d'un assassinat* (Yann Piat, Chronicle of a Murder, Canal+, 2012) is the story of a Députée du Var (a Member of the National Assembly from the Var region, south-eastern France). She was murdered in 1994 by Mafia developers. The purpose of this film was to demonstrate the close and corrupt links between politics and crime and to show how, especially in wealthy areas of the country, politicians find it hard to resist the pressure from criminals who use bribery, threats, menaces, illegal methods and even murder to gain control over valuable lands, properties and financially rewarding assets. This film was also intended to pay tribute to politicians, like Yann Piat, who pay for their integrity with their lives.

Another similar case was the previously mentioned *Notable donc coupable*, about a prominent figure in the city of Toulouse who was wrongly accused of sex-trafficking. From the broadcaster's point of view, this type of production answered the need to inform the population; from the filmmaker's point of view it was meant to fulfil the need to redress injustice, whether journalistic or judicial. It relayed a feeling of extreme anger. The film was shot while the investigation was still underway, which provides a good example of trial by media. The revisiting of resounding legal cases touches upon the romantic and very popular notion of putting right what was wrong, of redressing miscarriages of justice and defamation by the press which did not respect the presumption of innocence. *Notable donc coupable* was a rare instance of political docudrama broadcast on state-owned television channels which are normally, as I have said, chary of dealing directly with politically sensitive affairs (and even less likely to do so in prime time). A possible explanation for this is that many in the political milieu felt guilty for having helped to fuel a case against a political enemy they knew was not guilty. Rumour and defamation seriously damaged the image of this man, which benefitted his opponents. Yet, it went too far and something had to be done to redress the past wrong.[12]

Film treatments of unsolved crimes, controversial verdicts and barbaric murders, then, have proved their worth to French television broadcasters. Docudramas on recent history, however, have been slightly trickier to make in previous times because they often break a prevailing silence. This silence has been a burden for the oppressor, who has to continually close off avenues of investigation, and a frustration for the oppressed, who have an interest in the facts and information. From the point of view of the broadcaster, dealing with controversial subjects in the public interest answers the requirement of educating the population. For filmmakers, such docudramas can often be a means of releasing a personal feeling of rage against the covering-up of something. This is especially true for the treatment of politically embarrassing issues, like the one of the contaminated blood transfusions in the 1980s (*Facteur VIII*, Canal+, 1995), the sinking of the Greenpeace ship (*L'Affaire du Rainbow Warrior*, Canal+, 2006) or the consequences of the mismanagement of second-generation immigrants in the ghettoized suburbs of big cities: *L'Embrasement*.

A diachronic survey of docudramas reveals that *Facteur VIII* was groundbreaking in many ways. This fiction incorporates several features usually associated with docudrama and dramadoc.[13] It is a highly political drama about the infecting of thousands of people with the HIV virus following the health authorities' deliberate decision to allow transfusions with blood from infected donors in the early 1980s. Originally, France 3, one of the state-owned channels, was to produce the film but it eventually decided to pull out of the project as a result of pressure from the government of the time. A week before the crew started shooting the film in state-owned hospitals, the Assistance publique—Hôpitaux de Paris (the National Health Authorities) forbade them to do so despite agreements reached months earlier; it was a sudden and unexpected twist proving that whenever the subject matter is politically sensitive there will always be political pressures for the project to be aborted.

Facteur VIII followed a distinctive docudramatic protocol by using the minutes and official written records of the trial. All characters may have been invented, but they were easily identifiable (as in many films labelled 'factions'). What had been a tragedy up until 1992, the year in which the trial was held, became a scandal when it was revealed that, from 1984 to the end of 1985, infected blood had been used for transfusions with the assent of the health authorities. Doctors and national authorities received heavy fines and even prison sentences. None of this, however, sufficed to stop the wave of indignation from the public. The broadcast of this docudrama in 1995 took place a few years after the trials of those involved in the poisoning, and preceded those of the Prime Minister and of the Minister of Health concerned in this matter (these trials were held in 1999). The latter case resulted in two acquittals, which allowed the incriminated to draw a fine line between guilt and responsibility, the ministers declaring themselves 'responsible but not guilty'. This film fuelled the general public's interest in a case still under examination at court. It offered those who watched it an insight into the trial of public cases. The political dimension of this kind of production lay in the indictment of public figures and pointed to a demand for more responsibility and greater commitment from politicians. However, pressure from politicians made it impossible for this kind of production to be broadcast on either public channels or channels with a large audience so *Facteur VIII* was aired on the subscription-based Canal+.

The 'Rainbow Warrior' incident is another instance of the resurrection of a political issue through docudrama. This affair also concerned the mismanagement of public affairs. *L'Affaire du Rainbow Warrior* tells the story of the sinking of the Greenpeace ship in the Bay of Auckland in New Zealand by French government officials in 1985. *Rainbow Warrior* docked at Auckland while on its way to Mururoa in the South Pacific, where it was due to protest against the military nuclear tests about to be carried out there by the French military. To stop Greenpeace from protesting and from interfering with the nuclear tests, the Direction générale de la Sécurité extérieure (the Intelligence Services), prompted by Charles Hernu, the Minister of Defence, ordered the sinking of the ship. A member of the Greenpeace group, a photographer, died during the raid. *L'Affaire du Rainbow Warrior* is a film by a British filmmaker, Michael Tuchner, who worked for the BBC in the 1960s–1970s. He produced the film in New Zealand in 1995. However, his film was not broadcast in France, neither then, when it would have been relevant to do so, nor even later. The subject matter was sensitive enough to be avoided by the public service channels and once again it was Canal+ which decided to commission and broadcast a French rehashed version of Tuchner's film. *Le Rainbow Warrior* was produced in 2005 and aired a year later, but 21 years after the events. Planète, a channel specializing in documentaries and owned by Canal+, broadcast a repeat of Pierre Boutron's film on 15 December 2008. Only Canal+ and Planète, with their limited viewership, were able to do this. The film was not a hit and although i-Télé (Canal+'s 24-hour national and global news coverage channel) ran a programme about it in its magazine programme, *Le Journal des médias*, on the day of the first broadcast, the viewership of *Le Journal des médias* was also very limited. Because of the chronological distance between the event and the broadcasting, the film lost much of its political relevance. Had the film been broadcast a couple of years after the event it would have had the impact of a bombshell.[14]

Injustice at the hands of the state authorities is also the subject matter of the 2007 *L'Embrasement* about the 2005 riots which erupted after teenagers, who were hunted down by the police, took shelter in an electric power station where all but one died. Alex, a young Belgian journalist, arrives in the city full of scepticism. With the help of the lawyers of the victims' families, he decides to investigate via a reconstruction of the tragedy. His investigation uncovers a social and political reality that he could not imagine existing. Philippe Triboit, the filmmaker, had already made politically and socially committed films, and here he chose to follow the precise chronology of the events, while opting for the introduction of fictional characters. These evolve in the story alongside characters that reference real people involved in the event. Yet, he never mixes the two categories within a scene, so the fictional characters never meet the real ones in any given sequence. By this means he aimed to avoid a feeling of manipulation that could undermine the journalistic dimension of his film. The filmmaker wisely used the grammar of the docudrama (in particular the identification of emblematic and strong characters) to explore, with subtlety, the personal dimension of the distress experienced by the young protagonists.

The only survivor alleged that the police were responsible for the teenagers' hiding in the power station. Nicolas Sarkozy, Ministre de l'Intérieur (Home Secretary) at the time, denied all the allegations on the evening of the incident. As a consequence, anger escalated in the suburbs and the first cars were set on fire, marking the beginning of three weeks of riots. The film's point of view is that of the victims of the incident, and it was based on reports provided by the protagonists and witnesses, and on the police's own accounts and reports. When broadcast, it aroused controversy: the topic was highly controversial because it was about the suburban ghettoes in cities like Paris, and about the mismanagement of the population living in them by politicians and the authorities. *L'embrasement* has the merit of exploring a political affair from a social angle, something the wider media carefully avoided. It forcefully puts forward a long-denied piece of evidence: that a man-hunt did take place and representatives of the state lied to uphold the image of the police.

For many suburb-dwellers, the events recounted in *L'embrasement* were a repeat of those depicted in a film mentioned earlier, *Nuit Noire*. Both films focused on the difficulties of integration in France. In 2005 *Nuit Noire* told the story of the murders by the police of hundreds of Algerian-born Frenchmen, following a demonstration to support independence in Algeria. It is about how the war in Algeria was brought into mainland France. *Nuit Noire* meant the revisiting of history from a polemical point of view. Like much classic docudrama it treats a recent historic event in order to mount some form of challenge to the official version of events. Alain Tasma's film, the only TV film about this period, stands as a good example of the relevance of docudrama's ability to revisit recent history. Although the events treated in this film occurred before all those at the heart of the other films mentioned above, its treatment of a sombre passage in French history was vital because it had been inadequately dealt with by history books.

The anniversary of this tragic incident, which occurred on 17 October 1961, now sees magazines and newspapers openly discussing the death of 200 French people, but at the time of Tasma's film something more needed to be done to get people to understand what had happened. Tasma chose to develop his film by using a 'choir structure'[15] which allows for the introduction of several differing points of view: that of the French-Algerians, that of the police, that of the politicians and that of the rest of the metropolitan population. The quick pace of the editing aptly renders the electric atmosphere and the excitement at the time, increased by the choice of black-and-white images that heighten the feeling of opposite and irreconcilable points of view.

TREATMENTS OF POLITICS OR HAGIOGRAPHY?

Although fiction films on French TV channels in general do not exhibit either political relevance or fierce opposition to those in power,[16] over the last years efforts have been made to remedy this situation. An apt example of this new trend is *L'École du pouvoir* (The School for Power, Canal+, 2009),[17] a highly critical investigation into the education of today's French political elite. As an example of a rather offbeat and unheard-of genre for people at the time, the film helped docudrama earn a reputation of excellence. The genre became a favoured one to which people became accustomed. TV channels, too, have begun to take great pride in producing films such as this. It shows how students of the École nationale d'administration (ENA—one of the most prestigious French graduate schools and the training ground of future politicians) are actually somewhat cynical and career-obsessed. The sole concern of these megalomaniacs is shown to be their desire to occupy the most prestigious and most financially rewarding positions available to French society. Broadcast on Canal+, the political relevance of this film derives from its student characters being thinly disguised portraits of some of today's most prominent politicians. None of them held prominent positions at the time of the broadcasting, but François Hollande (winner of the 2011 Presidential Election), Ségolène Royal (mother of his four children and presidential candidate in 2007) and several other prominent politicians can be clearly identified in the film, and their ambitions are unmasked.

L'École du pouvoir holds a very special place amongst French docudramas. Even though it is about prominent current politicians there is more to it than a blend of short biopics. It is anything but laudatory; on the contrary, it is very critical about people who use politics as a means to financially rewarding ends. The film is something of a French equivalent to Peter Kosminsky's docudramatic work in the UK.[18] It is no surprise either that Raoul Peck, the distinguished Franco-Haitian filmmaker, should have taken over the challenge of making the mini-series. He had already shown an interest in fact-based drama. *L'Affaire Vuillemin* was his, and he has also made films about, for example, Patrice Lumumba—indeed, he is one of the few filmmakers in France who has exposed the flaws of French diplomacy in Africa.

Ever since the success of this mini-series, Canal+ has kept on investing in political docudrama. For example, it commissioned *L'Affaire Gordji: Histoire d'une cohabitation* (The Gordji Affair: The Story of 'Cohabitation'

(2002) which examines the dysfunctional management of the country that followed a socialist president's having to team up with a right-wing government (termed 'cohabiting' in France). This film explores how politicians can sacrifice national interest and lie to achieve their own personal purposes. This affair took place during François Mitterrand's second presidential term, which was the first post-World War II socialist presidency. The so-called 'Gordji case' had to do with a wave of terrorist attacks in France by terrorists from Iran, used by Mitterrand to engineer a repeat victory at the 1988 presidential election. In 1987, Iran was holding French hostages and, to put pressure on the Iranian authorities, François Mitterrand accused Wahid Gordji, a diplomat officially working as a translator at the Iranian embassy, of being behind a series of terrorist attacks in Paris. The hoax worked, the hostages were released (and so was Wahid Gordji). But during the debate held between the two rounds of the 1988 Presidential election, Mitterrand lied in front of the cameras. He accused Jacques Chirac, then Prime Minister and also presidential contender, of knowing that Wahid Gordji was a dangerous terrorist, thus discrediting him. The lie was revealed after Mitterrand's victory, and it severely undermined the status of both the President and the politics in general.

Formerly, politicians in office did not allow the press to criticize them. In 1974, President Valérie Giscard d'Estaing even forbade the broadcast of a documentary on the presidential election though he was neither the only protagonist, nor the intended subject matter of the programme. Factually based treatments of the lives of presidents have been made since—the 2006 mock-documentary *Dans la Peau de Jacques Chirac* (Being Jacques Chirac being one example—but recently, docudrama has ventured even further into exposing political corruption with *La Conquête* (The Conquest, Canal+, 2012). In *La Conquête*, the run-up to the presidential elections, which witnessed Nicolas Sarkozy's victory in 2007, is closely scrutinized. Considering that up until then the person holding the highest office of state had been protected from appearing on the small screen, the release of *La Conquête* on Canal+, a week before the presidential election which witnessed the victory of François Hollande, was either a case of boldness or of political intent on the part of the broadcaster. The media had been the target of repeated attacks from the outgoing president, so it was perhaps both. At the time, French public opinion thought that at last they would have the type of scathing political docudrama about a politician in office so familiar to British viewers, and that Nicolas Sarkozy would bear the brunt of the critique. Unfortunately, the film failed to provide any real criticism. One of the reasons for this is perhaps to do with the fact that there will always be a tendency to empathize with protagonists in realist docudrama—an empathy that comes with closeness to the lead figures, and which absolves them to some degree. Perhaps fear of accusations of exaggeration, even defamation charges, inhibited the makers, or perhaps any alternative to the realist dramaturgy was too daunting and too ambitious to consider.

By contrast, French TV docudramas that combine history and the biography of important historic figures are often closely associated with the project of public service broadcasting, and correspond to a reprocessing of mainstream popular culture. The national myths they are associated with are conveniently called upon and revisited in an effort to strengthen national cohesion. Yet, few are the consensual figures that can rally a very large audience. One such is Jean Moulin, a hero of the World War II resistance movement and undoubtedly the person who has inspired some of the most memorable docudramas. Two films were made recently tapping into Jean Moulin's all-too-brief life, the focus being inevitably on the even fewer years he spent in the Resistance. *Jean Moulin, une affaire française* (Jean Moulin, a French Affair, 2003), highly fictionalized and not very faithful to historical evidence, was produced by TF1, the privately owned channel; it reaped a record 35 % share of ratings, 8.5 million viewers, along with the criticisms of both *Le Monde* and historians. The other one, *Jean Moulin* (France 2, 2002), attracted 5.5 million viewers or 26.5 % of ratings. This comparison illustrates the fact that viewers turn to television mainly for entertainment, and that being true to reality does not necessarily pay off in terms of audience numbers. The good results garnered by both films also confirm that, whatever the topic, fiction is a very convenient way to provide information.

Another important nationally cohesive figure is, of course, General Charles De Gaulle, whose appeal echoes that of the more ancient icon Joan of Arc.[19] Productions featuring these two figures are numerous. As for President François Mitterrand, though his name still needs exposure to the test of time, and despite some rather murky and controversial periods in his life, he created his own personal myth as the modern figure of social progress, the one who attempted to update the ideals of the Popular Front. Analysis of *Le Promeneur du Champ de Mars* (Canal+, 2005), released under the title *The Last Mitterrand* in Britain and other anglophone countries, will illustrate some of the problems inherent in what I am calling 'embedded biography'.

LE PROMENEUR DU CHAMP DE MARS AS EMBEDDED BIOPIC

Essentially, this film is about the relationship between François Mitterrand and his biographer during the last years of the President's second and final term. The film is based on Georges-Marc Benamou's 1997 biography *Le Dernier Mitterrand* so, even though there is some fictionalization in Robert Guédiguian's film, there are clear documentary intentions. The most personal aspects of the political life but also of the personal life of the former President are tackled, and even though the protagonist is always referred to by his function as 'President', never by his actual name, viewers cannot but identify him as François Mitterrand.[20] Mitterrand had a very old-fashioned perception of image, partly because of the fact that he knew he did not come out well on television. Unfortunately for him, charisma has much to do with image, and appearance in front of cameras is vital in today's political sphere. Image problems partly account for his loss to Valéry Giscard d'Estaing, the right-wing contender, in the 1974 presidential election.

For Mitterrand, there was more to image than flat projections on a screen; he believed in image as a combination of form and substance. Near the end of his life, image turned into a full-time preoccupation for him and gradually he became obsessed with it. The plot of *Le Promeneur du Champ de Mars* follows the chronology of events until the fatal day of his political 'death'. The image that is conveyed of Mitterrand is all in all a positive one: he is shown as a learned man, very clever, if Machiavellian— an intellectual who, on the eve of death, was still fighting the ghosts of his murky past and fighting for a place in history. Empathy is increased by the choice of Michel Bouquet as Mitterrand, one of the country's most acclaimed actors—and one sure enough of his talent to cross media and genres and act in TV films and in docudramas, as was the case in Robert Guédiguian's film. The François Mitterrand of the film seems totally engrossed in the project not only of leaving an imprint on French history but of leaving a positive image. As the film develops, this leads the character to be dishonest about his feelings and about events in his life. He constantly corrects what he says about himself according to the good image he wants to convey of himself. Consequently, he is shown pretending and deceiving. He fictionalizes his life, anticipating the posthumous image he would like people to remember of him. A key episode that takes place in the Royal Basilica of Saint Denis, where most French kings were buried, is very explicit about this. Mitterrand goes to this iconic location to reflect upon his own power as a leader, and to ponder over how he is going to be remembered.

The function of this sequence is complex. It is designed to show how desperate he was to be remembered as the buried kings have been, and how to some extent he wanted to be part of such a lineage. He is shown as pathetic, claiming at one point that after all he will be remembered as a great leader because he is the one who has remained in power for the longest period of time since Napoléon III—even longer than his rival for twentieth-century longevity, De Gaulle. Though he is clever enough to know that fame has nothing to do with this, his hubristic obsession with leaving a memorable trace in history blinds him to this glaring truth: it is De Gaulle who will inevitably be remembered as the great French statesman of the last century. The scene gives viewers access to his way of thinking, and this facilitates a process of identification. It is a process of mind-reading conducive to empathy, and ultimately to the alignment of the viewer's perception to the filmmaker's own. This clever man, a man with a past that he understands, better equipped than anyone to make sense of the present, can be seen in a positive light—from his own point of view at least. Once the visit to the tombstones of the Royal Basilica of Saint Denis is over and once he is outside in the broad daylight, reality prevails: he realizes he will never be king. To comfort himself, he declares that in the future he will at least be seen as the last President, his collection of successors being mere financiers and accountants rather than politicians. This constant movement between the past and the future shows his lack of interest in politics at the end of his second-term presidency. His mind seems no longer mobilized by domestic issues but by the need to bolster and revamp his image. His biography—his legacy—has become a propaganda tool.

The main interest of this film, from a stylistic point of view, lies in the several instances of what I am calling 'embeddedness'. The word is chosen to reference the 'embedded journalists' placed with armies in recent Middle East actions. Journalists should aim to be unbiased, yet their very embeddedness within army units, some have argued, must compromise this. *Le Promeneur du Champ de Mars* has a number of instances that throw light on the tension between reality and fiction that follow from embeddedness, and which foster considerations of representation, image and propaganda as a form of audience mobilization. *Le Promeneur du Champ de Mars* is a biopic built on embeddedness, and co-dependent fictions. There is the biographer: someone who, though supposed to provide some sort of record, fictionalizes the life being written about; then there is the President, who also fictionalizes his life. Then, of course, there is the director using the biography as the basis for a film. Trying to be true to reality, Mitterrand does consider the darkest moments in his life. But he also chooses to brighten them up. This in turn causes the biographer to ponder over them and to wonder about the boundaries between fiction and reality.[21] This sets up a constant tug of war in the film. Mitterrand's biographer and the filmmaker, also a biographer of sorts, betray their sympathy with their subject. The more they learn about Mitterrand the more they fall under his spell. This is the core of one of the subplots, about accusations against Mitterrand that he collaborated during World War II. In this, another instance of embeddedness, the biographer is shown trying desperately to clear Mitterrand's name, fighting those who accuse Mitterrand. In one of the final scenes, the biographer offers Mitterrand a letter of explanation, intended for the media, which would help him clear his name. Mitterrand pretends to consider it, but soon discards it disdainfully. Empathy for subject meets subject's propaganda here, and the biographer could be accused of rewriting history in order to fit into the positive view he has of the President. Conversely, the latter prefers not to get involved in countering the smear campaign, and wishes to leave things as they are without dispelling the doubts that exist about his readiness to join the wartime Resistance.[22] Even though both filmmaker and biographer have a commitment to the truth, then, ultimately their choice of useful episodes from Mitterrand's life which serve their purpose demonstrates that they follow his line. The biographer in the film becomes aware that he has been cheated and that he has been given access only to the social man, the social self, and not to the man himself. He even begins to wonder whether Mitterrand, as a career politician, ever was himself and not the image that his position required from him. Viewers learn about these thoughts from a voice-over which says: 'What he had just shown me was the ultimate stage, the petrified stage. The body of the President had become our body, a body belonging to the nation.' Gradually, Mitterrand becomes a kind of character both for the biographer and for himself: no longer himself but the image he would like to present, he has become alienated from his own self.

In *Le Promeneur du Champ de Mars*, there is plenty of documentary evidence drawn from the written biography, used to access the private thoughts and feelings of Mitterrand. The filmmaker's embedded biopic makes central the relationships between the official biographer, then a young journalist, and Mitterrand himself. The biographer has several functions within the film; first as a recorder of the president's life, of course, but also as a confidant, and to some extent as a psychoanalyst. From time to time the president happens to forget about his presence and divulges personal details which the biographer is seen recording. In talking to his biographer, Mitterrand is actually addressing the future readers of his biography—and, of course, the audience of the film. Thus the on-screen biographer is also an extension of the viewer. As the project of the biography becomes a means to try and understand the man—who he really was and what prompted him to do what he did—so the audience share in the frustrations of the biographer, who gradually finds himself at cross purposes with Mitterrand. While the biographer wants to be a psychoanalyst who attempts to get the President to think about his past, Mitterrand is actually working for his future, his legacy in public memory. The biographer gradually feels himself to be in an inferior position because of Mitterrand's overweening attitude, just like spectators do when watching a film which, in a similar way, leads to projection and empathy.[23] Because he is a politician, then, the Mitterrand of *Le Promeneur du Champ de Mars* does not present himself as a person but as an archetype, a paragon. Paradoxically, the more archetypal he is, the harder identification becomes, since no one is really a paragon of virtue. The more human he is, however, the more identification is possible.

For Robert Guédiaguian, the purpose of the film was undoubtedly social mobilization for socialism in France. He has always been an avowed socialist and wanted to rekindle the flame of the movement with this film about a socialist President. In 2005, the year the film was released, the need to mobilize around socialism was felt keenly, because this was a period that had been marked by more than ten years of right-wing governments. Socialists were anticipating and fearing this would be followed by another five-year right-wing presidency if Nicolas Sarkozy were to win, which he did. The success of *Le Promeneur du Champ de Mars* is also one for docudrama, a genre now sufficiently successful to move into the realm of feature cinema production. Guédiguian's wish to increase socialist mobilization before general elections was, perhaps, undercut by the focus on a man and his obsession with the place he would leave in history, rather than on the same man's actual ideas and achievements. To some extent, this film actually says more about Guédiguian, the filmmaker. Although a staunch socialist, he never really forgave Mitterrand for having abandoned the working class in his policies. More generally, Mitterrand's shortcomings, failures and renunciations bespeak similar features of 15 years of socialist governments. *Le Promeneur du Champ de Mars* also affords fertile perspectives on the links between fiction and reality, between past and present, all issues which stand at the core of discussions of docudrama. The film raises questions which reach beyond the links between Mitterrand's past and present, between facts and memory, between real lives and the narratives made to tell them, to interrogate the relevance of docudrama's ability to investigate history.

NOTES

'Docudrama' will be used in this chapter as the generic term for the variety of hybrid film creations utilizing fact—see Derek Paget's justification for this (2011—see in particular Chap. 3).

2. In 1964the second state-owned channel was created and 1967 saw the broadcast of the first colour programmes. The first half of the 1980s corresponded to a large increase in the number of broadcasters and to the birth of the current audiovisual ecology.

3. All translations from the French are mine.

4. Many explanations have been put forward, all hinging on Drummond's double status as a famous biochemist and spy. His killing was an act of retaliation for his activity as a spy for the British, and possibly American, secret services, which he had been engaged in since World War I. One of the most probable theories relates to Drummond's zealous postwar involvement, as a spy for the British Intelligence Service, in the exfiltration of former Nazi scientists to the West and in particular to the USA. This affair was a serious bone of contention between the Eastern Bloc and the West at the time. West Germany, at the end of the 1950s, protested against this 'brain drain' which severely damaged the recovery of its industry (see Pierre Carrias, Yves Thélen, Jean Teyssier and Roger Pacaut, *Dominici: De l'accident aux agents secrets*, Paris: Editions Cheminements, 2003).

5. This phrase corresponds to Tobias Ebbrecht-Hartmann's concept of 'historical event television', which he outlines further in Chap. 2 of this book. My phrase, however, has a distinctively French inflection because the idea of 'patrimony' is fundamental to French national identity.

6. *Moloch* is a book about a Madame Preud'homme, who criminally pretended that her daughter was suffering from organic disorders so that she could inject her with heavy doses of insulin. These eventually proved fatal.

7. The airing, in 2004, of *The Last Days of Pompeii*, a BBC production broadcast 20 years earlier in Great Britain, garnered 32.5 % of viewers,

which was one of the highest records of the year. See: http://www. strategies.fr/actualities/medias/r79297W/france-a-battu-tf-dimanche-soir-avec-les-dernieres-jours-de-pompei.html

8. To be precise, the official viewing figure was 8.74 million.

9. In the present paper, 'realism', when applied to aesthetics, refers to what John Fiske and John Hartley in *Reading Television* define as 'the mode in which the fictional story is presented [...] the natural representation of the way things are: a story may be fictional, but the way it is related tells it like it is'. As for realism, when it is used to refer to the subject-matter of a film or a novel ('a realistic film'), it is to be understood as being a careful description of everyday life. See Fiske et al. (2003, pp. 129).

10. Olivier Marchal, the former policeman and scriptwriter, tapped into his decennial professional experience in the police to write this screenplay. The title is the actual address of the Paris police headquarters.

11. 'L'Affaire' is best translated in all these legal instances as 'Case'; in non-legal examples the English word 'affair' can be used.

12. Chapter 2 of Paget 2011 deals with the various legalities associated with British and American television (particularly concerning docudrama). Many regulations are designed to try to avoid 'trial by television'. The same work needs to be done in respect of French television, but space does not permit this in the present chapter.

13. Again, for further detail on terminology, see Paget (2011).

14. In a sense, *L'Affaire du Rainbow Warrior* could be said to be the French equivalent of Peter Watkins' *The War Game*, made in 1965 for the BBC, finally screened on UK television in 1985.

15. 'Choir structure' is my translation of the French term *film choral*, which refers to films with a large number of characters but without a main protagonist or prominent characters.

16. British TV channels have often broadcast docudramas offering fierce criticisms of political leaders—even when they are still in office. For example, two quite recent teleplays were highly critical of Tony Blair (*The Government Inspector*, C4, 2005, and *The Trial of Tony Blair*, More4, 2007).

17. This is the literal translation. A more idiomatic one would be 'Fast Track to Power' or 'Fast Lane to Power'.

18. Canal+ has broadcast a number of Kosminsky's radical films to French audiences in recent years.

19. Recently, a docudrama was made about Charles de Gaulle, *Le Grand Charles* (2002) produced and broadcast by France2. It would take too long to list all the films on Joan of Arc, the first one being *La Passion de Jeanne d'Arc* (dir. Carl Theodor Dreyer, 1928) and the latest one being *Jeanne d'Arc* (dir. Luc Besson, 1999), with Milla Jovovich as Joan of Arc.

20. Of course, instant recognition of the identity of the protagonist was unlikely when the film was shown outside France, hence the naming of Mitterrand in the English title.
21. The biographer is a thinly disguised portrait of Georges-Marc Benamou who, at the time, was a young journalist François Mitterrand was well acquainted with, and whose company he appreciated.
22. The subject of François Mitterrand and wartime resistance is well-documented in Gérard Guicheteau's *François Mitterrand: La Résistance et Vichy* (2008). See also Michel Winnock's *François Mitterrand* (2015).
23. For more details, see Jean-Louis Baudry in Mast et al. (1992, pp. 703–704).

CHAPTER 6

Spanish Docudrama: Of Heroes and Celebrities

Victoria Pastor-González

INTRODUCTION: NARRATIVES OF CONSENT

If we had to choose a word to define the presence of docudrama on Spanish television, it would be intermittent, with sudden bursts of production followed by years of scarcity. The aim of this chapter is to analyse the latest phase of this trend—roughly corresponding to the period from 2008 to the present—the most significant period so far in terms of the number of productions, variety of topics, and interest in audience reception.

Unlike some other European countries, Spain was a latecomer to the world of television docudrama. Analysing the national production of programmes 'based on real events', Jaime Barroso argues that the cultural isolation Spain was still experiencing in the early 1960s made it difficult for television professionals to be aware of the creative experiments taking place in other European countries such as Great Britain, where docudrama was already a recognisable genre.[1] Moreover, and given that the country was still under a dictatorship, he argues that it would have been inconceivable for Spanish television to 'welcome an emerging genre such as docudrama, so much linked at that time to the disclosure of social injustice and bent on giving voice to less privileged communities frequently ignored by the machinery of the State' (Barroso 2004, p. 178).[2]

Lacking this investigative journalistic influence at its very inception, Spanish docudrama bypassed the first phase of the developmental model

© The Editor(s) (if applicable) and The Author(s) 2016
T. Ebbrecht-Hartmann, D. Paget (eds.), *Docudrama on European Television*, Palgrave European Film and Media Studies,
DOI 10.1057/978-1-137-49979-0_6

that Derek Paget outlined in his seminal work *No Other Way to Tell It* (2011, p. 180). As a consequence, subsequent Spanish productions of the 1980s–2000s are stylistically closer to the Anglo-Saxon docudramas of the third phase, where the 'form that started out as a response to real-world events located in documentary practices gradually became a response to a public situation articulated principally through the codes and conventions of film and television drama' (2011, p. 182). The case studies in this chapter will show that contemporary Spanish docudrama is still moving through this third phase and finds itself at some distance from the 'creative hybridisation' that characterises Paget's fourth phase of docudrama in the Anglo-Saxon tradition (2011, p. 264). As a norm, Spanish docudrama is fairly conservative in its narrative and visual strategies, and tends to look to drama and melodrama for stylistic inspiration.

Going back to the earlier decades of Spanish television, Barroso mentions some examples of programmes from the 1970s—*Crónicas de un pueblo* (Village Chronicles, TVE 1, 1971–74) and *Vivir cada día* (Living each Day, TVE 1, 1978–82 and 1983–88).[3] These could be inserted within the spectrum of dramas based on real events, but are stylistically closer to fiction drama (and the British category 'drama-documentary'). We have to wait until the 1980s to experience the first significant but short-lived wave of Spanish docudramas in the form of biopics produced during Pilar Miró's term as General Director of the state-owned channel TVE (1986–89). A filmmaker closely related to the new socialist party that came to power in 1982, Miró imposed a policy of quality over quantity and encouraged national productions whilst limiting the acquisition of US exports. This resulted in an increased number of mini-series, both literary adaptations and more importantly biopics. In the opinion of Manuel Palacio, these productions reflect on the one hand 'the will of the new government to translate socialist ideals into television images' and on the other a desire to 'support world-class productions' (2008, p. 159). Thus, Spanish television biopics of the 1980s become arenas in which it was possible to reclaim, or create, icons for an infant democracy. This was achieved through recasting historical characters (*Teresa de Jesús*/St Teresa of Avila, TVE 1, 1984), recovering censored cultural icons (*Lorca muerte de un poeta*/Lorca, Death of a Poet, TVE1, 1987), or simply by creating a contemporary myth (*El Lute: camina o revienta*/El Lute: Run for your Life, TVE 1, 1987). There was even a sense that television had a moral duty to become the stage on which historical and social constructs could be recreated and reassessed. As Josefina Molina, director of *Teresa de Jesús*, explained:

[this biopic] is very important, if only because we need to be aware of our own history, unravel and interpret its facts in order to learn a practical lesson for our own times. And nowadays, who best to take up that challenge but television? (Pérez Ornia 1982)

However, in the 1990s, neither the public channel TVE, nor the new private channels Antena 3, Telecinco and Canal+ showed any interest in answering this call, and the production of dramas based on real events— historical or otherwise—withered. With social and technological changes having a deep impact on the industry, all the television channels in Spain chose instead to try to win sport-related broadcasting rights, and to foster the production of indigenous fictional drama and comedy series.[4]

Docudrama emerges from these shadows in the early 2000s with the release of Antena 3's mini-series *Padre Coraje* (Father Courage, Antena 3, 2001—more on this later in the chapter). But only later in the decade did the real explosion of docudrama production extend to the entire television network. Once again, a combination of social and economic factors played a pivotal role in the rebirth of the genre; most significantly the passing of the new Ley General de la Comunicación Audiovisual (Law of Audiovisual Communication) in March 2010. This was an ambitious project by the socialist government of José Luis Rodríguez Zapatero that, according to its supporters:

> would provide the sector with an adequate legislative framework to respond to recent social changes and to acknowledge the new business models born out of strong and unstoppable technological advancements. (España 2009)

As was the case with previous legislation, the 2010 law regulates the financial support that national and regional channels (state-owned and private) must provide to European film production.[5] It states that private channels must invest 5 % of their profits in the film industry (6 % for state-owned channels). A fifth of this must be devoted exclusively to produce films/mini-series for television. A brief survey of the TV movies released in the past decade reveals that almost 80 % were produced in 2010 or after, and many of them were programmes based on real events. A further consequence of these legal factors is that the term 'docudrama' is virtually absent from the Spanish television ecology. Most contemporary programmes based on real events will be classified under the labels *mini serie basada en hechos reales* (mini-series based on real events) or 'TV movie'.

Around 2010 newspapers and specialist websites started discussing this new trend. Unsurprisingly, financial incentives were frequently mentioned, but critics and television executives also commented on the added value of docudrama production in terms of programming strategies and artistic quality. For Mercedes Gamero (Director of Antena 3 Films), TV movies in general and docudramas in particular offered a powerful tool when it came to building a schedule in an increasingly competitive sector. She observed that 'audiences recognize these programmes as exclusive products: a unique event that creates expectation' (Fernández 2009). Mikel Lejarza (President of Antena 3 Films) also welcomed the new interest in docudrama, but he cautioned against 'producing them in excessive numbers because they will eventually lose that aura of uniqueness' (Pérez-Lanzac 2010). Channels seem aware of this risk and have made significant efforts to expand their docudrama portfolio in terms of topics, formats, and even production values. They have also been adopting a variety of scheduling strategies, sometimes using docudramas as key weapons in a programming battle. This shows the level of confidence that schedulers have in these programmes' capacity to draw and retain audiences.

Television executives tend to boast about the production values of the new breed of docudramas, and the fact that they have caught the interest of professionals who have previously worked exclusively in film. Having prestigious directors such as Benito Zambrano and Daniel Calparsoro attached to these projects has undoubtedly helped the artistic quality (and credentials) of many television docudramas. Equally, well-known names from the Spanish star system (Carmelo Gómez, Emma Suárez, Marisa Paredes, Blanca Portillo) have taken up the challenge of interpreting real-life characters. For Eduardo García Matilla, President of Corporación Multimedia and now a member of the Comisión Nacional de los Mercados y de la Competencia (a regulatory body for the audiovisual sector in Spain) TV movies could be 'a hothouse for new ideas and an engine to develop the audio-visual sector' (Fernández 2009).

This engine has certainly been fuelled with generous budgets. It has been reported that Antena 3, one of the most prolific producers of docudramas, would normally invest between €1 and €1.5 million on a two-part mini-series. This amount will usually be paid to an independent production company for an 'all-inclusive' package, covering script, creative team, and production management (EFE 2010). However, some budgets can be as high as the €2.5 million spent on RTVE's *23F: El día más difícil del Rey* (23F: The King's Most Difficult Day, TVE 1, 2009) or the €3 million of

Tarancón, el quinto mandamiento (Tarancón, the Fifth Commandment, TVE 1, 2010). As David Cotarelo, Associate Director of Telefilms for RTVE, has observed, TV movies became a life raft for small production companies that used to work exclusively in feature films, when demand from that sector shrank (EFE 2010). Given significant investment, it is not surprising that channels aim for the best possible return, whether this takes the form of publicity or financial gain. Networks such as Mediaset and Atresmedia have developed special sections on their websites to showcase their TV movies/mini-series production. And although some of these programmes are accessible online free of charge, a number of them are only available on DVD or through pay-per-view.

In addition to this corporate support, docudrama has wowed the Spanish audience. Data shows that the 15 most popular docudramas shown there between 2007 and 2014 achieved audience shares of between 16 and 33 %.[6] In a country where the annual list of the most viewed programmes is consistently topped by football-related events, to achieve such high audience ratings is truly significant. These numbers place docudramas in a similar league to homegrown popular drama and comedy series such as RTVE's *Cuéntame cómo pasó* (Tell Me How it Happened, TVE 1, 2001–present) and Telecinco's *La que se avecina* (This is What's Coming, Telecinco, 2007–present), and demonstrate that Spanish audiences are attracted to the genre's conventions and narratives. Many Spanish television executives explain the appeal of docudrama as placing the audience in the position of witness to an event of social relevance or a story of human interest. Fernando López Puig (RTVE's Head of Drama) argues:

> Audiences experience recent events through the prism of news reports but when you fictionalize the events you also reinterpret them. The spectator extracts pleasure from reliving the events and also because we all enjoy knowing about the gruesome details; we all expect to see something new that takes us by surprise. In our programmes we always try to include the unexpected or some little-known detail. (Pérez-Lanzac 2010)

López Puig's words mirror Steven N. Lipkin's observation that 'docudrama offers effective television programming material because it is "rootable", "relatable" and "promotable"' (Lipkin 2002, p. 55). But this statement also confirms that within the Spanish television ecology, docudrama is more valued for its capacity to elicit an emotional response than for its journalism. Highlighting its entertainment value also casts doubts on the capacity of docudrama in the Spanish context to launch what Lipkin calls 'persuasive argument' and may even undermine the moral authority that the narrative gains from its proximity to the actuality it references. The close connection with tabloid television is also picked up on by other media professionals who have identified docudrama production as an effective strategy with which to respond to audience fragmentation in the subgenre of gossip and celebrity chat shows.

Historically, Spanish television has served as the natural environment for the tabloid. Especially popular are talk shows focusing on minor celebrities and controversial issues. Confessional interviews and life debates form part of this mix, particularly on the private channel Telecinco, where the style of hosting alternates between the patronising and the confrontational, and where verbal fights are actively encouraged. Critics seeking to improve the quality of Spanish media regularly cite this style of celebrity television—its growth and endurance—as the worst malady that afflicts the country's television industry. In addition to these negative views, producers now face significant fragmentation in television audiences. Thus, new formats are required that may engage their traditional audience (mainly middle-class women aged 45–65—see Gay 2007) whilst attracting new audiences not so interested in gossip shows. Producing docudramas on the lives of celebrities, aristocrats, and artists seems like a natural progression, where melodramatic excess and the unveiling of secrets are packaged in a high-quality product, marketed as a television event and presented as unique and prestigious. Aside from celebrity biopics, audiences have also turned their attention to docudramas dealing with historical events, a phenomenon that may be a consequence of the financial instability of the early 2010s. As the political analyst Gutiérrez-Rubi suggests, 'audiences faced with an uncertain future look back to real historical events to provide them with emotional and experiential stability' (Pérez-Lanzac 2010).

The escape into the past is by no means exclusive to the Spanish context. Milly Buonanno argues that many countries in Europe have been influenced by the 'temporal turn which at the beginning of the third millennium, has fostered, in televisual story-telling, a widespread trend of a "return to the past"' (Buonanno 2012a, p. 174). In recent years, Spanish society has engaged in a process of reassessment and memorialisation of its recent past which in the television context has translated into very successful drama series and docudramas addressing key historical events such as the years after the Civil War and the transition from dictatorship to democracy. I will argue that within the Spanish context, historical docudrama has been effective in putting forward persuasive arguments, but this has only been achieved through narratives of consent rather than dissent. Spanish audiences have so far trusted historical docudrama as long as its message functions within a commonly accepted version of events. Historical docudramas dwelling on conspiracy theories are generally observed with suspicion, and tend to perform poorly in terms of audiences. Docudrama in the Spanish context is valued for its capacity to establish an emotional connection between the spectator and historical events, but it is not perceived as a space for historical reassessment or investigative journalism.

The combination of financial incentives, industry challenges, and sociocultural factors have contributed to bring about a Golden Age of docudrama production in Spain. What started as a rare occurrence in the early 2000s became an outpouring of programmes by the end of the decade. In the last four years production has stabilised, as the form has gradually evolved into a regular feature on television schedules. This enthusiasm for docudrama guaranteed that within a timeframe of less than ten years, Spain gained an extensive and varied corpus, which enables me to map Spanish productions against Lipkin's 'arenas' of docudramatic performance: the representation of noteworthy individuals; the representation of noteworthy events; and the representation of the events of war (2011, p. 3). This categorisation helps to place Spanish docudrama production in a wider context, alongside longer established traditions, and also allows for the case studies to demonstrate national specificities. Finally, at the centre of Lipkin's model lies the basic concept of docudrama as a mode of address whose main objective is to launch persuasive argument. Observing Spanish docudramas through this prism will lead in the following sections to important questions about the value and impact of docudrama in the Spanish television ecology.

Exemplary Lives: The Representation of Noteworthy Individuals

In her analysis of made-for-TV movies on US cable channels, Erin Copple Smith argues that in addition to their 'considerable economic and industrial advantages [...], the made-for-TV movie arguably delivers equivalent—if not greater—value as an opportunity for channel branding or establishing prestige' (2009, p. 146). This statement could certainly be applied to the collection of TV movies and mini-series about noteworthy individuals produced in Spain in the last decade. Analysis of these docudramatic biopics not only reveals how the genre has adapted to respond to national specificities but it also serves as an index of the production models, cultural identities, and branding strategies of national television networks. Just browsing the names of the protagonists of recent examples reveals that RTVE, the state-owned channel, has produced almost exclusively portrayals of social reformers, no doubt because this fits its public service remit. Private channel Antena 3, by contrast, has opted for a more diverse portfolio of characters: politicians, members of the royal family, and a large number of entertainers. The common denominator, however, and a distinctive characteristic of this channel's films, is a seriousness in the treatment of the events, with narratives that highlight the professional achievements of the protagonists over the fact that they are also celebrities. The third player, Telecinco, has also considered individuals from different areas of activity, including lawyers, members of the aristocracy, and entertainers. The tone of these biopics is largely sensationalist and a high percentage of the protagonists are closely linked to the complex financial networks and cultural structures that sustain tabloid media.

According to Lipkin, contemporary biopics exist to explain the fame, the notoriety, and/or the noteworthiness of their main subject: to do this, 'they must re-create as vividly as possible a sense of their subjects' extraordinary abilities and/or accomplishments' (Lipkin 2011, p. 134). This is certainly the principle at the heart of the biopics produced by the public channel RTVE, four of which will be considered in this section: *Tarancón, el quinto mandamiento, Vicente Ferrer* (TVE1, 2013), *Clara Campoamor, la mujer olvidada* (Clara Campoamor, The Forgotten Woman, TVE1, 2010), and *Concepción Arenal, la visitadora de cárceles* (Concepción Arenal, The Prison Visitor, TVE1, 2012). These films feature individuals who have distinguished themselves as instigators or facilitators of social and political change. The main protagonists of the films engage in exceptional acts of bravery, facing up to restrictive social convention and reactionary institutions in an attempt to fight for justice and in the hope of a better world. A classical narrative of conflict and resolution drives the action. However, emphasis is placed on the commitment of the protagonists to democratic and/or egalitarian principles. Placed in an arena of action, such as a trial or an encounter with an antagonist or an uncooperative superior, the resolution of the conflict is always achieved through dialogue or legal means.

A second element common to these biopics is the presence of the Catholic Church as an entity to be reckoned with, or an ideology to be followed, criticized, or openly opposed. This is perhaps not surprising in a country where a high percentage of nationals (71 % according to the latest statistics—CIS 2014) identify themselves as Catholics, and where religious rituals and practices are frequently closely and deeply linked to cultural manifestations. Nevertheless, the presence of the Catholic Church in these particular biopics is justified by the fact that historically this institution enjoyed privileged access to the mechanisms of the state, and for a long time had the monopoly of charitable enterprises, areas in which the protagonists develop their professional activities.

The best two examples are the biopics devoted to the Jesuit charity aid worker Vicente Ferrer and to Archbishop Vicente Enrique Tarancón, a controversial figure and leader of the Spanish Episcopal Conference 1971–81—the decade marked by Spain's challenging transition from dictatorship to democracy. A distinctive feature of films dealing with religious figures is the absence of references to the more transcendental elements of religion (miracle-working, visions, mysticism). The Ferrer and Tarancón biopics leave the spectator in no doubt as to why they have been deemed worthy of treatment: it is because of their social and political achievements—guided by the Christian principle of caritas—and not because of saintly attributes, moral rectitude, or spirituality. Even though both characters dress as members of the clergy, neither is shown preaching nor even inside a sacred building for more than a few seconds. Both side with the poor and the sick, have close relations with the Jesuits (traditionally viewed as a progressive religious order), and clash repeatedly with more conservative sections of the Catholic Church.

The performances that we see are of a man, Vicente Ferrer, working with the 'untouchables' in India, and a person of authority, Tarancón, fighting to extricate the Catholic Church from the ideological sphere of the Francoist regime. For a non-religious viewer it is easy to bypass the religious context and identify with their personal struggles; for the Catholic viewer there is the recognition of a series of common personal beliefs and cultural values. In addition, *Vicente Ferrer* and *Tarancón* are paradigmatic of production and promotional strategies that have characterised Spanish televisual biopics in the last decade. Both are co-productions with the Basque and Catalan regional channels. This financial arrangement is in fact common to almost 90 % of the docudramas produced by RTVE. Private channels prefer to use independent production companies, and generally opt for the all-inclusive package already mentioned.

Both characters are played by well-known television actors: Pepe Sancho (Tarancón) and Imanol Arias (Vicente Ferrer). Although both have had a regular presence in the Spanish media for more than three decades, for younger generations they are first and foremost associated with their roles of Don Pablo and Antonio Alcántara in the enormously successful drama series *Cuéntame cómo pasó*. This illustrates an industry-wide strategy where films dealing with actual cultural, political, or social icons no longer require the presence of a high-profile film actor as was formerly the case. Whilst Spanish docudramatic biopic may share this trend with other media cultures with longer traditions of producing biographical films (see Moine 2014, p. 59) it also reveals the status that docudrama has attained in a relatively short period of time. As critics begin to praise some biopics (and some even receive national and international prizes), more television actors are considering docudrama as a quality vehicle. Furthermore, they see it as an arena in which to test or exhibit acting abilities that may be suppressed in other television genres.

RTVE has also promoted the lives of exemplary female characters. Whilst there is no shortage of female protagonists in contemporary Spanish biopics, most channels prefer to portray members of the aristocracy or entertainers. With *Clara Campoamor, la mujer olvidada* and *Concepción Arenal, la visitadora de cárceles*, the public channel has cast itself as the chronicler of the Women's Rights movement in Spain, viewed through the experiences of these two activists. These productions are also an example of how Spanish docudrama can be innovative in its approach to female subjects. Even though in both cases we have the conventional premise of a female protagonist standing against a patriarchal society, in neither case does this lead to victimisation and despair. Instead the activists are celebrated, and depicted finding satisfaction in activities commonly associated with men, such as public speaking or political activity. As Dennis Bingham observes:

> Female biopics play on tensions between a woman's public achievement and women's traditional orientation to home, marriage, and motherhood. In consequence, female biopics often find suffering (and therefore) drama in a public woman's very inability to make decisions and discover her own destiny. (2010, p. 213)

The Clara Campoamor and Concepción Arenal biopics address these genre conventions and expectations through a variety of strategies. First, the protagonists are introduced later in their lives, when romantic considerations and motherhood are not at issue. At the time of the events portrayed in *la visitadora de cárceles*, Concepción is already a widow with two children, who still remembers her late husband with fondness and who does not wish to marry again. Clara is introduced when in her early forties, single and childless because, as she says, she has 'no time for such things'. Other characters may comment on this unusual situation, particularly given the different historical contexts in which these two women lived (Concepción in the 1860s, Clara in the 1930s). But the films themselves refuse to present their lives as unfulfilled. Importance is given instead to other sources of emotional support, in particular female friendships or the relationship with close family members such as mothers, brothers, and sons. Clara and Concepción devote their energy to their causes: for Clara, achieving the right of women to vote; for Concepción, improving the conditions for female prisoners. Unlike other biopics dealing with professional women (where protagonists are rarely shown practising their occupations), Clara and Concepción are constantly placed in an arena of performance that requires a display of professional abilities (both women trained as lawyers and they regularly engage in debate and argument). Even in the domestic sphere, their professional endeavours are symbolically represented by the writing implements placed centre stage in their bedrooms, a space where we witness the conception of some of their more radical ideas.

The line taken about professional women in these films is more persuasive because male characters are not reduced to the simplistic level of romantic interest or antagonist. Key roles in the films are given to male characters that support the two women, sharing with them a passion for writing and the arts. It is true that the creative decision to include the characters of the (real) violinist Jesús de Monasterio (played by Xosé Barato) in *Concepción Arenal* and the (fictional) journalist Antonio García (played by Antonio de la Torre) in *Clara Campoamor* may be seen as injecting a faint suggestion of romance, thus providing a respite from the political and ideological intrigues that sometimes dominate the narrative. However, any romantic tension is carefully diffused, with melodramatic excess absent and no trace of emotional damage to the female protagonists. Instead their relationships develop into a mutually satisfying and intellectually stimulating friendship.

Both Clara and Concepción, then, enter the areas of ecclesiastical and civil law traditionally considered male, but their political activism does not diminish their femininity. In fact, the films incorporate genre devices that appear almost exclusively in the context of the female biopic, namely the use of fashion as a narrative trope. Clothes are presented as one of the few weapons available for women in a patriarchal society to express their personality or as a form of protest. This is however incorporated as a narrative device rather than a tool of characterisation. Neither Clara nor Concepción are defined by the way they look. In fact, they both favour elegant but practical fashions that mark them out as professional women. Fashion and sewing and dressmaking are also presented in the films as a form of liberation for other women. For the female prisoners in *Concepción Arenal*, receiving their first ever pair of shoes signals the start of their journey into rehabilitation. Concepción also suggests that embroidery and lace-making would be more suitable, dignified, and profitable activities for the prisoners, thus rescuing them from the backbreaking, demeaning, tannery work. The money they earn with their needlework becomes a symbol of hope and source of pride. In a defining scene, the now humanised prisoners refuse to lay down their crochet hooks and needles as a form of non-violent-protest against a prison governor who wants to force them back into their old work scraping sheep skins.

For Clara Campoamor the new fashion of shorter skirts and bras 'are doing more for the liberation of women than many politicians', and it is clear that for her these changes in fashion are visible evidence of the Republican spirit that was sweeping the country in the early twentieth century.[7] Dressmaking also becomes a way to create a connection between older and younger female generations. In a key scene, Clara stands in her underclothes, editing parts of the new Constitution, whilst her mother, a talented seamstress, takes her measurements for the new dress that she will be wearing for the opening of Parliament. Throughout this long sequence, the action moves back and forth from this domestic setting to the room where representatives from all parties are also working on the new Constitution. This intimate scene marks a moment of reconciliation between the two generations, as Clara agrees to have a new dress made by a mother who has always been very critical of her daughter's political activities. But it is also symbolic of how the work of the younger generation can bear fruit only if the older generation offers its support.[8] Moreover, the process of fitting and sewing the new dress is presented as of equal importance to the process of cutting and editing the articles of the Constitution. Female and male spheres are thus seamlessly joined, with the character of Clara acting as mediator.

Part of the unconventional approach to the figures of Clara and Concepción comes from placing a female director, Laura Mañá, at the helm of both projects. Reflecting on these biopics, Mañá describes her work in terms of a moral duty because 'we must remember heroines that have won their place in history, so men start showing some respect towards women' (RTVE 2010). In her assessment of biopics of professional women Ginette Vincendeau observes that 'to the spectacle of female competence and control, the films clearly prefer tragic romance, decadence, and ruin' (2014, p. 183). In the Spanish context the biopics of Clara Campoamor and Concepción Arenal offer a compelling alternative to this by presenting two women who are first and foremost humanists (as Clara actually defines herself).

CELEBRITIES AND PERFORMERS

It seems clear that RTVE views the production and broadcasting of these programmes in terms of prestige and as a way to fulfil its public service remit. It is therefore not surprising that once we move from the area of social activism into activities such as singing or acting, the public channel is conspicuous by its absence. Even the now seemingly defunct plan to produce a biopic of the singer Julio Iglesias was initially greeted by members of the channel's governing body with dismissive comments and fears that this was not in line with RTVE's public service commitment (ABC 2012).[9] Thus RTVE is out of line with other public service channels such as the BBC (still investing in high-quality biopics of figures from popular culture—Elizabeth Taylor, Kenneth Williams, Cilla Black).[10] In Spain, the private channels Telecinco and Antena 3 have taken on this kind of popular culture subject, so favoured by contemporary television audiences. As Raphaëlle Moine says of contemporary French biopics, 'more recent films tend to involve a "media heritage" that is more easily activated, in so far as the heroes and heroines belong to the recent past, to a rich world of available images' (Moine 2014, p. 59). What is undoubtedly particular to the Spanish case is that in a significant number of biopics of aristocrats or entertainers, this rich world of available documentary images largely originates in the tabloids, rather than in other documents such as televisual performances, professional interviews, or official occasions. The choice of the documentary visuals presented in the biopic in order to trigger memories has a deep impact on how the audience will read not just the character, but also the product itself. This raises the troubling question as to whether a film based solely on tabloid reports has the power to formulate and sustain a persuasive argument.

The level to which the performance of celebrity status is given prominence over the performance of artistic abilities or aristocratic obligations is perhaps more evident in the case of Telecinco, where the combination of content and promotional strategies places their biopics firmly in the territory of sensationalist television.

As Rueda Laffond argues in his analysis of *La Duquesa I & II* (The Duchess Part I & II, Telecinco, 2010–11) *and Alfonso el príncipe maldito* (Alfonso, the Doomed Prince, Telecinco, 2010):

> In terms of brand image, Telecinco puts forward a model based on the display of the private lives of celebrity figures, assembled and magnified by their own television programmes. […] This has had an impact on the handling and characterisation of the two protagonists of these biopics, something perceptible in the dramatisation of their private spheres, which may render the characters closer to the clichéd image generated by the media rather than to their own realities. (2014, p. 1040)

Sensationalism may be central to the promotion and selling of these programmes, but it cannot be denied that Telecinco does approach and market made-for-TV movies as a 'quality product' within its ample portfolio of gossip programmes. A clear example of this strategy is the website that the channel set up to showcase these productions. Here, the viewer can access free of charge 'making-of' featurettes, interviews, and image galleries in addition to the programmes themselves. These metatexts—with their references to the investment made on locations and costumes, or to the work of investigative journalism that underpins the script—contribute to impressing upon the viewer the concept that these TV movies are prestigious and trustworthy products. These messages are reinforced by careful scheduling. Both Telecinco and Antena 3 present TV movies as television events. This cost-effective and high-impact strategy is particularly suitable for biopics, which are introduced as the centrepiece of a special evening devoted to the protagonist, and are commonly advertised as '*La noche de...*' (An evening with ..,). The main feature is normally broadcast in the context of a discussion show where a wide range of special guests comment on the characters' lives and achievements. Archive footage may be used in illustration, but is also an excuse to comment on the production values of the film or the work of the actors. The schedule for the evening is rounded off with extra-textual elements such as documentary programmes, frequently drawn from the channel's own archives.

Given the large number of biographical docudramas that have been produced on entertainers and members of the aristocracy, I want briefly to focus only on two at the furthest ends of the spectrum in terms of the impact that celebrity status had on the portrayal of the characters: *Mi gitana* (My Gypsy, Telecinco, 2012) and *Raphael, historia de una superación* (Raphael, Against All Odds, Antena 3, 2010). Commissioned by Telecinco and developed in conjunction with the independent producer Mandarina, *Mi Gitana* is a three-part mini-series covering two decades in the life of the singer Isabel Pantoja.[11] The first half of the series narrates Pantoja's friendship and possible intimate relationship with the journalist Encarna Sánchez. In the second half, political scandals and corruption take centre stage when Pantoja falls in love with Julian Múñoz, mayor of Marbella. In terms of visual style, *Mi Gitana* aims for a naturalistic look, avoiding studio sets and shooting both interior and exterior scenes on location. The narrative is linear and captions are used to provide the audience with geo-temporal information. The temporal flow is sometimes interrupted by flashbacks used as a narrative device to recap previous events. Despite its apparent simplicity, the final product lacks cohesion and there is hardly any plot development. As one critic observed:

> Instead of building a narrative about the singer that would take us from point A to point B, this film is nothing more than a collection of her greatest hits. And not even that, for we do not see her professional successes or any happy moments, but a collection of scenes portraying the most controversial and miserable events in her life. (Onieva 2012)

Lucy Fife Donaldson argues that 'biopics about actors or musicians would be expected to dramatize the physical processes and achievements of acting/singing (in practice and rehearsals) and thus call attention to the constructedness of the star's image' (Fife Donaldson 2014, p. 106). However, in *Mi Gitana* the fictional Isabel is hardly ever on stage or performing, and when she does sing the voice is neither that of the actress Eva Marciel or the real Isabel, but the voice of an unseen performer, Mercedes Durán. Instead, Isabel is shown meeting with her agent, signing contracts, buying houses and becoming the ambassador of Marbella, a town growing rich on shady property deals. The few moments that we see Pantoja on stage act more like musical interludes to illustrate the impact that personal relationships had in her life. This is a film about celebrity, not artistry. But in showing the key events in the construction of Isabel's public image, it also becomes an interesting reflection on the mechanisms that Telecinco employs as a channel to create and nurture the characters that sustain its celebrity shows.

At the other end of the spectrum is *Raphael, historia de una superación*, an example of how Antena 3 approaches the treatment of the lives of artists and performers. Produced in partnership with the independent company Boca a Boca, *Raphael* is a stylistically innovative work detailing the popular singer Raphael's fight against liver disease. In a similar style to *La Môme/La Vie en Rose*, the 2007 Edith Piaf biopic, this period of illness is used as a framing device to explore in flashbacks Raphael's childhood, his early career, and the love story with his wife Natalia Figueroa. The film opens, as is the case with many musical biopics, with the artist performing on stage. This type of opening scene can be crucial in determining audience response, and therefore it is surprising that the performance chosen is not a regular concert, with Raphael wearing his trademark black shirt and suit. Instead the artist is on stage in Barcelona performing the Spanish version of the song *Confrontation* from the American musical, *Jekyll and Hyde*. Despite the heavy make-up that Raphael wears to play Dr Jekyll, the Spanish audience would immediately recognise his powerful and highly distinctive voice (his real singing voice is used throughout the film). This cleverly constructed opening scene bypasses the risk of having the tone of the biopic determined by a central performance that could very easily fall into parody in the hands of the wrong actor—a genuine concern in the case of Raphael because of the special reading of his performance likely in a Spanish audience. This audience is influenced both by knowledge of the real character and his artistic achievements, and by the countless imitations and parodies that Raphael's overdramatic style has inspired over the years.

The scene also foreshadows what the film is really about—not the conflict between the private person and the public artist, but the clash between Raphael's healthy and sick selves. Soon after the end of this performance, Raphael is diagnosed with liver disease, and this period of illness acts as a framing device to explore his childhood and career. This is done through flashbacks often triggered by moments of intense pain or crisis, when the singer finds refuge from a difficult present in soothing memories of his youth. Nevertheless, these scenes are much more than a lighter counterpoint to the intense drama of hospital visits and hepatic crisis. They offer a collection of key moments in the construction of Raphael the artist: how he based his overdramatic style on the work of classically trained actors, and how he came up with his stage name and his 'all black' dress code. In a sense, the viewer becomes witness to Raphael's second fight against all obstacles. If in the present he is fighting for his life, these flashbacks into the past show how this boy from a poor family used his talents to rise from poverty and achieve international stardom. Not all biopics produced by Telecinco are as sensational as *Mi Gitana*, and not all by Antena 3 are as deferential as *Raphael*, but these examples illustrate the general approach, and how the channels envisage the function of docudramatic biopics within their schedules and branding strategies. This extends even to the legal matters that surround docudrama. Telecinco will walk the thin line between the legal and the illegal, welcoming—indeed, utilising—any publicity arising from celebrities' complaints. References to possible legal actions against the channel, or to the exclusive deals that they have signed with the protagonists, often feature in their website articles, or are discussed in other shows. Antena 3 has so far steered clear of legal actions; it prefers to emphasise that its films are based on books or authorised by protagonists' families.

REAL CRIMES AND OTHER 'NOTEWORTHY' EVENTS

Reconstructions of real crimes have always being a favourite subject for docudrama worldwide, and Spain is no exception. Crime docudramas rival biopics in numbers produced, and films from all channels achieve good ratings. One of the most popular products has been the series *La Huella de Crimen* (Traces of a Crime, TVE1 1985, 1991, 2009). The first two seasons had six episodes each, the 2009 season three. With the slogan *La historia de un país es también la historia de sus crímenes* ('The history of a country is also the history of its crimes'), the intention was to dramatise criminal events within their social and historical contexts, thus presenting an arguably realistic portrayal of Spain in the particular era. Whilst the events recreated in the first and second season mostly took place in the relatively distant past (frequently the early twentieth century), more recent episodes have explored murder cases from the past twenty years which have already been extensively covered in the media. Even though the series never shies away from portraying the gruesome details of violent cases, the final product avoids cheap sensationalism, partly due to the significant number of prestigious directors and actors that producer Pedro Costa signed up for the first two series. In 2009, the series still delivered a quality product, but this time with new directors who had cut their teeth working on other television docudramas, and with a group of actors mainly recognisable from other television work or supporting roles in feature films.

Analysing the first two seasons, Luis Guadaño argues that *La Huella del Crimen* encouraged audiences to exercise their recently gained powers for democratic praxis. Using a variety of sources that very frequently question the credibility of the official documents and versions of the story, the series invites the viewer to reconsider the well-known events and maybe reach a new interpretation and/or conclusion:

> By presenting a narrative open to alternative interpretations, the series forces the viewer to analyse what they see; the viewers/citizens become an active part of a democratic narrative rather than passive subjects/receptors of the process. (2009, pp. 281–282)

This idea of allowing the viewer to pass judgement on events is somehow missing from the 2009 series. The focus on proven cases leads to rather straightforward treatment, with the central characters always the criminal and his/her associates. The influence of contemporary crime drama is evident in new narratives that detail police procedures or highlight the role of forensic teams and experts in criminal psychology. Nevertheless, the emphasis remains on exploring the social context of the crimes, a trait that it shares with the real crime docudramas produced by other channels like Antena 3.

As Lipkin argues, 'what characterizes the means of representation in an events docudrama and in the biopic might work in unison' (2011, p. 3), and this is the initial premise of most of the docudramas based on real crimes commissioned by Antena 3. The focus of attention shifts from the criminal and the crime to the victim's family. This fits well with Milly Buonanno's observations about the transition of the biopic from film to television. For her this transition had a deep impact in the choice of characters portrayed:

> Those being fêted were no longer the people who were respected for having achieved great things in a particular field, but ordinary people, who became the protagonists of TV biopics—'unremarkable' individuals who were suddenly and fleetingly pulled out of the anonymity of their everyday lives by some unexpected and disruptive event. (Buonanno 2012a, b, p. 174)

In *Padre Coraje* (Father Courage, Antena 3, 2002) and *Días sin luz* (Days of Darkness, Antena 3, 2009) the narratives centre on the fathers of two murder victims and on their extraordinary efforts to find the culprits. The process transforms them from ordinary citizens into media personalities. In the case of *Padre Coraje*, the protagonist infiltrates the criminal world of his home town in the hope of securing a confession from one of the suspects. Even though the film provides details of the crime and exposes at some length the blunders of the local police, this is explored through the prism of the protagonist's personal and emotional struggle to cope with the consequences of the murder. In a similar fashion, *Días sin luz* dramatises the investigation into the death of a five-year-old girl, but it also charts the progression of her father from humble origins to public figure fronting a national campaign demanding longer prison sentences for child abusers. As in *La Huella del Crimen*, these crimes are explored against the backdrop of a very particular social context, to the point that the programmes can be regarded as a cross between crime drama and observational documentary in the way they expose the reality of drug addiction, the daily routine of a working-class neighbourhood, or the norms and conventions of gypsy communities.

In addition to real crimes, docudrama in Spain has dealt with other topics that can be defined as being 'of social interest'—such as plane crashes, kidnapping, or piracy at sea. But even within these topics, audiences still favour stories of individual characters fighting their personal fights, rather than cases detailing the triumphs of civil society. Good examples are *Rescatando a Sara* (Rescuing Sara, Antena 3, 2012) and *Un burka por amor* (A Burqa for Love, Antena 3, 2009); in both a woman struggles against a repressive Islamic society. In the former, the protagonist travels to Iraq during the war in 2006, in an attempt to rescue her daughter Sara who has been kidnapped by her Iraqi father. In the latter, a young Spanish woman falls in love with an Afghan man and follows him to his country where she ends up living in a remote village under constant threat of the Taliban. The narrative centres on her struggle to cope with cultural shock and her efforts to escape the country with children and husband. In both, the action allows for an exploration of a foreign culture, initially portrayed as exotic (through the romance between the protagonists and their husbands), but later revealed as repressive, dangerous, and alien.

Few Spanish docudramas address issues that have a clear impact on the wider society. Moreover whenever such topics were given docudramatic treatment, audience ratings have been in general disappointing and critical reactions mostly negative. However, these programmes present an opportunity to observe and measure the capacity of this mode of address to launch persuasive argument and generate social mobilisation in the Spanish context. Docudrama's capacity to present and sustain persuasive argument lies at the heart of Lipkin's and other scholars' defence of this frequently maligned genre. In the Spanish context, docudrama is also extolled for its ability to accommodate controversial subjects. So what happens when a docudrama is not able either to convince or to shock its audience?

Many people posed this question after seeing the docudramas, *Vuelo IL8714* (Flight IL8714, Telecinco, 2010) and *11-M, para que nadie lo olvide* (11-M, Never Forget, Telecinco, 2011). The first deals with the 2008 Madrid plane crash that killed 154 people. The second narrates the events of 11 March 2004 (the Madrid train bombings) when a series of terrorist attacks on Madrid's commuter trains caused the deaths of 191 people and sparked nationwide demonstrations against terrorism. *Vuelo IL8714* was an important project for Telecinco. The channel saw an opportunity to demonstrate that, in spite of its reputation, it could also deal with 'serious subjects'. The project attracted star actors, Emma Suárez and Carmelo Gómez—even an international star, Joaquim de Almeida. However, its audience share was a disappointing 9.6 %. Its release attracted controversy because the families of the victims opposed it, even though all the names and even references to the details of the real flight had been changed for legal reasons. In fact the victims play a very minor role, as the real protagonists are members of the special unit that investigates the accident. In terms of visual and acting style the film is indebted to the popular US series *CSI: Crime Scene Investigation* (CBS, 2000–15, which has been showing on Telecinco for more than a decade). Characters replicated those of the forensic drama—a professionally detached head of investigation, an emotionally unstable rookie, a computer 'geek', a maverick, a steady female investigator. Impressive digital technology recreated the accident's possible scenarios, and cold forensic precision was the stylistic hallmark. Writing online about the movie in 2010, the critic David Trueba felt the low audience ratings were not the result of viewers finding it immoral to watch a film about the accident, but quite the opposite. He alleges that the absence of the kind of sensationalist approach and gruesome details viewers have come to expect from Telecinco might have been a factor: 'if you promise a visit to the morgue you cannot stop at the door'.

Considering the preconceptions that audiences and critics have about this channel, it is not surprising that the announcement that they were working on a docudrama on the Madrid bombings caused alarm in newspapers and on social media. Never known for its subtlety, and felt to have rather loose ethical principles, there was a fear that the channel would pile up the corpses and exploit numerous conspiracy theories surrounding the event. Victims of the terrorist attack had given the green light to the project and the producers claimed that the narrative would be based exclusively on the facts from the judicial process. None of this mattered; audiences, it would seem, approached the programme expecting to see the sensationalist treatment of facts that has become the trademark of a channel popularly known as 'Telecircus'. In the end the channel took a safe route and delivered a similar product to *Vuelo IL8715*. Audience ratings were much better, but critics once again felt that this was an 'un-dramatic docudrama'. Because the narrative followed the judicial facts, it almost ignored the presence of the victims and concentrated on the activities of the terrorists—with whom viewers found it difficult to identify. José Díaz noted online in 2011:

> If the intention was first and foremost to explain the sentence, they could have picked a better medium (a special report or a documentary). At times, the makers of this TV movie forget that this is a dramatization of events. Sometimes there is no plot, only a collection of facts that need to be listed.

He concluded that *11-M* and *Vuelo IL8715* brought nothing new to Spanish television drama. To this, we could add that neither have they managed to encourage audiences to engage in a significant discussion of the topics, other than the comment that such events 'should not be given fictional treatment'. We could argue that perhaps the capacity of these docudramas to launch persuasive argument was compromised by an excessive regard for factual data. Unable to dwell on the personal stories of the victims, the team behind *Vuelo IL8715* could only make the technical details more palatable by turning the docudrama into a forensic drama. Given the sensitive nature of the Madrid bombings, Telecinco could not afford to make it melodramatic, and instead delivered a didactic programme. In one way they made the judicial sentence more accessible to the general public, and the docudrama did have to compete with documentaries and special reports. All these had already considered the conspiracy theories related to this event thoroughly and extensively.[12]

Discussing the *raison d'être* of docudramas, Lipkin argues:

> The overall thrust of docudrama is neither exposition nor logical argumentation, but persuasion. Docudrama exists to create conviction. Docudrama

strives to persuade us to believe that what occurred happened much as we see it on the screen. (2002, p. ix)

When it comes to controversial subjects concerning civil society, Spanish docudrama seems to be caught in an expository mode, still unable, because of network politics, creative limitations, or legal issues, to offer persuasive arguments. This is, perhaps, the next frontier to be conquered in the evolution of Spanish docudrama.

The Representation of the Events of War (and Peace)

The third arena of docudramatic performance in Lipkin's classification is events of war. However this is the point where Spanish docudrama production differs markedly from that of other countries. Historical and cultural factors may explain why events from World War I and World War II—such popular subjects elsewhere in Europe—are virtually absent from Spanish docudrama.[13] More surprisingly, the Spanish Civil War has also been a marginal topic. The historical events of 1936–39 have inspired a significant corpus of feature films, but for television this is still very much uncharted territory. The prewar Republican years and the postwar era have been extensively explored in serialised period dramas such as *14 de abril, La República* (14 April, The Republic, TVE 1 2011) and *Amar en Tiempos Revueltos* (Loving in Troubled Times, TVE 1, 2005–12), and even a docudrama, *Carta a Eva* (Letter to Eva, TVE 1, 2012), but no series has yet focused exclusively on the years of the civil conflict.[14]

The production of these programmes seems to be intimately connected with the construction of a system of historical memory in Spain. Stimulated and encouraged by the passing of the controversial Ley de la Memoria Histórica (Law of Historical Memory) in 2006,[15] Spanish society and its media have for the past decade engaged in a critical exploration of the recent past. Whilst the law itself has striven for recognition and rehabilitation of the victims of the dictatorship, the current interest in the past is by no means restricted to the postwar era. Equally important is the exploration of the key years that marked the transition from dictatorship to democracy, a period commonly known as *la Transición* ('the transition', 1975–81). This general interest has crystallised into very successful fiction dramas such as the aforementioned *Cuéntame cómo pasó* and also *La chica de ayer* (The Girl from Yesterday, Antena 3, 2009). In the case of docudrama, events from *la Transición* are the inspiration for almost 80 % of all historical drama, with all channels offering their trademarked view of these key years.

In 2014, Telecinco stepped into this arena with its biopic *El Rey* (The King 2015) dedicated to the figure of King Don Juan Carlos I. As expected, the mini-series concentrated on the personal rather than the political, so the accidental death of his younger brother and fraught relationship with his father were to the fore. But some key historical events of *la Transición* had to be recreated, such as his Coronation Day. Antena 3, on the other hand, has been a diligent chronicler of *la Transición*. It was thanks to this channel that Spanish audiences first saw on their television screens fictional scenes clearly referencing dictator Francisco Franco and King Don Juan Carlos I in the docudrama *20-N, los últimos días de Franco* (20-N, the Final Days of Franco, Antena 3, 2008). This was followed by *Adolfo Suárez, el presidente* (Adolfo Suárez, the President, Antena 3, 2010), a biopic of the first democratically elected president. True to the channel's cautious approach to fact-based subjects, *20-N* casts a compassionate look at Franco in the final months of his life, inviting viewers to take pity on an old man plagued by illnesses and kept alive for political reasons. Equally, *Adolfo Suárez* offers a respectful, almost hagiographical, portrayal of the moderate politician, emphasising his efforts to construct an all-inclusive democracy and praising him for his conciliatory stance.

But of all historical docudramas, the most interesting are those dealing with the failed *coup d'etat* of 23 February 1981, when a group of armed officers seized Parliament and held MPs hostage for almost 18 hours. The significance of this event cannot be underestimated. In the public imagination this powerful narrative marks the moment when the young democracy was most publicly put to the test—and triumphed. It was also a defining experience for the new king, who delivered a powerful televised address declaring his unwavering support for democratic principles and exhorting the rebels to lay down their arms. So far, two channels have produced docudramas narrating the events of 23 February 1981 (known as '23F'): RTVE produced *23F*, whilst Antena 3 made *23F: Historia de una traición* (23F: Chronicle of a Betrayal).[16] Both produced in the same year, 2009, they were also broadcast on the same night. Audiences preferred the more conservative interpretation of the events, championed by the public channel, to the political thriller offered by the private network; *23F: El día más difícil del Rey* is the most popular docudrama in recent history with almost 7 million viewers.

   23F: El día más difícil del Rey embraces visual conventions and narrative codes that have delineated most televisual portrayals of *la Transición*, and this episode in particular. Spain is presented as country emerging gradually but securely from an exhausted dictatorship into a modern democracy, with the monarchy acting as guarantor of the process, and characterised as a symbol of political consensus. After the events of the coup, the king earns further recognition as a champion of this new state, a quasi-heroic figure controlling and restraining the military establishment through non-violent means—and does so through the relatively novel medium of television. The elements of this docudrama are carefully managed to fit a commonly accepted version of events. The action is confined to the few hours between the morning of the 23 February 1981 and the early hours of the following day, when the king recorded his televised speech. Filmed almost entirely on set, most of the action occurs in the royal residence.[17] Temporal and spatial constraints facilitate the construction of a narrative that 'complies with the conventions of a political and family drama of emotional implications, structured as a confrontation between an individual hero and a collective anti-hero, it is the King versus the military rebels' (Rueda Laffond 2009, p. 172).

   However, Don Juan Carlos I is by no means characterised as an unapproachable figure. In this docudrama, the viewer encounters a recognisable character that mirrors the public image of a professional but amiable king. He has cultivated this image over the years during official acts and in the media. The populist characterisation is also evident in the representation of other members of the royal household. Queen Sofía's portrayal fits with her discreet public image; she is a character in the shadows, interested in charitable enterprises, concerned about her children, always supporting the king throughout difficult events. The docudrama also focuses on the relationship between Don Juan Carlos and his son, Prince Felipe (the future King Felipe VI). In the opening scene, the king and his son (Lluis Homar and Lluis Bou respectively) are casually discussing the football results at the family breakfast table. The prince confesses he is struggling to complete a school assignment on what he wants to be when he grows up. He argues it is more difficult for him because he has no choice. The king suggests he should write about what it means to be king, and promises to help him later. This casual offer will reveal itself as prophetic, on a day when the strength of the constitutional monarchy and the new king's political abilities will be put to the test. The prince will be a visible presence at crucial moments of the drama, on the sidelines like the queen (Mónica López), but singled out by the camera in medium shots depicting a brave, inquisitive young boy intently watching and learning how a democratic monarch should act and behave. Under the unflinching gaze of the prince, the actions of the king in this docudrama gain in depth and relevance.

In the recreation of these historical events, the audience is offered an historical figure who enters the arena of the coup as a determined and professional democratic monarch. These principles are echoed and reprised in the recreated conversations that he holds with the prince, his successor. Thus, this docudrama actualises and perpetuates the values of that momentous night, whilst reasserting the legitimacy of the hereditary monarchy for a contemporary audience all too aware of the insistent rumours about Don Juan Carlos's possible abdication.[18] In deep contrast with this thoroughly modern and dynamic characterisation of the royals, the military rebels appear determinedly *ancien régime*. The docudrama offers well-rounded portrayals of the high-ranking officials involved in the uprising, with performances from established actors such as Pepe Sancho and Juan Luis Galiardo. Nevertheless, it is not so much their acts as their words (some historically accurate, some historically inspired) that can shock a modern audience. One character asserts that the coup was the last opportunity to save Spain from destruction, by imposing a military government 'as God intended'. Statements such as this have a ring of historical truth, but would certainly alienate contemporary viewers. The docudrama also plays up the fact that some of the rebels were friends of the king, and by engineering this coup they have betrayed that friendship and, by extension, the country.

The military establishment, friendships, and personal betrayal are also at the heart of Antena 3's interpretation of the events of 23F. However, its narrative is speculative, playing on the potential appeal of conspiracy theories. The many unexplained details surrounding the coup were something that Spanish television channels had already been exploring in documentaries.[19] Antena 3's docudrama *Historia de una traición* links the years of the coup with the present time through parallel stories spanning two generations. In the late 1970s two army officers, Antonio Leal and Ignacio Zarate, become friends; on the day of the coup they find themselves on opposite sides. In the present, their children, Gonzalo Leal and Arancha Zarate, are accidentally involved in the search for a mysterious dossier containing confidential and potentially damning information about 23F. With these elements, Antena 3 constructs an uneven romantic thriller, with formulaic characters and a positively anticlimactic finale. Unlike *El día más difícil del Rey*, *Historia de una traición* includes a limited number of historical characters and recreated historical events. The few archive images act as temporal indices rather than as a warrant of validity for the alternative theories suggested. As Rueda Laffond indicates in his analysis of the mini-series, this contrast between past and present, reality and fiction places *Historia de una traición* closer to fiction drama such as *Cuéntame cómo pasó* or *La chica de ayer* (2009, p. 196).

For audiences, the conspiracy theories of Antena 3 were no match for RTVE's authoritative historical reconstruction. Although audience reaction may have had much to do with the dramatic quality of these products, it is also true that the public channel version is in line with strategies adopted by successful historical docudramas elsewhere. Buonanno observes of the Italian case: 'historical drama has made its choices according to a logic of national reconciliation hinging upon the recognition of a common identity matrix and belonging' (2012a, b, p. 223). *23F: El día más difícil del Rey* is a clear example of this in the Spanish context. Its success gives an indication of Spanish audiences' preference, at least in the case of *la Transición*: the period is seen as an exemplary passage from dictatorship to democracy, and is thus a source of pride for Spanish citizens.

This does not mean that Spanish media recoils from testing the resilience of this historical construct. On 23 February 2014, private channel La Sexta broadcast a mockumentary, *Operación Palace* (Operation Palace, 2014) to coincide with the anniversary of the coup. This successful programme, watched by more than 5 million viewers, was the brainchild of journalist Jordi Évole, presenter of the news show *Salvados*.[20] The programme argued that the coup was a set-up, a farce orchestrated by politicians in collaboration with the public television channel to strengthen the image of the monarchy. The narrative combines archive images with a series of interviews with journalists, politicians, and film director Jose Luis Garci, interspersed with reconstructions of meetings at the Palace Hotel in Madrid planning the 'fake' coup. The pretence of reality is firmly held until the closing lines, when the voice of the narrator reveals that this version of events is just a fantasy, a fable. A live debate followed, with a discussion on the power of the media to manipulate audiences, whilst in parallel public figures and spectators expressed their views on social media. Whilst some critics praised the programme for being innovative—daring to point at the official secrecy that still surrounds the events of 23F—many viewers reacted negatively. Some felt angry at being deceived by a journalist of such calibre, whilst politicians such as Gaspar Llamazares questioned the morality of the experiment.[21] The popularity of this programme and the impact that it had on social media demonstrate that the events of 23F are still central to the foundational narrative that supports Spain's modern democracy. With much official documentation still secret, it is very likely that television networks will revisit this historical moment, perhaps with increasingly sophisticated strategies, in order to test it.

CONCLUSION

In December 2014, the painter Antonio López unveiled his portrait of the Spanish royal family. A massive 3×3 m², the work was initially commissioned in 1994, and based on pictures that were taken in that year. For two decades, the painter arranged and rearranged the figures, changing the colour of the shoes or the position of the hands. The result is an image that feels both old and modern, sporting the fashions of the day but suspended in a white, aseptic background. This image speaks not so much about the past as about the time that has passed, and the way these people and the institution of the monarchy have changed. Historical docudrama has played a similar role in contemporary Spanish television, zooming in on the past and inviting the viewer to evaluate Spain's journey from the momentous events of the late 1970s to the present. Like López's work, historical docudrama may have helped to coalesce into visible evidence the foundational narratives of Spain's democracy. As Colin McArthur argues 'all television (including drama) fulfils an ideological function and there will be a relationship between the popularity of a programme and the extent to which it reinforces the ideological position of the majority audience' (1981, p. 288). The great success of *23F: El día más difícil del Rey* confirms that. In a sense, only docudrama could capture the essence of a monarchy whose legitimacy is said to be based 'on symbols, metaphors, and, first and foremost, on storytelling' (Murado 2013).

From being a newcomer, docudrama has become a permanent fixture of the Spanish television ecology, showing an innate ability to respond and adapt to network trends and evolving consumer tastes. For television executives, docudrama was a golden ticket allowing them to take full advantage of new laws that paved the way for quality TV movies and mini-series, as well as a useful tool in lessening the impact of audience fragmentation in the celebrity television landscape. For audiences, these productions opened a unique space in which to experience historical memory and to engage in the construction of the Spanish 'media heritage'. But after the intense activity of the last decade, docudrama in Spain seems to have reached a plateau. Both Antena 3 and Telecinco are now keen to obtain further returns from their current stock before starting any new projects. Both channels are planning reruns of some docudramas, with Antena 3 also offering them on their pay-per-view service. It should also be noted that Antena 3 and RTVE hold a number of unreleased docudramas—from biopics of the popular singer Rocío Jurado and the nineteenth-century politician Prim, to a historical reconstruction of the 1936 military *coup d'etat*.

This decline in the number of productions speaks more of the normalisation of the docudrama genre rather than of its disappearance. Recent projects include a biopic of the hypnotist José Mir Rocafort, 'Professor Fassman', who rose to fame in the 1940s/1950s in Spain and Argentina, and a two episode mini-series on the life of St Teresa of Avila. Moreover, these projects come associated with actors and directors that in the Spanish context have become synonymous with docudrama. Whether it chooses to launch persuasive arguments about historical events, or to explore the emotional appeal of public figures, the industry of docudrama production is now sufficiently well-established to ensure a steady presence in schedules in the years to come.

NOTES

1. Barroso illustrates this point with reference to Ken Loach's seminal film *Cathy Come Home*. Whilst it reached most European countries soon after its release in 1966, in Spain it was shown ten years later (Barroso 2004, p. 178).
2. All translations from Spanish are mine.
3. Of particular interest are the ten episodes of *Vivir cada día* directed by Javier Maqua. His work exemplifies the formal experimentation that defined the second period of the programme, openly mixing elements of documentary and drama: 'a formula that was already well established in other countries but was still new to the Spanish context' (Moral 2009, p. 99).
4. See Palacio (2008, p. 165) and Diego (2010, pp. 83–116) for more detail.
5. Although there are examples of docudrama production at regional level, the present chapter considers only docudramas broadcast by the three national television channels responsible for the vast majority of productions. These channels sit within larger television networks or media

corporations: TVE 1 is part of the state-owned corporation CRTVE that regulates public television and radio in Spain; Antena 3 belongs to one of the most important media groups in the country, Atresmedia (comprising other television channels such as la Sexta and the popular radio station Onda Cero); finally, the channels Telecinco and Cuatro merged in 2011 and became the largest television network in Spain, Mediaset España Comunicación, owned by the Italian company Mediaset (Mavise 2014).

6. See García Hernández (2014) for a detailed list of programmes.

7. *Clara Campoamor* also exposes the internal conflicts that crippled the Second Spanish Republic (1931–39), as well as the questionable decisions and shortcomings of some of its politicians. This programme is the only docudrama dealing with the Second Republic to have been broadcast nationally. It has been suggested that the public channel RTVE holds at least 19 unreleased films dealing with the Second Republic and the Spanish Civil War. Questioned by the Spanish Parliament about this situation, the director of RTVE, Leopoldo González-Echenique explained that this was due to budgetary restrictions, not politics (Europa Press 2014). Of these films we should highlight the case of *La Conspiración* (Conspiracy, EiTB, 2012). This TV movie explores the role of General Emilio Mola in the military uprising of 1936 that culminated in the Spanish Civil War. A co-production by RTVE and the Basque regional channel, it was shown on Basque television in 2012 but it is still waiting for its national release. According to Manuel Morón (who plays General Mola), 'this is just a new form of censorship under the excuse of financial savings' (Taboada 2013).

8. This intergenerational address is frequent in Spanish historical docudramas of the last decade and fits well with the didactic approach that many of these historical programmes adopt. Using a variety of visual and narrative strategies, they invite the viewer to identify normally with the younger generation as they experience the past events through the actions or testimony of the older generation. For example, in *Concepcion Arenal*, we share the point of view of her son as she expresses the need for a prison reform. Equally, in *23F: El día más difícil del Rey* we experience some of the iconic events through the eyes of the young Prince Felipe.

9. In 2011, RTVE planned a biopic about the singer Julio Iglesias. Parts of the programme have been filmed, but as yet there is no release date. Iglesias has repeatedly expressed his discomfort at having someone other than himself narrating the events of his life (Iglesias 2012).

10. See David Rolinson's Chap. 8 for more detail on this development in recent British docudrama.

11. Born in Seville to a family of artists, Isabel Pantoja is a singer whose popularity soared throughout the 1990s and 2000s, Her extraordinary voice and stage presence earned her the title of 'Queen of *la copla*', a very

distinctive Spanish folkloric music genre. Her mix of traditional songs with more contemporary ballads made her very popular in the wider Hispanic world, and she achieved great commercial success. Despite her involvement in financial scandals (she was jailed for two years in 2014), and her dealings with the yellow press, she still commands the respect of commentators and the public as a great performer.

12. José Carlos Rueda Laffond and Carlota Coronado Ruiz have discussed these documentary programmes in their book *La mirada Televisiva* (2009, pp. 226–259).

13. The only notable exception is *El Ángel de Budapest* (The Angel of Budapest, TVE 1, 2010) a stirring portrayal of the Spanish diplomat Ángel Sanz Briz who saved the lives of thousands of Hungarian Jews during World War II.

14. An exception to this is the short-lived surrealist comedy *Plaza de España* (Spain Square, TVE 1, 2011). The plot centres on the residents of an isolated village in the mountains and on their efforts to carry on with their lives despite the military conflict. For more details see Chicharro Merayo (2012, pp. 202–208).

15. Recovering the lost or erased memory of the Spaniards who lost the Civil War (1936–39) has been a long lasting dream for left-wing politicians in Spain. After many years, and lacking conservative support, the socialist government finally passed the Ley de la Memoria Histórica (Law of Historical Memory) in 2006. The law covers, amongst many other things, recognition of the victims of political, religious, and ideological violence on both sides of the Spanish Civil War, and of Franco's regime; condemnation of the Francoist regime; and the removal of Francoist symbols from public buildings and spaces. Right-wing politicians claimed that the law will only reopen old wounds, but other sectors defended the decision as a sign that Spanish democracy had finally reached maturity.

16. In 2001, RTVE also produced *23F, la película* (23F, The Movie), a cinema-only feature film about the coup. This has not been shown so far on television.

17. These scenes where not recorded at the Palacio de la Zarzuela, the official residence of the royal family, but at the Palacio de Pedralbes, in Barcelona (*23-F: Recreating the atmosphere of 28 years ago*, 2009).

18. On 19 June 2014, King Don Juan Carlos abdicated in favour of his son, who became the new King Felipe VI. This came at a moment when the popularity of the institution was at an all-time low, following several public incidents involving the King and accusations of tax evasion against his daughter, the Infanta Cristina.

19. On the evening of the first episode of the miniseries, Antena 3 broadcast two of these previous documentaries, *Se rompe el silencio* (Breaking the Silence, Antena 3, 1994) and *Las cintas secretas del 23F* (Secret Recordings from 23F, Antena 3, 2006).

20. This news show has been described as 'a mixture of intrepid and sarcastic journalism that takes reality with a pinch of humour, with the purpose of entertaining' (Fórmula TV 2008).

21. On the night of the broadcast, Llamazares wrote on his Twitter account: 'The coup was something very serious, with accomplices from inside and outside the system, that's why pretending that it was just a farce could be foolish and dangerous' (Vertele 2014). Anger is a frequent and even natural reaction to mockumentary, as Roscoe and Craig point out in their analysis of the form (2001, p. 22).

CHAPTER 7

Swedish Docudrama: In the Borderlands of Fact and Fiction

Åsa Bergström

INTRODUCTION

Sweden is a comparatively small country with a dominant public service television broadcaster and the national traits of its television docudramas therefore need to be set in perspective. This article is a first step in the process of mapping the development of Swedish docudrama, with a survey approach prioritised over detailed analysis. An initial overview of the docudrama discourse and research in Sweden over time is followed by a summary of the Swedish television context. The examples discussed are chosen in order to offer wider perspectives on what is a multifaceted field of productions. In order to address some specific aspects revealed in more recent Swedish docudramas, three productions will finally be highlighted.

My selection of productions is based on three criteria: firstly, one of the productions has been highly praised while the other two have been heavily debated and criticised. Interestingly, the praised and award-winning production focuses on noteworthy events of higher international interest, while both criticised productions deal with events with a less international, more national or even local, focus. Secondly, the three docudramas represent different production and broadcast contexts—Swedish public service television, the commercial channel TV4, and international co-production. Thirdly, the most recent production potentially marks a shift towards to a fourth phase of Swedish docudrama. Furthermore, all

© The Editor(s) (if applicable) and The Author(s) 2016
T. Ebbrecht-Hartmann, D. Paget (eds.), *Docudrama on European Television*, Palgrave European Film and Media Studies,
DOI 10.1057/978-1-137-49979-0_7

three include stylistic devices highly relevant to a survey of the Swedish borderlands of fact and fiction, which also make them essential in relation to the European television docudrama context.

DOCUDRAMA DISCOURSE AND RESEARCH IN SWEDEN

The website of *Nationalencyklopedin* (*NE*—the official national encyclopaedia of Sweden), provides the following descriptions of 'documentary drama' and 'drama documentary':

> Documentary drama: theatre and drama that seek to reproduce documentary material in accordance with a defined ideology. For example: *Danton's Death* (*Dantons Tod*, Georg Büchner, 1834), *The Investigation* (*Die Ermittlung*, Peter Weiss, 1965) and *The Raft* (*Flotten*, Kent Andersson and Bengt Bratt, 1967). (NE 2015a)[1]

> Drama documentary: dramatized documentary film. The term is used mainly for television feature films and series built on real events and was introduced in the 1970s, although the phenomenon itself is about as old as the cinema. (NE 2015b)

The word 'docudrama' is not included in this encyclopaedia. Overall, the word generates very few hits in Swedish databases, books, and websites. In addition, productions generating hits are of a great variety, which often means that they are not even actual docudramas as understood in this book. The two major film and media sites in Sweden—the Swedish Film Database (SFDB) administered by the Swedish Film Institute (SFI), and the Swedish Media Database (SMDB) administered by the audiovisual media section (AVM) at the National Library of Sweden—are perhaps the most significant examples of this blurred labelling.[2] Neither the Swedish word 'dokudrama', nor the English word 'docudrama', generates any hits on the Swedish Film Database (SFI 2015a, b). Depending on whether the keyword is written in Swedish or in English on the Swedish Media Database, 'dokudrama' generates 20 hits, and 'docudrama' generates 49, all with little or no connection to docudrama (AVM 2015a, b). As to the Swedish word 'dramadokumentär', nine hits result on the Swedish Film Database (SFI, 2015c). Two of these, *Alfred Nobel—Mr. Dynamite* (SVT TV2, 1983, dir. Olle Häger and Hans Villius) and *Vägen hem* (The Religious Sect—A Murder Story, TV4, 2009, dir. Karin Swärd) can be considered relevant to this survey. Just as in the example of entering the

English keyword 'docudrama' on the Swedish Film Database, the English spelling 'drama documentary' generates no hits (SFI 2015d). The most significant change in number of hits is on the keyword 'dramadokumentär' on the Swedish Media Database, which has increased from 1638 to 2083 between 2012 and 2015 (AVM 2015c). However, a majority of the hits involve British or other international productions (AVM 2015c). Despite the many international productions included in the Swedish Media Database, a search for the English word 'drama documentary' only results in 344 hits, which in turn reveals an apparent lack of consistency in the attempts at standardised definitions (AVM 2015d). Thus, just as in the case of Great Britain, Sweden seems to have favoured the word 'dramadokumentär' (in English, 'drama documentary'), which also corresponds to the development of this mode of representation historically. In Sweden, the development of docudrama is related to the process in which certain investigative documentaries have gradually applied stylistic and narrative approaches similar to those of fictional drama.

Clearly, the search results reveal more about the limitations of Swedish docudrama discourse, and the lack of Swedish research in this field, than about the actual stylistic devices of Swedish film, television and theatre productions within the docudramatic mode. The compilation film *Vi mötte stormen* (We Met the Storm, 1943, dir. Bengt Janzon) can serve as a clarifying example here, especially because the characterisation of docudrama in *Nationalencyklopedin* is too narrow, and therefore not applicable in a discussion of Swedish docudrama (Svensk Filmdatabas 2015e). Produced in 1943, this film cross-cuts dramatised scenes of a fictional Swedish family from the upper-middle class and contemporary clips from a number of fiction films, newsreels, and documentary footage. The soundtrack primarily consists of dialogue performed by the actors, occasionally directed towards the camera, supplemented by a somewhat ideological voice-over emphasising Swedish social democracy and neutrality. Consequently, the interaction of fact and fiction clearly reproduces what *Nationalencyklopedin* describes as 'documentary material in accordance with a defined ideology' (NE 2015a).

Although Swedish research on docudrama is limited, a 2006 study by literary scholar Bo G. Jansson discusses what he calls 'faction' in literature, film, and television. The paratexts and focalisations Jansson defines in his Swedish and international examples are analysed narratologically, resulting in a limited textual focus. His study is in Swedish, but has an appendix in English (2006, pp. 215–237), and some of the examples overlap with docudramas discussed in my survey. Briefly, Jansson defines the 'faction' epic in relation to 'non-fictional' and 'fictional' epic (p. 9).[3] Under his umbrella term 'faction' he discusses both docudrama and drama documentary and acknowledges their differences:

> The drama documentary is more closely related to the documentary film and non-fiction than to the fiction film and the novel. This is due to the fact that the drama documentary, like the documentary film and the non-fiction narration, does not suppress its dependence on sources and documents but rather openly refers to these. Conversely to drama documentary, it is impossible for the docudrama to openly refer to sources and documents. Every attempt to do so immediately removes the historical events represented in the docudrama from the intradiegetic level to the hypodiegetic level, hence, transforming the docudrama to drama documentary. (p. 62)

This leads him to argue that if a potential docudrama openly refers to sources and documents—which from his perspective implies that these components are transferred from the intradiegetic to the hypodiegetic level—it is immediately transformed into a drama documentary. Consequently, Jansson challenges earlier research, not least when it comes to studies focusing on docudramas on film and television:

> Some writings on the faction phenomena are trying to define faction in a completely different way. Unlike me, these critiques, for example Derek Paget's, do not primarily use the paratextual and textual criteria, but the vantage point of to what extent the factual text relates to the historical reality. [—] Hence, Paget's use of drama documentary and documentary drama, as well as his definition of these two faction criteria, are quite different from mine and, according to me, less successful. (pp. 81–82)

On the one hand, then, Jansson emphasises the significance of the paratext when defining docudrama, hereby acknowledging the importance of contextualisation. On the other hand, however, his conclusions are primarily drawn from a narratological and therefore strictly textual perspective. Furthermore, the use of 'faction' as a wide umbrella term leads him into a vast area where the relationship between paratext and text is in focus for definitions of fact and fiction, where the potential boundaries not only are defined, but also fixed and unalterable. A consequence of this narrow textual focus is that the contexts outside the paratext, as well as the crucial performative aspects of docudrama—which are motivated by the actual embodiment of the text not least when it turns into performance on stage, film, and/or television—are more or less neglected. This limitation is problematic, especially since docudramas per se are representations of significant events and/or individuals (Lipkin 2011, p. 3), set in a specific period of time, and with an obvious connection to social, temporal, and productive contexts. Accordingly, I find it crucial to include the performative aspects as well as the contextual parameters of when, where, how, and by whom, when considering docudrama.

Another Scandinavian study with a primarily theoretical approach is to be found in the interdisciplinary Danish anthology *Fact, Fiction and Faction* (Johansen and Søndergaard 2010).[4] In the foreword the interdisciplinary approach is explained:

> The reason for approaching the distinction between fact and fiction (and faction) from an interdisciplinary perspective is the circumstance that their relationship, at the present time, has become somewhat complicated. [—] There are several reasons for this. The media present facts in a manner that makes them look like fiction, and conversely fiction is presented as if it were facts. (p. 7)

The editors emphasise that the 'collection of articles attempts to analyze important aspects of the complex relationships between fact on one side and fiction and faction, history and counterfactual history on the other in the contemporary world' (pp. 7–8). Even so, neither docudrama nor drama documentary is mentioned, consequently, no explicit references are made to actual research in this field.

Although research on Swedish docudrama is limited, discussions of specific docudramas are included in several studies and articles. Three of these studies are of special importance not only for their qualities but also because some of the examples overlap with docudramas discussed in my survey (Agger 2013; Jönsson 2008; Ludvigsson 2003). Thus, they will be applied throughout the forthcoming discussions. My own view is that Paget's reflection on attempts to standardise and set definitions of drama documentary and/or documentary drama is a valid one, applicable in the Swedish context. 'Ultimately', he notes:

> I regard all attempts to standardise definitions, including my own, as worthy but doomed. The two terms are routinely used (often shortened to 'dramadoc' or 'docudrama') in journalistic commentary about widely different

examples, as if they were the same thing. [—] But I believe now that 'docudrama' is effectively the term of choice for discussion of this subject—academic and otherwise—in anglophone cultures. (2011, p. 15)

Additionally, I find useful the four-phase developmental model Paget proposes for the histories of British and American docudrama. These are: first phase antecedents (during the immediate postwar period 1946–60); second phase developments (throughout the Cold War Period 1960–80); third phase co-production (during the period of détente, including an interregnum following the collapse of Eastern Communist states—about 1980–1996); and fourth phase hybridisation (circa.1996–) (see Paget 2011, p. v, pp. 171–296). The Swedish development of televised docudrama reflects these four phases up to a point, allowing for slight delays which need to be scrutinised. For example, the first phase is shortened in Sweden owing to Swedish television broadcast history (see below).

Finally, I find useful Steven N. Lipkin's consideration of docudrama as a mode of representation where the framing narratives, which he calls 'arenas', primarily include 'the representation of noteworthy events [...]; the representation of the events of war [...]; the representation of noteworthy individuals [...]' (2011, p. 3). In a broad sense, these arenas correspond fairly well to Swedish docudramas, although I believe the representation of crimes and court cases to be additionally pertinent in the discussion. This 'arena' is partly associated with the recent development and success of 'Nordic Noir'.[5]

THE DEVELOPMENT OF TELEVISION IN SWEDEN

Swedish public service television is so dominant it tends to manifest itself as an elephant in the room, foreshadowing all other discussion. In the early years, Britain's BBC constituted a model for Swedish radio. Within the framework of the company Radiotjänst regular television broadcasting commenced in September 1956. The new medium was considered to be in need of regulation and there was political unity about giving a single company exclusive rights to transmit. From 1956 to 1969, there was only one channel within the framework of the public service company Sveriges Radio. The programme service was regulated in an agreement with the state and production was, and still is, financed by a licence fee (Kleberg 1996, p. 182). Motivated politically by considerations of the value of diversity, a second channel was introduced in December 1969, featuring contrasting programming aimed at different audience interests (1996, pp. 196–197). The original TV1 was considered to be conventional and traditional while the new channel, TV2, was dominated by a serious documentary section, programmes for children, and a drama/theatre unit providing a Swedish theatre repertoire, sometimes with a socially critical approach. Early 1970s programming was characterised by a Swedish working-class focus and contemporary views of society, for example raising awareness of environmental threats and population explosion (Furhammar 1995, pp. 117–119). In the late 1970s Sveriges Radio was divided into four units, of which Sveriges Television (SVT) and Sveriges Utbildningsradio (UR) are of importance for this survey.[6]

This monopolistic two-channel system was abandoned in the mid-1980s, when cable and satellite systems began operating (Kleberg 1996, p. 182). At the same time, there was an urgent need to regulate cable transmissions and in 1986 The Cable Act was passed, which meant wider rights to install cable and establish cable networks (1996, p. 201). While satellites and cable stations were growing in number, a third terrestrial network was put in operation. Since TV3 already existed (a commercially financed Scandinavian company, broadcasting by satellite from London), the new channel was called TV4 (1996, pp. 201–203). While public services broadcaster SVT tends to be associated with cultural values, TV4's governing concept is business-orientated (Edin 2000, p. 159).

LATE FIRST- AND SECOND-PHASE SWEDISH DOCUDRAMA ON PUBLIC SERVICE TELEVISION

In the early phase of development, the films and TV programmes made by historians and filmmakers Olle Häger (1935–2014) and Hans Villius (1923–2012) constitute noteworthy examples. They are also crucial for understanding the gradual shift from the first to the second phase. Häger and Villius' historical documentaries were produced and broadcast from the mid-1960s onwards, and over the years Häger and Villius developed some of their productions as docudramas. The development of Swedish docudrama on television was initiated by dramatised scenes persistently accompanied by Hans Villius' slightly didactic voice-over, gradually leading on to full-length docudramas based on three-act dramaturgy and with scripted dialogue performed by actors. The lack of consistency in Swedish docudrama discourse is exemplified by the fact that only one of their productions, *Alfred Nobel—Mr. Dynamite* (SVT TV2, 1983, dir. Olle Häger and Hans Villius—about the Swedish chemist, inventor, and founder of the Nobel Prize) is listed as a drama documentary in the Swedish Film Database (SFI 2015f). Initially intended as a mini-series, this was broadcast in short film form by TV2. The film consists of scripted and dramatised scenes with actor John Zacharias as Nobel, cross-cut with Swedish and international archival footage, with both still and moving images, and contemporary footage emphasising Nobel's worldwide scientific impact. Häger provides the voice-over in some of the dramatised scenes, while Villius' voice-over links to the archival footage. In an attempt to clarify the filmmakers' own view of the reconstruction of historical events, David Ludvigsson quotes Villius:

> When it comes to history the concrete is rarely as interesting as the abstract. What was the meaning of that which happened? What were the motives of those involved? What was their world of ideas like and what were the consequences, etc.? It is not just a question of reconstructing the sequence of events and the external milieu, but one must also strive to get a deeper reality. (Villius quoted in English in Ludvigsson 2003, p. 290)

Ludvigsson reads Villius' statement as an explicit ambition with regard to interpretation, implicitly revealing that '[—] Villius thought that concrete looks of scenes and persons acting in them were uninteresting' (p. 291). Considering the fact that the mode of docudrama is commonly used, or even highly significant, in Häger and Villius' productions from the mid-1980s and onwards, Ludvigsson's interpretation is somewhat contradictory. In *Alfred Nobel—Mr. Dynamite* some of the lines, for example Nobel's monologues, are performed by actors, while the meaning and interpretation of time, events, places, and persons depicted are communicated through Häger's and Villius' voice-overs. In view of that, it is fairly obvious that the visual appearance of scenes and persons acting in them were not uninteresting to Villius, but were an important part of his '[—] pragmatic view on how documentary and drama could be mixed, although clearly he sought to reach the '"meaning" of events' (p. 291).

Additionally, some of Häger and Villius' television productions from the late 1980s are discussed as '[—] historical drama-documentaries [*sic*] dealing with events from Swedish political history' (p. 143). Ludvigsson argues that:

> First was the three-part *Sammansvärjningen* (1986) on the 1792 murder of King Gustav III and then *Fyra dagar som skakade Sverige* (1988). The

latter film, one of Häger and Villius's [*sic*] most ambitious productions, dealt with the Midsummer crisis of 1941 when Nazi Germany attacked the Soviet Union. (Ludvigsson 2000, p. 143)

With regard to the former, *Sammansvärjningen* (The Conspiracy, SVT TV2, 1986, dir. Per Sjöstrand) was produced by the drama/theatre unit at TV2. All three episodes are dramatised and the casting includes some of the most well-known Swedish actors from the mid-1980s. Apart from the prologue of the first episode, consisting of a written text providing the historical and biographical context of King Gustav III (1746–92, monarch from 1771 until his death), none of the episodes include explicit references to actual documents. In the epilogue, at the end of the third and final episode, the only voice-over of this production occurs. While the scene shows the deportation of the men convicted for the conspiracy that led to the assassination of King Gustav III, Villius' voice-over explains what happened to them when they arrived in Denmark. It is pertinent to note that Häger and Villius' productions not only gradually develop into docudramas but that they themselves occasionally also appear as historical characters. In *Sammansvärjningen*, Villius plays the part of Colonel Hästesko, condemned to death after opposing King Gustav III during the war between Sweden and Russia 1788–90, while Häger plays a prison warder guarding the suspected (later convicted) assassin Jacob Johan Anckarström.

On the one hand, *Sammansvärjningen* reveals Häger and Villius' gradual move towards docudrama. On the other hand, their priority of reaching the 'meaning of events' through the inclusion of documents and voice-overs is still present, yet manifests itself in a different way. A week before the first episode of *Sammansvärjningen*, another Häger and Villius production was broadcast. Produced by the factual/documentary unit of TV2, *Innan skottet föll—Bilder från Gustav IIIs och Bellmans dagar* (Before the Shooting—Images from the Days of Gustav III and Bellman, SVT TV2, 1986, dir. Olle Häger and Hans Villius) focuses on the historical and biographical context of King Gustav III's life, clarified by Villius' voice-over. Through the inclusion of late eighteenth-century paintings, the historical milieus and characters are not recreated but visualised and explained in voice-over. The transitions between now and then, here and there, are primarily made through the music of the songwriter Carl Michael Bellman (1740–95). At a number of different historically accurate locations, the well-known pop singer Björn Skifs performs the Bellman songs in obvious 1980s clothes and manner. Accordingly, this production works as an odd form of prequel to the docudrama, where Häger and Villius promote their view of the historical premises of the docudrama to come.

In *Fyra dagar som skakade Sverige—Midsommarkrisen 1941* (Four Days That Shook Sweden—The Midsummer Crisis in 1941, SVT TV1, 1988, dir. Olle Häger), Villius once again performs as himself and in voice-over. As Ludvigsson notes, this is one of Häger and Villius' most ambitious productions. He defines it as a historical drama documentary that deals with events from Swedish political history (2003, p. 143). The political and historical context is implied already in the subheading, where 'The Midsummer Crisis 1941' refers to the crisis which the Swedish coalition government faced when confronted with Nazi Germany's attack on the Soviet Union in June 1941. During that Midsummer, the Swedish government debated whether or not neutral Sweden should accept German transit transportations.[7] After a prologue, seemingly added after the first broadcast, where Häger and Villius discuss their own memories of the early 1940s, the first scene focuses on a young boy in a railway station, an explicit symbol for the transit transportations.[8] In line with this establishing scene, *Fyra dagar som skakade Sverige—Midsommarkrisen* 1941 primarily consists of dramatised scenes plus archival footage, as Nazi Germany propaganda films and newsreels are included. The actor Ernst-Hugo Järegård, famous for his film and theatre performances, plays the Swedish Prime Minister, Per Albin Hansson (1885–1946), and through remarkable make-up and performance Järegård becomes a Hansson lookalike. Through a metaperspective, initiated in the first broadcasts by a scene in which Villius introduces a middle-aged actor as a contemporary interviewer, the late 1980s is repeatedly woven into the narrative. 'The Interviewer' walks down memory lane in his 1980s clothes interviewing the actors, all in character as the renowned 1940s politicians. The last scene is set in the same railway station as the opening scene with two major differences. The 1940s is now replaced by the 1980s and the little boy is incarnated as 'The Interviewer'. Through his performative function as Häger and Villius' deputy in the narrative, the little boy's childhood memories have developed and matured. They have become an adult's insight into the political chain of events connected to the actual transit transportations. Hence, the docudrama widens individual memories from a specific time and place, establishing a Swedish collective memory of historically and politically noteworthy events. Subsequently, *Fyra dagar som skakade*

Sverige—Midsommarkrisen 1941 is stylistically situated somewhere in between *Alfred Nobel—Mr. Dynamite* and *Sammansvärjningen*.

In Swedish public service television, the educational unit Sveriges Utbildningsradio (UR) has a fairly long tradition of using docudrama with a pronounced educational and didactic approach (in some cases including the publication of teaching guides). An example is *Veckan då Roger dödades* (The Week Roger Was Killed, SVT TV2, 1981, dir. Staffan Hildebrand) based on the so-called 'punk murder' committed on 28 February 1981, when 16-year-old Roger Johansson was killed in the Stockholm metro. Ending with authentic film of Roger's funeral ceremony, this docudrama cross-cuts dramatised scenes and interviews with the victim's twin brother.

Three months after the murder, and immediately after the trial, the swiftly produced *Veckan då Roger dödades* was initially broadcast within the framework of the socially oriented program *Magasinet* (SVT TV2, 1981). The initial broadcast included a contextualising prologue and an epilogue, the latter consisting of interviews with a police representative, director Staffan Hildebrand, and two of the young actors as well as a reportage of the ongoing debate on the potential impact of violent videos. In May 1982, *Veckan då Roger dödades* was broadcast a second time, but with a new epilogue (SVT TV1, 1982). In this epilogue director Staffan Hildebrand and Dominik Henzel, playing the part of Roger, discuss the film and the reactions to the screenings as well as the lectures they have held in schools and youth clubs on themes such as escalating violence and drug abuse among young people (SVT TV1, 1982). The 1982 broadcast was part of a wider UR project called *Våld & värn* (Violence & Protection/ Shelter), accompanied by a publication with the same title intended as classroom material. As well as Lipkin's previously cited three arenas, the crime and court case focus in this educational docudrama seems to offer a foretaste of a fourth noteworthy arena in Swedish docudramas, which I will discuss later.

In the second phase of Swedish docudrama, two additional major productions ought to be highlighted, both of them produced during the mid-1980s. Initially intended as a broadcast in connection with the 40-year anniversary of Denmark's liberation after World War II in May 1945, the Swedish and Danish co-production *Jane Horney* (SVT TV1, 1985, dir. Stellan Olsson) was shown in both countries as a six-episode TV series in late 1985. Accused of espionage in Nazi-occupied Denmark, Swedish journalist Jane Horney mysteriously disappeared in January 1945. Still unsolved, her disappearance and presumed death, as well as her activities during the war, have led to speculation on whether she was murdered and, if so, by whom—the Danish resistance, the Nazis, or someone else? Initially the broadcast had to be postponed because of strong reactions from Danish authorities and private individuals who saw the production as accusing the Danish resistance movement of murder. Former Danish resistance man Arne Sejr found too many similarities between himself and the character Jonas in the docudrama, and argued that the series should therefore be censored.[9] Resemblance might in itself not seem an obvious ground for objection, but according to Olsson and Moen the witness Lily Kiær actually identified Sejr in connection to Horney's disappearance. In 1956 and 1985, she claimed that the day after the disappearance Sejr delivered Horney's bag and train ticket to her. Kiær also asserted that her mission was to act as the body double of Horney, and that she pursued the assignment by using Horney's ticket and carrying her bag on the train from Malmö to Stockholm (Olsson and Moen 1986, pp. 294–296). This witness theory hence connects Sejr not only to the activities carried out by the Danish resistance movement but also to the actual disappearance of Jane Horney.

In the docudrama bearing her name, newsreel footage and pages from Swedish newspapers describing noteworthy events from the ongoing war are recurrently included. These documents function as warrants of historical accuracy, sometimes commenting on what has happened, sometimes foreshadowing what is to come, sometimes giving a hint of the spatial transitions when the dramatised scenes shifts between Sweden, Denmark, and Nazi Germany. The fact that Horney occasionally worked as a journalist links the protagonist to these time-and-place-specific documents, which also underpins the docudrama's connection to newspapers and newsreels.

The reception given to the docudrama *Jane Horney* in Sweden and Denmark differed markedly. In Denmark the series generated a huge critical debate about its reliability. With the intention of discussing both sides of the controversy, public service television in Sweden broadcast an hour-long studio discussion, *Jane Horney—EPILOG* (Jane Horney—EPILOGUE, SVT TV1, 25 November 1985) in which moderator Lars Hansegård explained the necessity of having two sides to a studio debate that was to have included some representatives of the former Danish resistance movement. However, none of the invited Danes agreed to participate in the studio debate. The Danish side was still represented, however, through interviews with Danish journalists and historians. The Swedish scriptwriter and director of the docudrama also participated. The interviews essentially revealed a generational division of opinion. Younger Danes emphasised the importance of open archives in order to understand wider historical events as well as what the Danish resistance not only did but actually felt during the occupation; the older generation emphasised the docudrama's misrepresentation of events, and wanted classified documents kept in locked vaults.[10]

In 1986, hence shortly after the transmission of *Jane Horney*, Swedish public service television produced and broadcast a series focusing historical murders and court cases from the southern part of Sweden, more exactly in the region of Skåne. The five docudramas, thematically labelled *Skånska mord* (Scanian Murders), were all scripted by Max Lundgren, and realised by three different directors. Broadcast on SVT TV2, the series opened in February 1986 with *Vebereödsmannen* (The Man from Veberöd, dir. Jan. Hemmel), and over the rest of that year *Esarparen* (The Man from Esarp, dir. Richard Hobert), *Hurvamorden* (The Hurva Murders, dir. Jan. Hemmel), *Bessingemordet* (The Bessinge Murder, dir. Leif Krantz), and *Yngsjömordet* (The Yngsjö Murder, dir. Richard Hobert) followed.[11] The murders and court cases covered a period from the 1880s to the early 1950s, so the claim of authenticity—as well as the use of historical documents and media references—differed depending on the historical context. Nevertheless, trial transcripts and/or articles and headlines from newspapers play a central part in these docudramas.

Vebereödsmannen opens with an establishing shot over a windmill in a vast and dark winter landscape with the series title, *Skånska mord*, in capitals in the upper right-hand corner of the screen. The pervading theme of all five episodes (murders in Skåne) is hence established, and in the following episodes only the individual titles of the docudramas appear. Immediately after the first scene, which shows windmill owner Martin Svensson committing his first murder and arson, a characteristic Villius voice-over is heard. Over images of the victim's burnt-down windmill, Villius explains the crime was based on envy—perpetrator Svensson thought the victim, a business competitor, too popular among customers. Promoting the series' historical accuracy, Villius' voice-over supplies context to each windmillburning, and gives the verdicts in the last scene. As with the single early use of the series title *Skånska mord*, Villius' voice-over is only heard in this first episode. His well-established voice (as previously noted, a common feature of earlier Swedish documentaries and docudramas) thus functions as a kind of national seal of approval. It is nothing short of a warrant of historical accuracy for forthcoming episodes of *Skånska mord*.

Just as historical documents embedded in docudramas function as warrants of accuracy, the conscious casting of certain actors already connected to the docudrama mode can function as performative warrants, also emphasising historical accuracy. In common with most markers of this kind, they are predominantly intelligible and valid within a specific national context—only Swedes would respond to particular actors. In *Skånska mord*, this performative warrant is further emphasised by the fact that the same actor was cast as protagonist in three of the five episodes. Well-known actor Ernst-Hugo Järegård (Prime Minster Hansson in *Fyra dagar som skakade Sverige— Midsommarkrisen 1941*), plays protagonist/perpetrator in *Veberödsmannen*, *Esarparen*, and *Hurvamorden* respectively. A skilled professional, he occasionally speaks with well-established authority direct to camera, confronting the audience. His audience eye-contact is perhaps most significantly used in the last scene of *Hurvamorden*. Using verbatim the words from a suicide note written by serial killer Tore Hedin just before drowning himself, Järegård directs the murderer's confession straight into the camera, then walks slowly into a lake—thus mirroring the murderer's last act.

Through his performances in these three docudramas, I am arguing, Järegård functions as a performative warrant of accuracy. I further suggest that the authority thus established carried over to his performance as Prime Minister Hansson two years later. Furthermore, the director of two of the episodes of this series, Jan Hemmel, went on, over 20 years after the broadcasts of *Skånska mord*, to publish a book (also titled *Skånska mord*, Hemmel 2010) resulting from his research. All five crimes represented in the TV series are taken into account, and in addition he scrutinises eight other historical Scanian crimes and court cases, including the disappearance of Jane Horney (see Hemmel 2010, pp. 178–189). Here, trial transcripts and/or articles and headlines from newspapers are just as central as in the 1980s TV series, and the docudrama personnel underline their commitment to factuality.

THIRD-PHASE SWEDISH DOCUDRAMA ON PUBLIC SERVICE TELEVISION

In the 1990s and early 2000s, during what I am describing as the third phase of Swedish televised docudrama, two parallel traits are detectable. First, biographical representations of noteworthy individuals seemed to shift from historically, and or/politically, prominent individuals to individuals with a certain cultural impact. Second, the noteworthy events represented in docudramas were becoming dominated by crimes and court cases.

Apelsinmannen (The Man of Oranges, SVT Kanal 1, 1990, dir. Jonas Cornell) serves as an initial example of this third phase. Interestingly, it features corrupt legal practices, crimes and court cases, yet this is achieved by means of an autobiographical representation, the author/protagonist being additionally a culturally significant person. Based on the autobiographical novel (also titled *Apelsinmannen*, Stenberg 1983), in which the author includes personal reflections on the so called 'Kejneaffären' (The Kejne Affair), this two-part docudrama was broadcast in September 1990. The story concerns the unexpected consequences confronted by the young arts student Birgitta when she is drawn into the Stockholm underworld. In 1950, conspiracy theories such as rumours of a Swedish 'homosexual conspiracy' with links all the way up to the monarchy flourished in Sweden, and the title *Apelsinmannen* derives from the nickname Swedish media gave the person accused of attempting to killing Reverend Karl-Erik Kejne with poisoned oranges. The novel's author Brigitta Stenberg was on the periphery of these events and the story is told from her subjective perspective. The docudrama consists of dramatised scenes with little direct reference to actual documents, and the warrant of historical accuracy is primarily revealed in the prologue of both broadcasts. Once again, Villius, by this point in time strongly connected not only to historical documentaries but also to docudramas with high cultural values, appears and gives an historical background to the events.[12] In the prologues (identical in both episodes), Villius' strongly emphasises the subjectivity of the docudrama's interpretation of events, and adds that the aim of *Apelsinmannen* is to represent the 'Kafka-like' atmosphere of 1950s Sweden. As a warrant of accuracy, he accentuates the fact that during the 1950s conspiracy theories were common also among renowned Swedes, such as the author Vilhelm Moberg (1898–1973). 'Bizarre and peculiar' rumours, such as 'unfounded suspicions of murderers in the Swedish government' and 'conspiracy groups planning to abduct the sarcophagus containing King Gustaf V's dead body' (Gustav V, 1858–1950, was monarch from 1907 until his death), can definitely lead to widespread fear of state abuse and corruption, characterised by the 'Kafka-like' atmosphere Villius metaphorically describes. More captivatingly, the wish to describe this 'Kafka-like' atmosphere is explicitly stressed as the main aim of the production *Apelsinmannen* by Villius. This leads him not only to clarify but also to *motivate* some of the historical *inaccuracies* of the representation as artistic choices made in order to strengthen the eeriness required. Again, the docudrama carries the Villius' seal of approval, established through his recurrent functioning as historical warrant, yet his seal of approval here legitimises the historicity of the docudrama without using actual historical documents. Therefore, Villius here *approves and motivates* historical *inaccuracies*.

During this third phase, several other major docudramas representing crimes and court cases were produced by SVT. One such example is *Norrmalmstorg* (Norrmalm Square, SVT1, 2003, dir. Håkan Lindhé), which focuses on a hostage-taking in a Stockholm bank vault in late August 1973. The counter-intuitive strong emotional connection and identification between the hostages and the hostage-takers in this noteworthy crime generated the now well-established psychological concept 'The Stockholm Syndrome'. The dramatised scenes are anchored in the historical context through sequences of archival footage. These include footage from the police activity at Norrmalmstorg, broadcast news from August 1973, as well as footage of Prime Minister Olof Palme's speeches. The hostage-taking took place during the 1973 election campaign, and when Palme explicitly encourages Swedes to unite in condemning the hostage-taking, he also, implicitly, uses the appeal to encourage Swedes to vote for him and his Social Democratic party in the upcoming election.

As a part of the channel's thematically arranged programming for Saturday evenings, *Styckmordet* (The Dismemberment Murder, SVT2, 2005, dir. Anders Engström, Claes J. B. Löfgren, and Kristian Petri) was broadcast on SVT2, 14 May 2005. On this specific Saturday, the theme was the media's approach to justice. *Styckmordet* is based on the book *Döden är en man: Historien om obducenten och allmänläkaren* by the Swedish journalist Per Lindeberg (Death is a Man: The Story of the Pathologist and the General Practitioner of Medicine, Lindeberg 1999). Book and docudrama scrutinise the aftermath of the bestial dismemberment of Catrine da Costa in Stockholm in 1984. Over the years, this case has turned into a judicial scandal. In March 1988, a general practitioner of medicine and a pathologist were found guilty of the murder by a split decision of the district court. Since some of the lay judges involved had been interviewed by the press during the proceedings, the trial was declared invalid and a second one had to be performed.[13] This second trial began 30 May 1988 and in July the same two men were found guilty of the dismemberment. As a result of lack of evidence they were not, however, found guilty of murder. In accordance with Swedish legislation, molesting a dead body is considered as a separate crime called *brott mot griftefriden* ('violating the peace of the grave'), and in 1988 this special crime was statute-barred after two years of the crime taking place.[14] It was hence too late to convict the two accused for the actual dismemberment and although they walked free, their lives were ruined by the process. In *Styckmordet*, dramatised scenes are cross-cut with archival material and the judicial scandal is gradually revealed through interviews with witnesses, footage of documents such as legal protocols, pages from diaries, and pages from Swedish newspapers. Similar to the distribution of other Swedish docudramas with a strong social argument, the initial broadcast of *Styckmordet* was immediately followed by a televised debate on how media affects the rule of law.

The three-part mini-series *Lasermannen* (The Laserman, SVT1 2005, dir. Mikael Marcimain), broadcast on SVT1 in November and December 2005, was a major breakthrough for director Mikael Marcimain and cinematographer Hoyte van Hoytema. Preceded by the detailed and thorough reportage book *Lasermannen: En berättelse om Sverige* (The Laser Man: A Tale About Sweden, Tamas 2002), and followed by the documentary *Lasermannen—Dokumentären* (The Laser Man—The Documentary, SVT2 2005, dir. Gellert Tamas and Malcolm Dixelius), the mini-series was scripted by Ulf Rydberg. He kept the structure of Tamas' book more or less intact, focusing on the shootings which put Stockholm and the rest of Sweden in a state of fear from August 1991 to January 1992.[15] With a telescopic laser sight gun, John Ausonius (born Wolfgang Alexsander Zaugg), directed his random attacks at people with seemingly foreign characteristics such as dark hair and complexions, who in his view could be considered non-European immigrants. During this six-month period he shot and severely wounded 11, one fatally. The docudrama occasionally implements televised news footage from the decade (such as the 1991 televised election night party, headlines, and close-ups of newspapers in which photos of actors in the series are added, intertitles giving dates and places). However, the series recreated the atmosphere of the 1990s primarily through painstaking *mise en scène* and not through the inclusion of archival footage from the 1990s. Thus, the actions of Ausonius and other time-specific events in Sweden are recreated in dramatised scenes. In February 1991, the right-wing conservative, populist, and xenophobic party Ny Demokrati (New Democracy) had been formed and after the national elections of 15 September 1991, they entered parliament. The interrogations of the shooter Ausonius (actor David Dencik) are cross-cut with dramatised scenes about Ausonius' childhood and youth, the crimes committed, and the investigation that led to his arrest, trial, and conviction. The docudrama series was highly acclaimed, not least for its aesthetic values, where the overall *mise en scène* and the footage by Hoyte van Hoytema contributed to the impression of historical accuracy. Mats Jönsson argues that '[—] Marcimain indirectly also responded to many of the demands for realism, "faction" and docudrama that flourish in today's media landscape' (2008, p. 38). Moreover, Marcimain's achievements in implementing these 'demands for realism' seem to have worked as a warrant of accuracy in which has been transferred to the expectations for, and interpretations of his forthcoming productions.

Swedish public service television has a long tradition of producing and broadcasting TV drama. Some productions are timetabled in specific slots, and at least one major production a year is broadcast during the Christmas and New Year period. In the late Decembers of 2005, 2007, and 2008, these TV dramas broadcast on SVT1 focused on culturally noteworthy individuals who were so well known that the titles of the three biographical docudramas simply consisted of their first names. The 2005 two episode docudrama *Lovisa och Carl Michael—En dag i makarnas liv* (Lovisa and Carl Michael—A Day of Their Lives, SVT1, 2005, dir. Leif Magnusson) is about the life of the composer Carl Michael Bellman (1740–1795), and features a representation of eighteenth-century Stockholm.[16] The key references to historical documents in this acted dramatisation are found in Bellman's music, with some of his songs performed by actor Tomas von Brömssen (playing Bellman). The series also features Bellman's family, in particular (as indicated by the title), his wife Lovisa. The main issue arising from this docudrama was the accuracy of the 'Old Swedish' used in the dialogue and the extended focus on Bellman's wife Lovisa. In several interviews the actors emphasised their initial mixed feelings about the dated language, but stressed that they ultimately considered its use a key performative tool (Collin 2005; Kronbrink 2005).

Two years later, SVT1 produced and broadcast the two-episode docudrama *August* (2007, SVT1, dir. Stig Larsson), scripted by Peter Birro and promoted as the major Christmas TV drama of 2007.[17] *August* is, of course, about Swedish author and playwright August Strindberg (1849–1912). Set in the late 1870s, the production was explicitly described as a combination of fact and fantasy (Collin 2007). The fantasy element is best exemplified by the fact that some characters from Strindberg's novel *Röda rummet* (The Red Room, 1879) are brought to life in the docudrama.

Theatrical and performative traits are further emphasised by the *mise en scène*. When the modern Stockholm locations lack historical accuracy, sets are supplemented by painted backdrops. Similar to *Lovisa och Carl Michael—En dag i makarnas liv*, women also play a major part in the narrative. Actress Siri von Essen (1850–1912) is a central character. She married Strindberg in 1877, had three children with him, and then divorced him in 1893. Subsequent discussions about historical accuracy were primarily directed towards aesthetic and performative aspects, such as Jonas Karlsson (playing Strindberg) being a Strindberg lookalike. Several articles and reviews of the docudrama stress the fact that Karlsson grew a moustache like Strindberg's and even used the same sort of wax to shape it (Collin 2007; Djurberg 2007; nummer.se 2015a).

The two-part docudrama *Selma* (2008, SVT1, dir. Erik Leijonborg), scripted by Åsa Lantz, was produced, broadcast, and promoted as the Christmas TV drama in 2008. SVT described it as fiction, but it was also claimed to be based on the private correspondence of famous Swedish author Selma Lagerlöf (1858–1940). Similar to the Christmas TV dramas *Lovisa och Carl Michael—En dag i makarnas liv* and *August*, *Selma* is structured as a biographical drama, yet incorporates a few historical documents. References to reviews and articles in contemporary newspapers were actually of crucial importance to the argument, and an article of that time promoting August Strindberg as a more appropriate winner of the Nobel Prize than Lagerlöf is fundamental to the narrative. The first episode opens with a text from the Swedish Penal Code of 1864, where §18:10 states that any person committing unnatural fornication, including bestiality, is to be convicted and sentenced to up to two years' penal servitude.[18] In an interview, Lantz explained that the narrative emanates from Lagerlöf's correspondence with the two loves of her life, Sophie Elkan and Valborg Olander. Lantz also stated that the production team was somewhat cautious in their treatment of the material, even omitting certain details (Trus and Niklasson 2008). The first episode takes place in 1895, and begins with Lagerlöf (Helena Bergström) and Elkan (Alexandra Rapaport) on a trip to Sicily, while the second episode focuses on 1909, and the Nobel Prize Ceremony. Some critics approved of the revisionist portrayal of Lagerlöf, and praised SVT for finally making a Christmas Drama featuring a culturally important woman—released from the closet by the docudrama (Gentele 2008). Along with some of Lagerlöf's descendants, other critics saw the docudrama as a misrepresentation and considered it deeply problematic that what they saw as a false portrayal marked Lagerlöf as homosexual—and in her own time a criminal (Trus and Niklasson 2008).

THIRD-PHASE SWEDISH DOCUDRAMA ON COMMERCIAL TELEVISION

My discussion of docudramas produced and broadcast by Swedish commercial channels lacks many examples primarily because the development of Swedish televised docudrama has occurred first and foremost on public service television. Nonetheless, in 2009 the commercial channel TV4 produced and broadcast *Vägen hem* (The Religious Sect—A Murder Story, TV4, 2009, dir. Karin Swärd). This production is for many reasons essential for discussion of third-phase Swedish docudramas.

In January 2004, the small village of Knutby, indeed Sweden itself, was shocked by the brutal killing of Alexandra Fossmo and the attempted murder of her neighbour Daniel Linde. It emerged that the assassin, the young woman Sara Svensson, was influenced and driven to become a murderer by anonymous SMS messages from the Pentecostal pastor Helge Fossmo—husband of the female victim. Fossmo's indoctrination of Svensson convinced her that the anonymous SMS messages were being sent by God. Consequently, the Knutby drama has been discussed as Sweden's first SMS-murder, maybe even the first SMS-murder in the world (Sjöberg 2005, p. 12; Lapidus 2007). Helge Fossmo was a highly influential pastor of the Pentecostal Congregation in Knutby, to which all individuals in this tragic chain of events belonged. He also had ongoing sexual relationships with Daniel Linde's wife as well as with Sara Svensson. Additionally Fossmo's wife was the sister of another highly influential pastor of the Pentecostal Congregation in Knutby, Åsa Waldau. During the crime investigations Waldau became known by the sensational name of 'The Bride of Christ'. The crimes and the inner structure of the congregation triggered a huge furore in the Swedish news media. Soon after the actual drama in Knutby, a TV documentary ((*Skotten i Knutby*, A Fall from Grace, TV4, 2005, dir. Phil Poysti and Karin Swärd) was produced and broadcast by TV4, focusing on the Knutby congregation and the crime investigation. This documentary later became the base for the TV and film docudramas mentioned below. Several books with slightly different approaches to the events were also published (Bergstrand 2007; Cristiansson 2004; Essén 2008; Loe 2009; Lundgren 2008; Nilsson 2005; Nordling 2004; Sjöberg 2005; Waldau 2007).

Finally, the Knutby drama spawned docudramatic representations on television in the three-part TV series *Vägen Hem* (The Religious Sect—A Murder Story, TV4, 2009, dir. Karin Swärd), in the cinema with *Vägen Hem* (The Religious Sect—A Murder Story, 2009, dir. Karin Swärd), and also on the stage with *Knutby* (Uppsala Municipal Theatre, 2009, dir. Eva Dahlman). Much of this work resulted from commercial channel TV4's team (writer/director Karin Swärd and photographer/director Phil Poysti) being the first media outsiders to be accepted by the Knutby congregation. All three episodes of *Vägen hem* include verbatim aspects of the material. The TV series proclaimed itself based on real but reconstructed events, with dialogue based on interviews and minutes from the crime investigation.

The most curious fact of the production in terms of docudrama is that the actors mime to original recordings of the dialogue, in scenes including sermons and telephone interceptions. This had never before been a feature of Swedish docudrama.[19] Swärd's and Poysti's work on the initial 2005 TV4 Knutby documentary *Skotten i Knutby* generated a significant metaperspective and an interesting media perspective more generally. Both functioned as warrants of accuracy in their later docudrama. During the crime investigation, Swärd and Poysti were filming their documentary, and their interviews with people in the congregation play a central part. Hence, Swärd and Poysti became characters themselves played by actors in the docudrama. Re-enacted scenes give a perspective on the commercial channel's coverage of the Knutby tragedy, achieved through the performative warrant of actors playing reporters and journalists. Notwithstanding all this, the Knutby congregation itself was heavily opposed to the docudrama *Vägen hem*, arguing that Swärd and Poysti had misled them as to how the initial documentary material was to be used, or reused. It is more than possible to assert that their strong reactions also had to do with the short time span between the actual crimes committed in Knutby, the consequences thereof, and the many representations of these events that followed.

THIRD-PHASE SWEDISH DOCUDRAMA—INTERNATIONAL CO-PRODUCTION

As a part of SVT's thematically arranged Saturday evening programming, a Swedish and Polish co-production, *Ninas resa* (Nina's Journey, 2005, dir. Lena Einhorn), was broadcast on SVT2 on Holocaust Memorial Day,

27 January 2007. The film is based on an interview with Holocaust survivor Nina Einhorn, cross-cut with archival footage such as moving images from the Warsaw Ghetto and dramatised scenes with Polish actors. During the production process, scriptwriter and director Lena Einhorn, Nina's daughter, was in doubt about the financing of the film. As she was eager to go public with the material, she started writing a book based on the same interview (Ninas resa: En överlevnadsberättelse/Nina's Journey: A Story of Survival, Einhorn 2005). The actual result was an almost simultaneous publishing of the book and opening of the film. In 2005, the book was awarded the 'August Prize' in the category 'Best factual/non-fiction' category. The film was also released in 2005, and won two 'Guldbaggar' in the 2006 'Guldbaggegala' (one in the category 'Best Film', the other 'Best Script'—both in competition with fiction films).[20]

Most significant in this film is the strange effect of the inclusion of certain archival footage, more specifically sequences produced by the Nazis in the Warsaw Ghetto in May 1942. For example, on the soundtrack, the elderly Nina explains:

> Up until the summer of 1942, the 400,000 Jews in Warsaw tried to live some kind of normal life, if you can call life normal when you are so cut off from the outside world. Concerts were given in Warsaw, there was theatre in Warsaw, I remember lighter moments. I remember New Year's Eve 1941, which I spent with my friends.[21]

Here, Nina's voice-over accompanies archival footage showing people indoors as well as outdoors in the Ghetto—there is food, the general mood is good, and venues like restaurants and theatres are evident. In *Ninas resa*, then, archival footage is used as a warrant of historical accuracy. However, we know that the propagandistic films produced by the Nazis were staged like fiction films, in order to make the ghetto appear better than it was. An unintended effect of the inclusion of them in *Ninas resa*, perhaps, is that Holocaust survivor Nina suddenly seems to agree to this. This ghetto sequence is also used in *Shtikat Haarchion* (A Film Unfinished, 2010, dir. Yael Hersonski), with at least one major difference. In her effort to reveal the conscious staging of the original ghetto films, Hersonski inserts interviews with some of the survivors from the Warsaw Ghetto as well as extracts from real diaries and from the reconstructed verbatim trial testimony of Willy Wist, one of the cameramen of 'The Ghetto Film', Willy Wist.[22] The propagandistic entertainment and dining scenes most obviously now create brutal contrasts to street scenes showing starving and dead people, with the explicit message that some of the ghetto's inhabitants only survived at the expense of others.

In major Swedish film and television productions, Scandinavian co-producing is common, and accordingly *Ninas resa* is not the only co-production discussed in this survey. Yet, *Ninas resa* stands out as the only international co-production with an explicit transnational approach to history. That a docudrama about the Holocaust is of greater international interest than docudramas dealing with domestic Swedish history is also revealed by the international recognition and awards the production received when it was distributed cinematically, and by the fact that the English version of the Swedish Film Data Base emphasises *Ninas resa* as a 'Promoted film' (SFI 2015g).[23] None of the other docudramas included in this survey are promoted as such in the Swedish Film Database.

FOURTH-PHASE SWEDISH DOCUDRAMAS—TOWARDS A POLITICAL AND AFFECTIVE DOCUDRAMA

Almost 30 years have now passed since the assassination of Swedish Prime Minister Olof Palme on 28 February 1986. Recently, a number of productions focusing on aspects of Palme's political deeds, personal life, and death have appeared both in cinemas and on television. They have at least one thing in common—they all mediate strong affective engagement. Being a high-profile politician both domestically and internationally, Olof Palme was of course represented in Swedish film and television productions even before the political and affective turn I am proposing as the fourth phase of Swedish docudrama. For instance, in the docudrama *Norrmalmstorg* (Norrmalm Square, SVT1 2003, dir. Håkan Lindhé) discussed earlier, Palme is represented through verbal references in dramatised dialogue and through archival footage of a broadcast speech condemning hostage-taking and commenting on the ongoing drama in the bank vault. In 2012, however, enough time had passed since his assassination to select him, the still unsolved murder, and the Swedish political context of the late 1970s and early 1980s as main topics in docudramas with extremely diverse approaches and receptions. The development and emergence of a political and affective turn, here suggested as a potential fourth phase of Swedish docudrama, has to be scrutinised in relation not only to the development of docudrama but also to the overall development of political representations on Swedish film and television.

In September 2012, the documentary *Palme* (2012, dir. Kristina Lindström and Maud Nycander) opened in cinemas. During the Christmas period in 2012, SVT1 launched a longer version of the documentary as a three-part television series (*Palme*, SVT1 2012, dir. Kristina Lindström and Maud Nycander). This biographical documentary series was promoted, broadcast and received as the major Swedish public service television event during Christmas and New Year 2012. Through interviews and official archival footage as well as private footage provided by the Palme family, the two versions of the documentary provided a highly positive picture of the sometimes controversial Palme, which was generally very well received by critics and audiences.

Two months after the opening of *Palme* in November 2012, the film *Hassel—Privatspanarna* (Roland Hassel, 2012, dir. Måns Månsson) opened in Swedish cinemas. This somewhat peculiar production can be described as a spin-off based on the fictional character Roland Hassel, protagonist of around 30 crime novels and short stories by the author Olov Svedelid. During the period 1986–92, SVT produced ten adaptations of Svedelid's work with the actor Lars-Erik Berenett playing the part of Hassel. In the 2012 film, and 20 years after the last TV adaptation, Inspector Roland Hassel was still being played by Berenett. The much older Hassel is retired, bitter, and depressed, yet stubbornly obsessed by an increasing desire to solve the case of the assassination of Olof Palme. This obsession has led him into a deep involvement with a group working on re-enactments of the murder. The film ends with the 'Twenty-Fifth Anniversary Re-Enactment' on location at Sveavägen in Stockholm. Hassel now takes a totally distant position—not actively participating but watching and recording—as if he is expecting finally to solve the murder by studying a role play with affectively engaged re-enactors.

Based on Leif G.W. Persson's literary trilogy *Välfärdsstatens fall* (Fall of the Welfare State, Persson 2002, 2003, 2007), SVT1 produced and broadcast a four-part TV series in January and February 2013 (*En pilgrims död—Mordet på statsminister Olof Palme*/Death of a Pilgrim—The Assassination of Prime Minister Olof Palme, SVT1 2012, dir. Kristoffer Nyholm and Kristian Petri). It tells a story of espionage, abuse of state power, conspiracy, murder, and international conflict, and features a discussion about democracy and the decline of the Swedish welfare state.[24] The story incorporates connections to the author's earlier novels, where *Grisfesten* (The Pork Party, Persson 1978), and the film adaptation of it, *Mannen från Mallorca* (The Man from Majorca, 1984, dir. Bo Widerberg), are of specific interest. Persson works with recurring characters, investigators and police officers as well as politicians and criminals.[25] For example, in *Grisfesten*, and in the adaptation *Mannen från Mallorca*, both written and produced before the murder of Olof Palme, a corrupt policeman robs a post office. More than 20 years later this character reappears. In the literary trilogy *Välfärdsstatens fall*, as well as in the adaptation *En pilgrims död—Mordet på statsminister Olof Palme*, this former robber is not only connected to a political conspiracy but also revealed to be Olof Palme's assassin. On SVT's website, Christian Wikander (legally responsible for the production) states that the series is pure fiction originating from the assassination of Palme, and director Kristian Petri acknowledges that the borderland of fact and fiction needs to be discussed (SVT 2015a). In Sweden, Persson is a very well-known criminologist, author, and media commentator, and in his novels he explicitly elaborates what he refers to as 'the coincidence between author's imagination and empirical truth' (Persson 1978, p. 7). Moreover, while Persson's 'Foreword' to *Grisfesten* asserts that absolutely everything in the novel is 'just lies', he also claims that the quotation cited above is the title of a work by 'the famous American media sociologist Bartlett K Schuhheimer' (pp. 6–7).[26] Amusingly this 'famous media sociologist' only seems to exist in Persson's narrative, which adds yet another layer to the mixture of fact and fiction. Despite Persson's claim, the basic fact is that the novel *Grisfesten*, hence also the film adaptation *Mannen från Mallorca*, portrays the Swedish Minister of Justice as a corrupt user of prostitutes, which mirrors an actual chain of events in the mid-1970s. Moreover, Persson got his novel accepted by the publisher on 8 May 1978, and just 24 hours later the proportions of the actual chain of events mentioned above burst open generating the so-called 'brothel debate' (Persson 1978, p. 6). This leads directly to the last docudrama example in my survey.

The film *Call Girl* (2012, dir. Mikael Marcimain), depicts how two 14- and 15-year-old girls ended up involved in prostitution and drug abuse in a corrupt mid-1970s Stockholm. Scripted by Marietta von Hausswolff von Baumgarten, directed by Mikael Marcimain, with footage by Hoyte van Hoytema (both mentioned already in relation to the 2005 docudrama *Lasermannen*) and with a cast including several famous Swedish actors, the production of *Call Girl* initially generated great expectations. However, the initial positives soon turned into a controversy that escalated before the film's opening on 9 November 2012. On the poster, the film is described as 'a political thriller', and its opening caption states: 'This is inspired by actual events. Incidents, characters and timelines have been changed for dramatic purposes.'[27] Despite its disclaimer, the film is more or less a blueprint of the 1970s so-called 'Geijer Affair', connecting the Swedish brothel-keeper Doris Hopp to several prominent Swedes such as Minister of Justice Lennart Geijer.

In brief, Hopp organised call girls in Stockholm. She was arrested in 1976, and the police investigation revealed that many of her customers were well-known politicians and other prominent national figures. In November 1977, the newspaper *Dagens Nyheter* published allegations about the Minister of Justice being one of Hopp's customers. The reporter, Peter Bratt, claimed as his source a classified report in which the Chief of Police Carl Persson had informed Prime Minister Palme about a delicate problem: politicians involved in a prostitution scandal in the midst of an ongoing election campaign. Palme strongly denied all allegations and the newspaper was forced into a retreat, giving the Minister of Justice an official apology. Years later, it emerged that the revelations had actually been fairly correct, and over the years there has been much speculation regarding the identities of those who were on Hopp's list of customers (Johnsson 2004).

The book *Makten, männen, mörkläggningen: Historien om bordellhärvan 1976* (The Power, the Men and the Cover-Up: The Story of the 1976 Brothel Scandal, Rauscher and Mattsson 2004), focuses on the 'Geijer Affair', and includes the story of two young girls, who in the book are called Liv and Emelie. Co-author Deanne Raucher also worked as a researcher on *Call Girl*. Apart from compressing the timeline and either changing or excluding real names, *Call Girl* follows the story of the two girls more or less in detail. Opposition to the film was primarily generated by one scene, discussed as 'The Hotel Scene', in which the Swedish Prime Minister is shown paying for sex with one of the young girls—in Sweden then and now, a criminal act (Jönsson 2012; Lumholdt 2012; Kastner 2012). The production team immediate responded to the critique, claiming the film to be 'plain fiction with no connections to any real persons' (von Hausswolff von Baumgarten in Jönsson 2012; Marcimain in Lumholdt 2012). The possibility of associating the supposedly 'fictional' Prime Minister in *Call Girl* with Olof Palme, Prime Minister at the time, caused the Palme family to send a defamation notice to the State Attorney (who recommended the family not to press charges—see Gustafsson 2012; Viklund and Nilsson 2013). Instead a negotiation took place with the consequence that the criticised scene was re-edited. 'The Hotel Scene' is still in the film, but the part showing the Prime Minister with a young girl has been removed (Nordström 2013). After a long delay, the cut version was released on DVD in July 2013, and in the future this will be the only version allowed to be broadcast and screened—both in Sweden and abroad (Larsson 2013). In fact, *Call Girl* was not broadcast by its co-producer SVT until 1 January 2015, and it seems obvious that the controversy was a possible cause for over two years passing before *Call Girl* appeared on SVT1.

Interestingly, the first version of the trailer is still available on the web, with the voice of the actor playing the Prime Minister heard encouraging the young girl to 'come closer' as she enters the room in the now edited 'Hotel Scene' (YouTube 2015a).[28] Considering the fact that the production company explicitly labels the entire film, and specifically the censored scene, 'plain fiction', while the Palme family considers it defamation, both sides would seem to agree on the docudrama's lack of connection to real events and persons. It must be said, however, that scenes that really do imply a connection between the Prime Minister in *Call Girl* and Olof Palme have been of less interest in the controversy. The most obvious example is a scene in which the 'Prime Minister' is shown being interviewed by a woman described as 'a foreign guest, a unique star' in a TV show called *Kvällsöppet*. This very obviously links the narrative to the Swedish television programme *Kvällsöppet* and an interview Shirley MacLaine did with Olof Palme in May 1977 (*Kvällsöppet*, SVT TV2, 3 May 1977—see YouTube 2015b).[29]

As discussed earlier in relation to his *Lasermannen*, director Marcimain has over the years been highly acclaimed,particularly for the historical accuracy of his productions. The expectations and reception of *Call Girl* seem to have been highly influenced by an extensive trust in Marcimain's earlier accomplishments, not least when it comes to meet today's 'demands for realism' by historically accurate productions. Similar to *Lasermannen*, the historical accuracy is mediated in *Call Girl* through meticulous *mise en scène* and zeitgeist footage, yet with no references to actual documents. The critical debate generated by *Call Girl* thus indicates that the production team's view of the film as 'plain fiction with no connections to any real persons' (von Hausswolff von Baumgarten in Jönsson 2012; Marcimain in Lumholdt 2012) is overshadowed by the previously established perception of Marcimain as a performative warrant of historical accuracy. Accordingly, even if the production team stresses that *Call Girl* is 'plain fiction', the film still tends to be perceived as a detailed and above all true representation of real events and individuals.

CONCLUSION—'DEMANDS FOR REALISM'

The development of Swedish docudrama can be seen according to three significant phases, with a potential fourth phase just having emerged during the last few years. Also, it is apparent that Swedish docudramas correspond fairly well to Lipkin's docudramatic representational arenas (2011, p. 3), with the important national variation of the 'noteworthy events' contained in historical as well as recent crimes and court cases. Accordingly, I am suggesting that these representations constitute a fourth arena, partly related to the development and success of 'Nordic Noir'. A tentative conclusion might suggest that this somewhat populist choice of topics would be more common in docudramas produced and broadcast by commercial channels like TV4 than in docudramas produced and broadcast by Swedish public service television. This is, however, not the case. On the contrary, this tendency is in fact more common in docudramas produced and broadcast by Swedish public service television. Recent Swedish docudramas are also increasingly based on affective themes, politicians, and political controversies, where the director Mikael Marcimain's achievements in implementing today's 'demands for realism' in productions such as *Lasermannen* seem to have worked as a performative warrant of historical accuracy which has been transferred to the expectations and reception of his later productions, not least *Call Girl*. As for the controversy caused by the interaction of fact and fiction in *Call Girl*, it is obvious that this film, regardless of how the production team labels it, is perceived as a representation of specific noteworthy events and individuals rather than as a fictional political thriller dealing with corruption and the abuse of power more generally. If the question '[h]ow can we be sure that what we are seeing is true and not fiction?' (Cowie 2011, p. 19) is still haunting documentary, *Call Girl* definitely has raised an opposite query at least as important and valid: how can we be sure that what we are seeing is fiction and not true?

NOTES

1. All translations from the original Swedish are mine.
2. In relation to the research for this survey, the first experimental searches on all the keywords discussed, entered on both websites referred above, were

performed on 2 May 2012, while the last were performed on 5 February 2015.

3. In Swedish, Jansson uses the concepts 'faktionsepiken', 'den ickefiktiva epiken', and 'den fiktiva epiken'.

4. The articles are in English and were 'originally presented at a seminar organised by the Institute of Literature, Media and Cultural Studies the University of Southern Denmark in March 2007' (Johansen and Søndergaard 2010, p. 7).

5. 'Nordic Noir' (also called 'Scandinavian Noir') has its roots in Scandinavian crime fiction. Characterised by a realistic style and a morally complex mood, focusing on the day-to-day work of the police, with protagonists who are far from heroic detectives, 'Nordic Noir' has become a genre in its own right, influencing screenwriters far beyond the Scandinavian Peninsula. Recent 'Nordic Noir' productions such as *Brottet* (The Killing, 2007–), *Wallander* (2008–), and *Bron* (The Bridge, 2011–), are related to the development of Scandinavian crime novels, film, and television dramas more generally. Wallander can serve as a clarifying example. From 1991 to 2013, the Swedish author Henning Mankell published crime novels with Inspector Kurt Wallander as protagonist, and from 1995 to 2007 these novels were adapted as Swedish film and television dramas. In 2005, the character Wallander also started to appear in Swedish spin-off film and television dramas based on developments of the character and not on the actual novels. In 2008, the progression continued with the British adaptation of Mankell's novels (2008–), in which Wallander is played by Kenneth Branagh. While the earlier-mentioned Swedish spin-off versions have had their prime success abroad (not least in Germany) the British adaptations are quite successful in Sweden.

6. This shift is frequently described as taking place during the period 1978–79 (see, for example, Furhammar 1995, p. 193).

7. The 'transit transportations' (in Swedish 'transiteringstransporter' and/or 'permittenttrafik') refer to the controversial German transports of soldiers through neutral Sweden from July 1940 to August 1943 (see, for example, Zetterberg 1986, pp. 97–118). These trains were labelled 'tysktåg' ('German Trains') and the transit transportations were heavily debated and criticised not only during the 1941 'Midsummer Crises'.

8. The prologue is, however, not included in the first SVT TV1 broadcast of the docudrama (1988). My presumption is that it was added in connection to the release of the Häger and Villius DVD *Andra världskriget och Sverige* (The World War II and Sweden, 2008), including the docudrama *Fyra dagar som skakade Sverige—Midsommarkrisen 1941* (Four Days that Shook Sweden – The Midsummer Crisis 1941, SVT TV1,1988, dir. Olle Häger) as well as two other Häger and Villius productions dealing with aspects and

consequences of the Second World War, *G som i hemlig* (G as in Secret, SVT Kanal 1, 1994, dir. Olle Häger), and *Sista båten till Jurkalne* (The Last Boat to Jurkalne, SVT TV1, 1991, dir. Olle Häger).

9. Agger (2013, pp. 233–251), Jansson (2006, pp. 71–73), Olsson and Moen (1986), and Peyron (1986) all discuss the TV series *Jane Horney* from different angles. Sejr, however, is only mentioned in Agger, Olsson and Moen, and Peyron.

10. With 70 years having passed since the disappearance of Jane Horney, these classified Danish documents ought to be made public (Olsson and Moen 1986, p. 322).

11. A previous film on the murder in Yngsjö was *Yngsjömordet* (The Yngsjö Murder, 1966, dir. Arne Mattsson). This adaptation is based on the novel *Yngsjömordet* (The Yngsjö Murder, Lyttkens 1951). Its script is by the actress Eva Dahlbeck, probably most recognised for her work with Ingmar Bergman. Initially produced for cinematic distribution this film was not broadcast on Swedish television until 1992, six years after the broadcast of the TV series *Skånska mord*.

12. These presentations are generally cut when the docudramas are released on DVDs and/or when they are made available on the Swedish public service open access website.

13. Swedish courts use a different judicial system to, for example, British courts, and don't use an actual jury. It is difficult to find a good translation of the Swedish term *nämndeman/nämndemän* (who, for example, also has/have the right to oppose a verdict). Having had 'layman judges' suggested, I have settled on 'lay judges' as most accurate.

14. Since 1993, in Sweden the crime *brott mot griftefriden* (violating the peace of the grave) has a limitation time of five years.

15. Jansson discusses Tamas' book as a drama documentary and Marciman's mini-series as a docudrama (2006, pp. 183–188).

16. Carl Michael Bellman is already mentioned in relation to Häger and Villius' *Sammansvärjningen* (The Conspiracy, SVT TV2, 1986, dir. Per Sjöberg) and *Innan skottet föll—Bilder från Gustav IIIs och Bellmans dagar* (Before the Shooting—Images from the Days of Gustav III and Bellman, SVT TV2, 1986, dir. Olle Häger and Hans Villius). In these productions Bellman appears as an already renowned, yet poor, fringe figure.

17. In Sweden, Peter Birro is primarily recognised as scriptwriter of televised fiction drama series with a social realistic approach, who uses the city of Gothenburg as a recurrent setting.

18. The Swedish Penal Code has of course been reformed several times since 1864.

19. Miming to recordings of the actual voices of those involved was also used in the British production *The Arbor* (2010, dir. Clio Barnard), portraying

the late playwright Andrea Dunbar. It was, however, produced 5 years after Swärd's *Vägen hem*.

20. 'Guldbaggegalan' (The Golden Bug Gala) is the Swedish film industry's equivalent of the American Academy Awards. Instead of an Oscar the winner of each category of the Guldbaggegala is rewarded with a 'Golden Bug'.

21. Quotation from the DVD version of *Ninas resa* (00.32.26–00.33.07). Nina's voice-over, above in my translation, is here accompanied with archival footage from the Warsaw Ghetto.

22. In these reconstructed scenes the actor Rüdiger Vogler plays the part of Willy Wist, primarily in voice-over. For further discussions of *A Film Unfinished* see, for example: Böser (2012), Liebman (2011), and Prager (2015).

23. International recognition and awards for *Ninas resa*: 'Yad Vashem Award', Yad Vashem, Israel (2006); 'Best Director', Golden Rooster Film Festival Hangzhou, China (2006); 'Best of Fest', Palm Springs International Film Festival, US (2007); 'Best International Dramatic Feature Film', Vancouver Jewish Film Festival, Canada (2007); 'Best Narrative Feature', Atlanta Jewish Film Festival, US (2008) (SFI 2015g).

24. All three volumes in Leif G.W. Persson's literary trilogy *Välfärdsstatens fall* (Fall of the Welfare State) have the subheading *En roman om ett brott* (A Novel about a Crime). See: *Mellan sommarens längtan och vinterns köld: En roman om ett brott* (Before Summer's Longing and Winter's End: A Novel about a Crime, 2002); *En annan tid ett annat liv: En roman om ett brott* (Another Time, Another Life: a Novel about a Crime, 2003); *Faller fritt som i en dröm: En roman om ett brott* (Falling Freely, as in a Dream: a Novel about a Crime, 2007).

25. Persson's character Evert Bäckström has also been transformed into Everett Backstrom in the American TV series *Backstrom* created by Hart Hanson and broadcast from 2015. On the poster Fox describes Backstrom as 'brilliant detective, total dick'.

26. After the quotation, which is in Swedish, Persson includes a bracketed reference to Schuhheimer: '(Schuhheimer, Bartlett K; Poetry and Reality: The Case of Coincidence between Authors' Imagination and Empirical Truth; Hammond & Leslie, New Jersey 1975, cit s 263 ff)' (Persson 1978, p. 7).

27. Quotation from the DVD version of *Call Girl* (00.00.03–00.00.05).

28. The official trailer of *Call Girl*, presently available on YouTube.

29. The programme, *Kvällsöppet*, broadcast by SVT TV2, 3 May 1977, is presently available on YouTube.

CHAPTER 8

British Docudrama: New Directions in Reflexivity

David Rolinson

INTRODUCTION: BRITAIN'S TELEVISION ECOLOGY AND THE DOCUDRAMA

This chapter explores developments in British docudrama in the twenty-first century, in particular the strategies of reflexivity and hybridization which have engaged instructively with the nature of the genre and extended its reach and grasp. A brief survey of the industrial practices and cultural values of British television reveals their long-term impact on the characteristics of British docudrama. Public service broadcasting played a formative role in the world's first regular high-definition television service, launched by the British Broadcasting Corporation (BBC) in 1936. Its first Director-General, John Reith, instilled classic public service values such as a drive to 'inform, educate and entertain', still invoked in British television policy today. BBC Television, the only channel until 1955, originated 'dramatised story documentaries' post-war which dramatized field research in studio re-enactments. This practice resulted from early television's limited ability to record on location, but was seen by programme makers as a strength, generating a 'distinctive aesthetic' and 'particular dynamics of narrative' (Corner 1996, p. 31), and enabling 'audience identification' – these would become familiar parts of the ongoing 'defence for mixing documentary and drama' (Paget 2011, p. 186). This period tallies with Derek Paget's description of docudrama's 'first phase' from 1940 to

© The Editor(s) (if applicable) and The Author(s) 2016
T. Ebbrecht-Hartmann, D. Paget (eds.), *Docudrama on European Television*, Palgrave European Film and Media Studies,
DOI 10.1057/978-1-137-49979-0_8

199

1960, in which documentary – claiming 'probity and sobriety' valued by audiences – was uppermost (2011, p. 181).

The BBC was and remains a publicly owned broadcaster funded by the licence fee; in 1955 its monopoly was broken by the advertising-funded Independent Television (ITV) network. Concerns that ITV's more populist appeal would dilute Reithian values motivated the award of the third channel, BBC2, to the BBC in 1964 ('the BBC' became BBC1). However, the period of BBC/ITV duopoly was built upon a shared public service ethos.[1] Radical docudrama developed in this period, which tallies with the 1960–80 duration of Paget's 'second phase docudrama' (2011, p. 180). Docudrama formed part of a culture of politically and aesthetically radical drama which was the product of industry and policy frameworks that stressed that serious broadcasting 'must be challenging, controversial, and even transgressive' (Caughie 2000a, p. 85). BBC1's *The Wednesday Play* (1964–70) and *Play for Today* (1970–84) remain the best known platforms but a comparable culture existed at some of the regional companies that comprised ITV, such as Granada.[2] This was also the period in which docudrama studies began to flourish, and politically radical docudramas such as *Days of Hope* (BBC1, 1975) were central to debates in the film journal *Screen* on the attainability of ideologically progressive form.[3]

Although this current chapter uses the term 'docudrama' (after Paget 2011) for all work in the field, Caughie's proposal of two categories in 1980 has been highly influential because it instructively signals techniques and televisual contexts. The 'documentary drama' is essentially a dramatic fiction whose documentary case lies in its research and is validated as a truth representation by documentary or quasi-documentary visuals: for instance, Ken Loach's approach to *Cathy Come Home* (BBC1, 1966) presented writer Jeremy Sandford's research into homelessness as scripted drama, which generated an affective response. For Paget, Loach's 1960s techniques:

almost define second phase British docudrama: a pronounced social critique (usually focused through 'underdog' protagonists); filming techniques that placed a premium on immediacy (from which documentary authenticity could be inferred); and acting styles that stressed underplaying and appeared improvised (even when they were not). (2011, p. 208)

The sense of the dramatized documentary as primarily journalistic, indeed 'the journalism of last resort' (McBride 1999, p. 114), remains a strong part of British docudrama's DNA. It was a defining element of Granada's output under Leslie Woodhead, a direction he sought after an experience in which he had wanted to tell a story as a journalist but had 'found there was no other way to tell it' than to dramatize it (Woodhead 1999, p. 104). The journalistic intentions underscoring Granada's Eastern Europe docudramas such as *Three Days in Szczecin* (1976) and *Invasion* (1980) meant, according to producer David Boulton, 'no dramatic devices owing more to the writer's (or director's) creative imagination than to the implacable record of what actually happened' (Paget 2011, p. 217). Their evidential base was displayed on screen in 'captions and voiceover supplying details about the provenance of information' (p. 217), and the 'disclaimer' opening captions which they pioneered remain central in British docudrama regulation, albeit treated playfully by some makers, as we shall see.

However, Paget's second phase (1960–80) was a period in which 'the documentary claim within docudrama began to be doubted and interrogated' (2011, p. 182). John Hill has observed that '"radical" political expression' was possible at the BBC but in a contested space operating under 'ideological and institutional' constraints (2013, p. 132). Several docudramas were criticized or banned, including *The War Game* (1965) and *Scum* (1977). Programme makers felt that 'objections which were primarily about the substantive content and viewpoint expressed were strategically displaced into becoming objections about the unacceptability of the form itself' (Corner 1996, p. 39).[4] For instance, though *Scum* uncovered abuses in the borstal system,[5] the BBC publicly questioned the validity of its narrative compression of different cases, its use of a realist style too convincing in its immediacy, and its tough social commentary lacking the balance required for factual programmes. Docudrama makers contested that claim, as debates on docudrama practices became – and remain – a source of mainstream discussion in dedicated programmes.[6] Though controversies were occasionally described as a failure in labelling, programmes with detailed disclaimers also got into trouble, such as *Death of a Princess* (ATV/WGBH 1980) and *Hostages* (Granada/HBO 1992 – see Rosenthal 1999b, pp. 192–193; Paget 2011, pp. 98–99). The principle of giving journalism a wider social reach continued into landmark pieces such as *Who Bombed Birmingham?* (1990), in which Granada continued their current affairs strand *World in Action* (1963–98)'s investigation into the conviction of the Birmingham Six.[7]

In Paget's 'third phase' (roughly 1980–96), though 'the fact-rich British tradition continued to inflect' the genre, the hitherto less critically respected 'American-style' docudrama 'became formally dominant' (2011, p. 180). The arrival of Channel 4 in 1982 reinforced British television's shared public service values – with a remit for innovation and diversity supported by ITV assistance with its advertising income – but its status as a 'publisher', required to commission programmes from independent production companies, 'publishing' rather than making them in house, was extended to the BBC and ITV (with commissioned programmes constituting 25 % of their output). The old terrestrial channels were thus subjected to internal and external competition which changed the 'ecology of television production' (Bignell 2010, p. 196). This was one result of the 1990 Broadcasting Act, the first of several pieces of transformative regulation.

Along with deregulation, multi-channel television (pay-TV and free-to-air) has grown, not only through Channel 5's arrival as the last new commercial terrestrial network in 1997 but also through digital satellite, digital cable, digital terrestrial and internet television. All five national networks expanded into multi-channel television. The BBC created new channels with original programming to fulfil a public service requirement to drive digital uptake before switch-over from analogue signals (completed in 2012). These services have generated new sites for docudrama such as BBC3 (2003–), BBC4 (2002–) and Channel 4's More4 (2005–). The BBC and Channel 4 remain associated with public service broadcasting but ITV – its former regional structure centralised in 2004 – has been freed from many of its former requirements. This summary reminds us that texts are partly shaped by institutional contexts.

The docudramas covered in this chapter were made in this latter period of change. The argument takes a lead from Paget's suggestion that debates on the 'blurring' of boundaries have given way to a 'fourth-phase hybridisation' in which 'the "porous" boundary between documentary and drama has produced highly creative treatments of the serious and the social, the historical and the public, the personal and the collective' (2011, p. 287). The political and campaigning docudrama, so long the focus of academic discourse, has continued in the work of practitioners like Peter Kosminsky (*The Government Inspector*, C4, 2005), but this chapter tells a less often told story.[8]

The first two sections explore biographical docudramas about entertainment personalities, identifying characteristic devices, in particular reconstructions of fictional and non-fictional texts, to reveal an underestimated discursive complexity. These texts are placed in their institutional contexts, as mostly 'BBC4 biopics' or as examples of anniversary branding. The third section explores new developments in what has been described as the 'conditional tense docudrama'. All sections explore reflexive or postmodern practices, ranging from intertextual address to the questioning of discursive strategies, in order to establish the ways in which docudrama 'has mutated into a wide range of forms and formats, with a range of modes of address and aesthetic tone' as part of 'a larger process of negotiation, experiment and competition with related fictional and factual television forms' (Bignell 2010, p. 196). This reflexive concern with the limits of docudrama and other media is a strength of fourth-phase hybridization and is, arguably, specific to British docudrama.

'A Real But Half-Remembered Place': Television's Television Biopics

Early in *Marvellous* (BBC2, 2014), a caption proclaims: 'BASED ON A TRUE STORY'. This phrase and variations on it form 'disclaimers' which 'label' docudramas to stress the inevitability of creative treatment in the process of dramatizing research (Paget 2011, p. 99). The phrase 'based on a true story' acknowledges its own tensions – non-fiction's own narrative structures and the amount of latitude that 'based on' permits – but does not automatically resolve them: as Paget noted, disclaimers don't necessarily *anchor* films *to* the 'out-of-story world', which potentially weakens 'the mixed form's efforts to gain weight from an adjacency to fact' (2000, pp. 189, 200). *Marvellous* is one example of a new direction in British docudrama that actively draws attention to such tensions. Many docudramas present disclaimers as white text against a black background, a marker of seriousness and, given the approach's near-ubiquity, a marker of genre; however, this text is in bold capitals against a yellow background, signposting *Marvellous*'s joyful celebration of the unlikely but true life of Neil Baldwin, a man with learning disabilities who has served as a registered clown and in roles at a university and in British professional football. *Marvellous* opens with a more compelling disclaimer: the real Baldwin tells us, 'This is my story!', and actor Toby Jones, in character as Baldwin, adds: 'Right!' This simultaneously marks Baldwin's involvement, writer Peter Bowker's respect for Baldwin *and* the programme's dramatic treatment. This supportive but qualifying disclaimer prepares us for later scenes, such as Baldwin's appearance within the diegesis to deny that the previous scene happened – he did not, in fact, score a goal for Stoke City in a friendly amidst frenzied celebrations. However, the incredible fact that he *did* play as a substitute made that knowingly excessive version in its own way truthful. These approaches are characteristic of a distinctive reflexive trope in contemporary British docudrama's handling of real lives.

Current British docudrama shares with other European countries an interest in recent lives in politics and entertainment: as Belén Vidal observed, biopics have moved from historical subjects to 'historicizing the present by focusing on living subjects, or figures and events embedded in the recent collective memory' (2014a, b, p. 21). These first two sections focus on docudramas about television performers or programmes, events in the collective memory that are placed in wider institutional and cultural contexts. Observing trends across a number of docudramas, in particular shared approaches to performance and reconstruction, these sections support Paget's argument that hybridization promotes 'intertextual relationships with a variety of different sense-making factual and fictional entertainments' (2011, p. 286). The sections address two types of docudrama. In one, the 'living subject' is as much a programme or brand as a person. *The Road to Coronation Street* (BBC4, 2010) and *An Adventure in Space and Time* (BBC2, 2013) show the difficult births of the Granada soap opera *Coronation Street* (1960–) and the BBC science fiction series *Doctor Who* (1963–), while celebrating their fiftieth anniversaries and continuing popularity.[9] In the other type, there is an interest in the private lives of performers, which is at times symptomatic of the 'dark side of celebrityhood' approach noted by George Custen as being a feature of 'made-for-TV biopics' (1992, p. 223), but sometimes raises deeper questions about docudrama practice.

An Adventure in Space and Time and *The Road to Coronation Street* reconstruct scenes from programmes and the making of those scenes, within television's shifting institutional discourses and its production and office spaces, making their creative environments sites of cultural memory. *An Adventure in Space and Time* focuses on outsiders: an undervalued genre; a young female producer, Verity Lambert (Jessica Raine); a young, gay, Anglo-Indian director, Waris Hussein (Sacha Dhawan); and a Canadian, ex-ITV populiser Head of Drama, Sydney Newman (Brian Cox). In addition, the life of the first Doctor, actor William Hartnell (David Bradley), would change with this series. *The Road to Coronation Street* focuses on young, gay Northerner Tony Warren, creator and initial writer of *Coronation Street*, and Pat Phoenix, whose life will be changed by playing soap character Elsie Tanner. Granada executives Sidney and Cecil Bernstein are shown as wary of losing Granada's reputation for quality programmes but mindful of Granada's franchise requirement to reflect life in the north-west.[10]

The disclaimer that opens *An Adventure in Space and Time* marks its address as simultaneously historical and contemporary. Presented in the idiom of a period BBC continuity announcement (classic black and white station ident), it states:

> This is the BBC. The following programme is based on real events. It is important to remember, however, that you can't rewrite history. Not one line. Except perhaps when you embark on an adventure in space and time.

The docudrama was broadcast on BBC2 but refers to 'the BBC', which looks back (since *Doctor Who* started before 'the BBC' became BBC1) and forward (*Doctor Who* today is as important to BBC Worldwide and BBC America as it is to BBC1). The phrase 'based on real events' signposts docudrama's mediating strategies while stressing the truth claim of a 'based on' licence (Corner 1996, p. 42). This idiomatic presentation of disclaimers is a regular feature of these recent reflexive docudramas, from the false teeth that warn of 'naughty bits' in the manner of its subject, DJ and comedian Kenny Everett, in *Best Possible Taste* (BBC4, 2012) to the opening of political biopic *The Deal* (C4, 2003), which opens with captions including 'much of what follows is true'. This quotation from *Butch Cassidy and the Sundance Kid* (1969) intertextually signposts writer Peter Morgan's contested depiction of a leadership deal between the Labour Party's Tony Blair and Gordon Brown in a private conversation and reads their relationship.

The warning that 'you can't rewrite history. Not one line' invokes 'The Aztecs', a 1964 *Doctor Who* story which debates time travel ethics, and echoes twenty-first-century *Doctor Who*'s paratextual tagline 'time *can* be rewritten'. As well as introducing the docudrama's interest in reconstruction, the reference playfully combines time-travel and docudrama ethics. *The Road to Coronation Street* begins with the old Granada Television frontcap (the slogan 'from the North' stressing Granada's status as the ITV network's North West region).[11] *An Adventure in Space and Time* places *Doctor Who*'s collaborative authorship in the institutional context of the BBC.[12] At crucial moments of crisis and success, compositions stress the centrality of Television Centre, for decades the BBC's administrative and production centre in London. This reconstruction of the past is haunted by our present, since the docudrama was shot in the increasingly derelict spaces of Television Centre, which was sold as part of the BBC's response to a 2010 financial settlement with the government.

The reconstruction of studio sets is a major part of television-themed docudrama. Studio space is doubly (re)constructed: Tony Warren (David Dawson) responds emotionally to the set of the Tanner family's house, the first tangible sign that he can reflect and reach his community. Similarly, the interior of the TARDIS (the Doctor's time machine) is a place of wonder for characters in *Doctor Who* and beyond. Fan/reporter Gary Gillatt stared at the docudrama set 'in slack-jawed wonder' with a 'primal' feeling as if 'someone has rebuilt a real but half-remembered place from your own life – your childhood bedroom, your first classroom at school – down to the last detail' (2013, p. 33). There are multiple levels of reflexive re-enactment here: the TARDIS set stands in a working 1963 studio, built within a working 2013 studio. Using the original Marconi cameras, producing black-and-white images on 405-line TV monitors, the production reconstructs a long multi-camera sequence using a 1963 camera script, even replicating mistakes. In its re-enactments of stories, the docudrama moves between its HD coverage and images on monitors, and actors move from playing actors to playing those actors playing characters. These layers coalesce at key moments, such as in a re-enacted scene from 'The Massacre' (1966) which yields to the docudrama's visual and affective language as the Doctor's lament for his departed friends in-story becomes Hartnell's lament for *his* departed friends in fact. His near-breakdown is conveyed by a lens change which makes the TARDIS studio space seem even more uncanny.

The docudrama's insight into multi-camera electronic recording reconstructs these specifically televisual spaces, celebrating the programme's innovative 'abuses of the television studio' (Potter 2007) and charting practices that have been the subject of reconstruction in practice-led academic research.[13] The docudrama's use of film shorthand helps contemporary viewers but also serves an affective purpose: by inaccurately showing standing sets (when rehearsals in fact took place in a church hall with sets marked by tape on the floor), it provides *Doctor Who* backdrops for vital *behind-the-scenes* moments, such as Lambert bidding farewell to Hartnell on the TARDIS set. This blurring of production and fiction departures is ratcheted up emotionally by the presence among the extras of some of Hartnell's actual 1960s co-stars.[14]

Indeed, real cast members, or images of them, often appear in docudramas about television, with complex results. At the end of *The Road to Coronation Street*, the camera tracks from the first episode (shown on a vintage set) to photographs of *Coronation Street*'s real original cast. Captions stress the series' subsequent longevity. *An Adventure in Space and Time* reverses this: captions give biographical futures but form alone conveys the series' future. A track across the reconstructed television studio gallery celebrates an impossible museum-like standing-set collection of *Doctor Who* icons. The current Doctor in 2013 (Matt Smith) impossibly appears on Hartnell's TARDIS set, so Hartnell sees his legacy just as he shoots his final scene. The docudrama 'reinforced the BBC's reputation for high-quality historical reconstructions' of which docudramas are a key exponent (Hills 2015, p. 44) and it joined a series of paratexts, events and texts (such as the record-breaking 2013 global simulcast of 'The Day of the Doctor') through which the fiftieth anniversary served simultaneously to maintain a flagship global brand while seeking to 'performatively sustain a public service agenda' (Hills 2013, p. 159).

THE CURSED COMEDIANS: ENTERTAINER DOCUDRAMAS

The docudramas discussed above are unusually celebratory for docudramas about television. This section will now assess the representativeness of their tropes by comparison with five docudramas that, though separate, cover interconnected comic actors and writers, most of whom worked together: *Cor Blimey!* (2000), *Fantabulosa!* (2006), *The Curse of Steptoe* (2008), *Hancock and Joan* (2008) and *Hattie* (2011) – all were broadcast on BBC4 except *Cor Blimey!* (ITV). The latter depicts an affair between actors Sid James and Barbara Windsor when performing in the *Carry On* film comedy series (1958–78, 1992). *Fantabulosa!* focuses on actor Kenneth Williams, including his work on the radio and television *Hancock's Half Hour* (1956–61) with actor Tony Hancock and writers Ray Galton and Alan Simpson. *The Curse of Steptoe* covers the making of Galton and Simpson's next comedy project, *Steptoe and Son* (1962–74), starring Harry H. Corbett and Wilfrid Brambell. *Hancock and Joan* covers Hancock's dark later years, including his affair with Joan Le Mesurier, third wife of his friend (and former *Hancock's Half Hour* co-star) John Le Mesurier. *Hattie* covers a long affair that Le Mesurier's second wife, Hattie Jacques, had before his marriage to Joan provided a discreet resolution.

These docudramas too make substantial use of reconstructed texts, both fiction (their subjects' films, television dramas and comedies) and non-fiction (their television appearances as themselves). These reconstructed texts partly address the 'spectator's sense of remembrance and participation in a shared popular culture' (Vidal 2014a, b, p. 22), but they also symbolize notions of performance and the authenticity of self. For example, many of these programmes have climactic sequences in which their subjects appear in television interviews in which there is a claim to reveal the private, 'real' self, but in a (re)constructed public performance that draws its meaning from the hybrid discourses afforded by docudramatic address. All reconstruct texts, but with instructive differences in their methods of integration. *The Curse of Steptoe* re-enacts scenes from *Steptoe and Son*, drawing parallels between characters and actors. Corbett (Jason Isaacs)'s first sight of the Steptoes' home is another moment of wonder, referencing his theatrical background: 'This is a fantastic space. Just the right feel. Claustrophobic'. The claustrophobic psychodrama of first episode 'The Offer' heightens these parallels through technique: camera movements take us from the studio floor to the reconstructed programme on the monitors, but the docudrama's own reverse-field cutting takes us into Corbett and Brambell's performance space.[15] Re-enactments from later episodes select moments to stand as double meanings about the docudrama's contested interpretation of the actors' personal issues and sense of being trapped by these roles, with close-ups of spectators whose laughter is drowned out by non-diegetic music that positions those moments as disturbing. The blurring of character and performer identities in *Carry On* re-enactments is handled differently. *Cor Blimey!* largely shows scenes from the film studio floor, though Sid (Geoffrey Hutchings) first falls for Windsor (Samantha Spiro) in her on-screen persona at a dubbing room screening of *Carry On Spying* (1964). *Hattie* attempts a seamless integration of diegetic looks, taking us from the making of *Carry On Cabby* (1963) into the film itself in one camera movement that shifts to black-and-white and adds diegetic music.

Hancock (played by Ken Stott in *Hancock and Joan*) and Corbett's statements on performance chime with notions of authenticity in docudrama. Just as docudrama actors value performance over impersonation of their subjects, so *The Curse of Steptoe* contrasts the 'absolute searching for truth' that Corbett found in his Theatre Workshop work under Joan Littlewood with the danger of repeated tics and pratfalls in comedy. In *Fantabulosa!*, Hancock (Martin Trenaman) shows dissatisfaction at

Williams's performances in re-enacted radio recordings of *Hancock's Half Hour*. *Fantabulosa!* reconstructs an already self-aware passage from 'The Emigrant' (1957) in which Kenneth Williams (Michael Sheen)'s 'Snide' character singles out 'that bloke with the funny voice' (himself by proxy) as the only good thing about Hancock's radio series. Off-stage, Hancock criticizes Williams's reliance on funny voices and 'playing to the gallery' rather than seeking acting purity. Williams speaks in comparable terms later – 'comedy and tragedy are only two sides of the same coin. However broad the performance might be, an audience will come with you *if* they believe you' – but Sheen's performative cues punctuate the argument: a snide grin at the end of the first sentence, an exaggerated rolling of his 'r's on 'broad' and pointedly clear enunciation of the final words. Comparing authentic and excessive representations of Williams is difficult: Sheen noted that 'I've never seen more information coming off a person [...] all these things that his body is saying, there's just so much of it, it was like white noise'. He wondered how to take 'someone who is already almost a caricature, a parody of themselves, but play them in a way that is totally believable' (*The South Bank Show*, ITV 2007). For Williams, the private is performance: 'never remove your mask', he advises. He even saw his diaries (their writing is also reconstructed docudramatically) as 'what the self wants to say'.

The interweaving of many elements – types of performance, rehearsal, characters building characters (including themselves), public and private selves – makes these figures complex docudrama subjects. The recurring device of doorway framing purports to take us into private space or observe personal moments from outside. *The Curse of Steptoe* and *Hancock and Joan* aired in a season called 'The Curse of Comedy', with its markers of the biopic's 'warts-and-all' mode (Bingham 2010, p. 17) and revelation of 'feet of clay' (Custen 1992, p. 223). The tears-of-a-clown approach seems an odd fit for BBC4, which was marketed as the BBC's intellectual channel, but docudrama was featured from its first night (the experimental and inevitably surreal 2002 Salvador Dalí piece *Surrealissimo*). Covering figures from British popular culture ranging from Shirley Bassey to Enid Blyton, the 'BBC4 biopic' became such a recognized strand that the press noted its passing when *Burton and Taylor* (2013 – about the stormy relationship between Richard Burton and Elizabeth Taylor) became BBC4's final drama owing to BBC cuts.

Perhaps docudrama 'equalizes these entertainers by bringing us up close to their tragedies', but the multiple nature of their subjects raises productive tensions: encountered 'through the world of TV' before they are 'encountered through the world of TV biography', these figures are '[m]ediated already' (Custen 1992, p. 230). This is particularly pronounced in these programmes' shared device of building to a climactic interview, non-fiction appearances which 'emphasise moments of crisis or transformation' (Bignell 2013, p. 227). These diegetic interrogations become part of the text's claim to reveal the private, 'real' self but do so within a (re)constructed public performance. *Hattie* provides a complex example of this. In 1963, Jacques was the subject of an edition of the television programme *This is Your Life*.[16] Her husband, John Le Mesurier, paid tribute to her running of the home as 'a jolly neat trick', a statement that could simply mean that Jacques balanced her busy work life with her husband and children. However, docudrama viewers know that Jacques (Ruth Jones) has moved her lover into the family home and Le Mesurier (Robert Bathurst) into a spare bedroom. *Hattie* unpicks public and private discourse by interweaving re-enacted *This is Your Life* footage, shots of the watching lover and subjective shots of Jacques's discomfort, both in close-up and in quick, distorted point-of-view images of guests greeting her. Authenticity comes in our insight into the subject: drama reveals the private self, whereas non-fiction shows the projected, performed, self. Uncovering the story behind such broadcasts does not destabilize factual forms' truth claims so much as incorporate forms and claims into its hybrid discourse. Jacques's actual *This is Your Life* was even repeated on BBC4 to add to the mix. If docudramas textually reference the ways in which '[a]rchival images and sounds form the textures of memory, whether individual or collective' (Vidal 2014a, b, p. 22), such scheduling affirms it as experience.

In comparable television interviews in *Fantabulosa!*, Williams discusses suicidal thoughts with Mavis Nicholson and speaks uproariously to Terry Wogan (in both cases, Sheen-as-Williams is intercut with the real Williams interviews). Acted-Williams later watches the Wogan interview in a shot/reverse-shot pattern as if in a revelatory exchange between his private and public selves. Dialogue between selves recurs in *Hancock and Joan*, which opens with Hancock (Ken Stott) waking in hospital as a result of his alcoholism and seeing himself in a confessional television appearance. The recreated Hancock watches the recreated Hancock apparently revealing his private self in public on television, but again the non-fiction coding of revelation through interiority compares unfavourably with the docudrama's own. The key intertext here is Hancock's appearance on *Face to Face* (BBC 1959–62), whose interviews 'attempted to penetrate more deeply than the standard conventions of television conversation allowed' (Medhurst 1991, p. 64). The programme largely excluded shots of interviewer John Freeman in favour of 'uninterrupted scrutiny of the subject' as if in 'a psychiatric session' (Fisher 2008, p. 273). Hancock's brother and agent Roger Hancock called the programme 'the biggest mistake he ever made', because the sort of '[s]elf-analysis' it required 'was his killer' (Fisher 2008, p. 272). In *Hancock and Joan*, on the night of his suicide Hancock hallucinates a confrontation between himself and his television self, the Homburg hat-wearing Hancock he had self-destructively tried to escape. If this is a meeting of public and private selves, which, an audience is invited to ask, is which? The docudramatic quotation of interviews presupposes a revelation of self but Hancock's desire to strip down the *Hancock's Half Hour* Hancock fulfilled *Face to Face*'s functions as if the *Face to Face* Hancock was himself a media construct. As Lucy Fife Donaldson has argued elsewhere, 'performance on the stage becomes performance of self' (Donaldson 2014, p. 109).

Imagery thus emphasizes the recurrence of multiple selves in an extended conceptual reflexivity. In *Fantabulosa!*, Williams often studies his reflection, and the re-enactment of a performance on the BBC radio show *Round the Horne* (1965–8) doubles him in refracted reflections in glass – as he performs the coded homosexuality of the 'Julian and Sandy' sketches. This adds poignancy to his own description of his sexuality as 'the paradox of my own nature: the thing that I am being the thing which I despise'.[17] Multiple selves acknowledge the difficulties of indexicality. At the end of *Fantabulosa!*, two characters move off-screen to find Williams dead in his flat, but the camera's movement continues to a photograph of the actual Williams. At the start of *Cor Blimey!*, photographs of the real Williams and James transform into photographs of the performed ones (Adam Godley, Geoffrey Hutchings). Part tribute, part acknowledgement of mediation, such moments encapsulate tensions in docudrama's newly sophisticated interweaving of private life, public performances, performed texts and (the performance of) the making of those texts.

If re-enactment is 'the act of imaginative recreation that allows the spectator to imagine they are "witnessing again" the events of the past' (Burgoyne 2008, p. 7), these programmes imaginatively recreate the imaginative creation of images which were witnessed by the spectator while their making was not. Paratexts emphasize the accuracy of their re-enactments, and these television-themed docudramas' imaginative recreations of widely known texts within the discourse of interior and investigative revelation shed light on Lipkin's 'logic of indexical iconicity' (2002, p. 4). Docudrama 'draws upon direct, motivated resemblances to its actual materials' to affirm 'the validity of its metaphors'. Lipkin relates the 'indexical' signs of documentary (with its discourse of sobriety) to the 'indexical icons' of docudrama, signs which are 'primarily iconic' but have 'direct, strongly motivated resemblances to their actual referents' (2002, p. 4).

'Proximity to pre-existing texts' has the referential claim of reproducing a verifiable record but this part of docudramatic address is one of a series of proximities that Lipkin posits as a nexus of ethical concerns (2002, p. 54). The laborious re-enactment of visual details does not excuse the mistreatment of essential facts, such as chronological alterations, problematic in *The Curse of Steptoe* to the extent that the BBC changed the programme for subsequent repeats, added a disclaimer – though insisting that disclaimers were not a '"blank cheque" for the indiscriminate and excessive use of dramatic licence' – and published specific editorial guidelines for biopics in Autumn 2010 (Corbett 2012, p. 448).

The approval of subjects does not mean that a docudrama will seek, let alone attain, mimetic referentiality. Indeed, biographical docudramas are often the site of postmodern concerns, problematizing their own depictions even while paratexts stress their fidelity of reconstruction. During a final scene between Windsor and Williams in *Cor Blimey!*, the real Barbara Windsor seamlessly replaces actress Samantha Spiro to play herself. Her involvement validates the representation but also reflects on the nature of the biopic by describing Heaven: 'You sit in front of your life [at a Steenbeck editing machine] and you're allowed to re-edit it – cut the rotten bits, loop the sex, montage the good moments, live it over [...] and eventually make it perfect'. Addressing reconstructed Williams (Godley), the real Windsor says, 'We were laughing, remember, the evening Sid died'. Though Windsor and Williams walk beneath a rainbow that is revealed to be a glass shot, this acknowledgement of mediation is itself couched in the recreation of a 1970s film set.

Windsor's displacement of Spiro resolves a theme in *Cor Blimey!* – Windsor's distinction between private Sid and public 'Sid' – but also forms one way of addressing the 'body too many' that Bill Nichols observed in the historical reconstruction of real people. As Paget explains, 'In the body of the actor [...] a kind of *excess* is enacted' (2011, p. 158). Belén Vidal noted that the subject and actor in the film *American Splendor* (2003) 'exist not in excess of each other, but visually side by side', which enacts the body too many with 'an emphatic duplication of bodies/subjects' (2014a, b, p. 15). This strategy is not new: Granada's *Invasion* (which uses transcripts to recreate the Soviet Union's 1968 invasion of Czechoslovakia) opens with the real Czech politician Zdenek Mlynar standing beside Paul Chapman, the actor who plays him. But if this doubling attempted to underline its strategy of reconstruction to stress its journalistic research and intentions, the 'beside-the-bodyness' in contemporary docudrama has been placed in the context of 'the deconstruction of the centred self' in postmodernism (Vidal 2014a, b, p. 15).

Recent British ('porous') docudrama of this kind embraces postmodern concerns with intertextuality and memory. The film *24 Hour Party People* (2002) has been influential. Its interruption of a scene to allow a represented subject to state that 'I *definitely* don't remember this happening' has equivalents elsewhere, including in *Marvellous. Cor Blimey!* partly resembles a *Carry On* film, in its opening titles and a scene with inopportunely timed, freakishly caused, discreetly realised group nudity; at such times, to borrow Lucy Fife Donaldson's observations of very different pieces, 'figures perform as characters in – and comment on – the plays/films/stage musicals they are known for, thus intertextually appealing to an (inferred) knowledge and enjoyment of their work' (2014, p. 104). *Holy Flying Circus* (BBC4, 2011) shows the potential for intertextual address to inform wider postmodern scrutiny. Its account of the controversy faced by the team behind *Monty Python's Life of Brian* (1979) is told in a *Monty Python* idiom, with rampant invention, animation, the doubling of an actor (Rufus Jones) playing both Terry Jones and his writing partner Michael Palin's wife, and parodies of BBC past and present, such as the depiction of the Head of BBC4 as a cocaine-snorter ordering 'some old footage of a barge' to fill his schedules. The result is 'sub-*Python* self-referential quasi-avant-garde posturing bullshit'... according to a contemporary viewer depicted in the programme itself. However, *Holy Flying Circus* also culminates in a re-enactment of a real discussion programme in which John Cleese (Darren Boyd) and Palin (Charles Edwards) struggled to defend the film against religious representatives. The Pythons took the debate seriously and were surprised that their opponents played to the gallery in a 'performance' (Palin 2006, p. 596).[18] These docudramas therefore do not deconstruct their own epistemological bases – they only destabilize modes to address a wider concern with the knowledge claims of various forms, in particular to stress that more valorized factual forms are themselves sites of performance.

'IT WASN'T A CASE OF *IF*': CONDITIONAL TENSE
DOCUDRAMA

Evidence for the argument that fourth-phase hybridization exhibits a 'new investigative energy and a new readiness to introduce performed elements into the structured mix' (Paget 2011, p. 274) can be found in the 'conditional (or "subjunctive") tense' docudrama or '"What If?" mode' (p. 278). Seeking new approaches to maintain docudrama's social and public service concerns, such texts are 'at the forefront of developments in the docudrama form' (Stewart and Butt 2011, p. 75). Set in the near future, these docudramas depict crises that are fictional but extrapolated from current trends and policies, often to assess the authorities' preparedness and the public's awareness. Critics have responded to the form's hybridity with various terms: 'future documentaries' (Mills 2011, p. 83), 'hypothetical' docudramas, 'hypothetical-catastrophe docudramas' (Stewart 2011, p. 251), 'mockumentary, docudrama, fake documentary, quasi-documentary, faux-documentary, pseudo-documentary, pretend documentary, faction, documentary styled drama, hypothetical docudrama, what ifs' (Stewart and Butt 2011, p. 73) or 'future-oriented docudrama' (p. 75). This chapter uses the definition that has gained the most traction: 'conditional tense docudrama', which Paul Ward usefully worked through (Ward 2006). Building on such antecedents as *You Are There* (1953–57), *It Happened Here* (1964) and *The War Game* (see Paget 2011, p. 278) in its methods of 'preconstruction' or 'pre-enactment' (Mills 2011, p. 84), the conditional tense docudrama has evolved in sync with tropes in factual television.

Some programmes take the documentary drama form as fictions whose claim on the real comes from journalistic research and a style influenced by documentary. They include: the BBC/HBO's *Dirty War* (2004), featuring a bioterrorist 'dirty bomb' attack on London; Channel 4's *Gas Attack* (2001), depicting racial tensions and a biological attack on refugees; and *Blackout* (2013), which combined factual and fictional 'found footage' to depict a long-term electricity blackout. Strictly speaking, conditional tense docudramas are presented in the style of contemporary history documentaries which 'address us from a *supposed future*, talking about a set of events in the *past* (i.e. past in relation to the future from which the story is told), while those events are still in our future' (Ward 2006, pp. 275–276). They are conditional in the sense that their imaginary events '*could yet* happen', a claim that they support by presenting those events 'as if they have *already* happened' (p. 273). Examples at the BBC include *Smallpox* 2002: *Silent Weapon* (BBC1, 2002), depicting the global impact of the release of the smallpox virus by one man in New York; *The Day Britain Stopped* (BBC2, 2003), depicting simultaneous pre-Christmas crises across the transport system in the crowded south-east of England; *The Man Who Broke Britain* (BBC2, 2004), predicting bank collapses and a global economic crisis caused by unregulated trading; and the *If...* series (BBC2, 2004–5), covering various disaster scenarios including a long-term electricity blackout. Examples elsewhere include More4/C4's *Death of a President* (2007), depicting the imagined assassination of George W. Bush, and Channel 4's *UKIP: The First 100 Days* (2015), which combined a fictional observational documentary with repurposed archive footage to hypothesize the consequences should a minor Eurosceptic party win that year's then-forthcoming General Election.

Michael Stewart observed that conditional tense docudrama 'mixes aesthetic modes and narrative registers in order to persuade viewers of the authenticity and veracity of its historical and disastrous prediction' (2011, p. 252). This section addresses two issues arising from this: how docudrama negotiates the rhetorical status of prediction, and the nature and extent of the mixture of modes and registers, given that conditional tense docudrama's 'core narrative action is imagined' (Stewart and Butt 2011, p. 75). This adds new weight to questions asked by John Corner in relation to docudrama's 'representation' issue:

> How does the programme look and sound? Is there an attempt to imitate the codes of documentary and thereby generate (if only 'in play') reportage values? Is there a mix of dramatic with more conventional documentary material? What are the possibilities for 'deception', for a viewer attributing an incorrect status to the depiction [...]? (1996, p. 42)

As Brett Mills noted, the makers of *Smallpox* 2002 felt that their approach was new, despite acknowledged antecedents, because of their 'deliberate decision to confuse the fact/fiction dichotomy in a manner not always clear to the audience' (2011, p. 88). The category therefore provides a useful test case for Paget's belief that new hybrid forms have 'promoted intertextual relationships' and that audiences, far from being 'duped', exercise 'innate media intelligence' (2011, p. 282).

Conditional tense docudrama imitates factual codes including: omniscient past-tense voice-over narration (created in imitation of documentary practice); CCTV footage (actual and created); home video and family photographs (actual and created); archive footage (actual, created, or actual but repurposed as if part of these future events); news coverage and reportage (actual and created); formal hindsight interviews on camera and in voice-over (featuring fictional characters or, less often, real people performing fictional or conventional testimony); satellite imagery/CGI/time-lapse photography; and other such material that is created here as it is in contemporary history documentary. However, the above list does not capture the variety and complexity of the form's discursive hybridity.

For example, *Dirty War* opens with a bioterror response drill that is simultaneously fiction, reconstruction from fact (research into emergency planning) and reflection upon fact and reconstruction: when a character realizes the difference in scale between their drill and the anticipated demands of that location during a real attack, she comments: 'It's not exactly realistic, then?' The potential reflexivity of a statement on the inadequacy of a pre-enactment at the start of a pre-enactment-based text is reduced by its status within docudrama's familiar discursive hierarchy: we witness the drill's profound flaws from the perspective of a fire-fighter, giving us experiential evidence against which the Minister's reassuring statements are flagged as PR reassurance. An interrogative zoom during her select committee evidence marks the programme's investigative rhetoric even though the character and events are fictitious: experiential evidence instils scepticism for official statements within – and, potentially, beyond – texts.

Further evidence of the conditional tense's distinctive mixture of discourses can be found in *The Day Britain Stopped*. The Galt family are introduced with aerial shots and graphics that bring us closer to them on the motorway and move us from the general to the particular. Voice-over and captions anchor events at a precise time and place (11.03 a.m.; Basingstoke, Hampshire) in line with docudrama's concern with verisimilitude-enhancing detail, on a day (19 December 2003) that is in the putative documentary's past (it looks back on events in 2003 and 2004) but in the viewer's future (broadcast 13 May 2003). The next shot comes from inside the car, from a home video shot by 12-year-old Thomas (Angelo Andreou). This shift in address invokes documentary discourse in complex ways that are characteristic of this form. The voice-over calls it 'a unique record of the day's events' and a caption labels it as a 'home video'. Viewed within the documentary idiom, these markers fulfil their standard function in acknowledging the technical inferiority and potential partiality of the footage while also stressing its importance as witness testimony in form (footage that gives hitherto-unavailable personal access to events) and empathetic narrative focus (experiencing those events with partici-pants). Of course, the footage is fiction, not a home video, but labelling here follows documentary practice: documentaries caption 'home video' footage but they also caption 'reconstruction' sequences or acknowledge dramatization, which this programme does not. The Galt family facilitate our witnessing of failures in the transport system, providing a personaliz-ing (re)constructed focus on 'individuals affected by the crisis or involved in trying to manage its effects' (Bignell 2010, p. 202).

The Galts therefore provide 'informational throughput', the proxemics of dramatization bringing us closer to 'the local human detail within the larger themes and sphere of action being addressed' (Corner 1996, p. 35). Corner contrasts this kind of effect with the 'distance' achieved by con-ventional documentary through observation and commentary. It is testa-ment to the power of intergeneric hybridization that this structural device is as characteristic of the contemporary history documentary as it is the docudrama. Over the 'home video' footage, the voice-over establishes the family's plan to travel from Basingstoke to Central London to Heathrow for their flight to Spain; the circumstances necessitating this unorthodox journey are explained by father Julian Galt (Steve North) in a formal inter-view, which at first we hear in sound only as a personalizing complement to the lead voice-over (Tim Pigott-Smith)'s distanced commentary. There are marked contrasts between the two putative sources: the home video moves constantly, its unstable framing supporting its aesthetic of imme-diacy as it records family members who interact with its amateur operator, while the professionally operated interview camera holds a static medium close-up of Julian, who addresses an off-camera interviewer. In this 'sober, reflective hindsight testimony', subdued lighting and dark clothing rein-force Julian's status as the only family member to survive the day's events. The power of the juxtaposition 'derives from the different ways in which the viewer relates to each type of footage: they are indexed distinctly' (Ward 2006, p. 280).[19]

The climactic plane crash presents a complex interaction of elements. A hindsight interview explains the increased workload of air traffic control-ler Nicola Evans (Joanna Griffiths) and the circumstances and procedures that culminate in two planes crashing. The programme constantly cor-roborates Nicola's testimony, with CCTV footage of her at work on that night, electronic displays of flight patterns, indicative images of locations, planes landing and aborting landings (either archive or constructed by the 'documentary', or constructed as archive by the 'drama'), an aerial satellite-type image and close-ups of details such as hands pressing buttons. The collision is anchored in disaster coverage's familiar witness address: the explosion appears in a home video whip pan from roadside football fans and in time-coded footage from two supermarket CCTV cameras. There is an optical zoom-in to a shocked Nicola, for which footage has been created to include real-world imperfections: this high-angle shot of the whole room needs to be manipulated to generate a medium close-up of Nicola which helps the 'documentary' to identify her and the 'drama' to heighten the moment. The programme thereby derives some impact from its 'interplay between indexical and indexically iconic materials', again to borrow Lipkin's terms.[20]

As Bignell noted, voice-over, extrapolation from research and the deployment of stylistic markers of actuality such as CCTV 'claim one kind of authenticity' in conditional tense docudramas but 'naturalistic performance claims another', both in the 'understated performance style' of the fictional characters and the 'matter-of-fact tone commonly used by professionals and experts' in factual texts (2010, pp. 201–202). Just as John Caughie influentially defined docudrama performance as a 'reversal' whereby 'the traditional skills of impersonation came to mean insincerity, and not quite knowing your lines meant you were speaking the truth' (2000b, p. 166), so the naturalistic performances contrast with the 'actorly voiceover' by Pigott-Smith (Paget 2011, p. 280). This feature paradoxically assists the programme's factual coding because it replicates the conventions of history documentary. In contrast, the programme's director, Gabriel Range, noted that witness interviews are 'unforgiving of an actor's performance' and so the actors immersed themselves in the experiences of people who had lived through similar situations and work duties, and improvised, in character, their answers to documentary questions (p. 279) with concomitant hesitancy and spontaneity. For Mills, 'the grain of truth which stops this being actorly improvisation and transforms it into documentary actuality is partly the result of the ways in which such stories are told to camera' (2011, p. 91). So Jane Newell (Nancy McClean)'s account of receiving the news that her pilot husband had been killed provides information that (plausibly) exceeds its narrative function in its affective rendering of a memory that seemingly surprises her: she was telephoned by 'a very, very softly-spoken man' (a performative sign which reinforces the scene's own performative function). For Stewart and

Butt, the interviews have 'a curious double quality' in that they are 'both hesitant and primed' (2011, p. 76), that is, melodramatic and affective but also 'ready and available' as testimony (p. 77). Such moments remind us that the skill of actors is the 'real key to this particular hybrid' (Paget 2011, p. 279).

Paratexts impact upon our understanding of the audience's position in relation to this rhetoric of witnessing. Scholars have debated whether the 'conditional tense' label applies for programmes like *The Day Britain Stopped* which 'recount events *as if* they are *from the past*', stressing that 'this *did* happen' (Ward 2006, p. 272), with voice-overs that 'transmute their predictions into history, with all the factual connotations which that process brings with it' (Mills 2011, p. 89). In contrast, *The War Game* 'imagines a *possible future*' (Ward 2006, p. 272), with 'tentative' phrasing (Mills 2011, p. 89), albeit with 'shocking and highly plausible images and sounds' that 'anchor the meaning' (Ward 2006, p. 276). The original broadcast paratexts make *The Day Britain Stopped* more complex than this summary suggests. One hour before broadcast, a continuity announcement and programme trail assimilated the text's past tense alongside other temporal and generic cues, describing it as 'a nightmare scenario in a drama to make you think', with hindsight audio ('It had been a dreadful day'), a future-tense graphic ('7 months from now') and an inelegant timeslot marker (*'The Day Britain Stopped...* in one hour'). Similarly, the continuity announcement stated: 'Now on BBC2, a drama set in the near future. Based on extensive research, this film looks back on the terrible events of one day in December 2003 – the day Britain stopped.'

To an extent this continues the 'labelling' function of 'disclaimers' that signpost a docudrama's research base while acknowledging the narrative structuring and creative treatment which have been necessary in the dramatization of that research (Paget 2011, p. 99) and serves to 'index' a text so that 'people will be watching *knowing* that the programme is what it is' (Ward 2006, p. 278). In a further paratext, an in-vision interview on the BBCi website and television red button service, co-writer/producer Simon Finch denied that the programme '*misleads* the audience in a fundamental way' because an 'attentive viewer watching for more than a few seconds' will realize their mistake if they initially believe that its events are 'actually happening in real time' (BBCi 2003). In the digital age docudramas are not merely pre-labelled but also (potentially) constantly indexed because of electronic programme guides and information on streaming catch-up services such as BBC iPlayer.

The text's opening voice-over cues a shift in tense from the paratextual introduction but does not resolve its tensions: 'On the nineteenth of December 2003, the failings of Britain's transport system were exposed as never before. Decades of neglect led to a day of disaster.' The past tense applies to the future event (the day of disaster) and to a documented past (failings and neglect). The past is a revelatory proposition built on research (*actual* failings led to this disaster) but it is hypothetical (these researched phenomena *will* result in disaster) and tentative (though the failings are real, they are exposed 'as never before' because they have never happened in the way we are about to see). Equally, taking place within schedules with paratexts and follow-up discussion programmes, a text can be in the conditional tense discursively even if it is not formally. *Dirty War* started with triple indexing: BBC1 contact details for the later discussion programme *Dirty War – Your Questions Answered*; a continuity announcement introducing *Dirty War*; and a disclaimer caption. There was also a BBC1 strapline at 10.00 p.m. to explain that the news would run later than usual, and a further trail for the discussion programme.

These docudramas are 'current, occurring events' (Stewart and Butt 2011, p. 81) which dramatize 'existing realities' *and* 'produce' and 'constitute' realities (p. 82). Their indexical claim is not to mimesis but to hypothesis, their ontological register not of the future but the present. In terms of social correspondence and viewer experience, they simultaneously generate the questions: 'Can anything be done to remedy the inadequacies of current planning and information provision that might lead to this?' and 'Which parts of the programme's evidence need to be discussed in the debates to follow?' While accepting Paget's point that 'the ideal spectator [...] actively engages in hypothesising the real', Stewart and Butt argue that this real is 'complicated and at least multiple', for instance through 'the pleasure of event-led action melodrama' whose viewers 'hypothesise on the nature of the fabula, or diegetic real' and speculate on 'when and how will disaster strike' (2011, p. 81). Viewers are therefore '*predicting* communities' as much as they are 'remembering communities' (Mills 2011, p. 94).

This textual and paratextual addressing of the audience as witnesses mobilizes 'warranting', on which depend perceptions of the effectiveness of a text's claims, texts and paratexts; these often stress that their 'events "really" happened', though subject to mediation (Lipkin 2002, p. 5). For instance, BBC1's continuity announcer introduced *Derailed* (2005) as 'a powerful and sensitive drama' which 'reveals the true story of the [1999]

Paddington train crash, told through the eyes of those most affected'. *The Day Britain Stopped* tells a hypothetical story but one that addresses prior incidents, which helps to address Lipkin's first warrant, that 'this story deserves to be told' (2002, p. 49). Range stressed that it was 'exploring important issues' (BBCi 2003); to an extent it works 'in the tradition of documentary investigation' in that it addresses 'institutional problems' in its researched depiction of pressures on, for instance, the emergency services (Bignell 2010, p. 202). A bigger challenge for conditional tense docudrama is Lipkin's 'second level of warranting', namely 'that the story must be told "this" way, through re-creation' (2002, p. 49). With conditional tense docudrama, this warrant must be addressed in two interconnected ways: firstly in terms of programmes' docudrama approaches and secondly in terms of their specific 'conditional tense' functions, which involve predictive 'creation' rather than Lipkin's 're-creation'. Answering the first question, Range thought that 'blurring the line' was 'absolutely legitimate' because of the 'power' it generates. Also, echoing the Granada tradition of dramatizing journalism because there was 'no other way to tell it', he noted that 'the dramatic element' encouraged interviewees to 'open up' with 'extended confidential briefings [...] that you don't generally experience as a documentary filmmaker' (BBCi 2003). The then BBC Head of Current Affairs Peter Horrocks argued on *Dirty War: Your Questions Answered* that they had made a drama rather than current affairs programme 'to try and bring a really significant issue to life for the public and to inform people'.

Hierarchical distinctions persist in discussions of hybridization, notably the association of documentary with the discourse of sobriety. For instance, BBC Transport Correspondent Simon Montague, presenting the BBCi interview, asked, 'What is the crucial, serious, journalistic point [...] you're trying to make?'[21] However, the conditional tense docudrama's hybridity destabilizes this discursive hierarchy. The verisimilitudinous function of actual newsreaders and channel branding is invoked as often by science fiction.[22] As Stewart and Butt observe, some critics of conditional tense docudramas 'seem unwilling to read them generically – that is, as action-melodrama' (2011, p. 81). Furthermore, the invocation of newsreaders and reportage values is queried by the texts' construction and their specific arguments. Although these programmes have been marked as 'not "just" fiction' with their 'documentary format and indexical appeal', they 'make truth claims' about real 'procedures and policies that have led the producers to hypothesise' (Stewart and Butt 2011, p. 75). Therefore, critics who measure the closeness of texts to reality, in thrall to 'the referential code' (p. 81), are missing some of this form's richness.[23]

Probability relates to an issue central to discussions so far: the conditional tense docudrama's 'might-still-yet-be' quality, the 'provisionality to the discourse' (Ward 2006, p. 273) which brings to mind Corner's definition of 'the "manipulation" issue': the accusation that 'viewers are encouraged to give truth status to unsubstantiated or purely imaginary events' (1996, p. 42). Ward rejects the idea that provisionality makes these pieces 'fiction', because they are 'most certainly documentary in *intention* and in their *reception*' (2006, p. 273), a claim supported by texts and paratexts. However, this does not entirely resolve Lipkin's second warrant. The form's hybridity makes it difficult to establish hierarchies, whether differentiating between fact and fiction, between 're-enactment and authentic footage' or between 'sequences that are evidence based and those that are not' (Stewart and Butt 2011, p. 75). But the very hybridity of *The Day Britain Stopped* contributes to the confidence of its prediction and its nature as political intervention. For Finch, the audience uses their 'familiarity' with 'the retrospective documentary form' to understand the programme's point: 'Look, this is sufficiently real, this *could* happen!' (BBCi 2003). Equally, the apparent excess of the fiction, the boldness of the hypothesis, is an index of the conviction of the research. What looks like a 'highly contingent causal chain', wherein one hypothetical emergency exacerbates others, stresses 'the social connections between things and people, the material relations' (Ward 2006, p. 275). Through such interconnections, the dramatic narrative takes an integrated overview of the transport system that the programme claims successive governments have not. The disaster-inflected prophetic fiction operates in the register of disaster planning: anticipating and learning from multiple previous incidents, this is a worst-case scenario stress test or, indeed, a war game.

The use of tenses is significant in terms of what Corner termed 'the "thematic" issue', texts' relation to '"official" positions and attitudes' and their '"debate" of ideas' (1996, p. 43). Conditional tense docudramas emphasize the plausibility of their hypothetical events by presenting them as if they have happened '*already*' (Ward's emphasis, 2006, p. 275), and they 'must convey a sense of authority and factuality which downplays their fictional elements and instead foregrounds the viability of the predictions', in particular to 'instigate debate' (Mills 2011, p. 84). This is true, but factual forms are also critiqued. A Sky News presenter blames chaos on the day's rail and underground strike.[24] The constructed hindsight interview by actual BBC Radio 5 Live traffic reporter Anna Rajan corrects those who blame the strike: 'in actual fact that only loaded about another 5 % of vehicles onto the road'. The phrase 'in actual fact' is simultaneously provisional (the 'actual fact' of a fictitious future event) and evidenced (past events). Rajan reinforces the programme's thesis: Britain's transport system runs at an intolerably 'high capacity', so 'it only takes the tiniest thing to bring everything to a grinding halt'. Others stress the lack of integrated planning and communication in transport and utilities 'since privatisation or deregulation'. The system is at fault, not an individual. This systemic focus contributes to these docudramas' aim 'to bring issues into the public arena where they can be debated', their recourse to 'the social function of documentary' (Mills 2011, p. 91). Although finding *The Day Britain Stopped* to be 'alarmist', Jim McGuigan described it as a 'critical intervention' in 'public debate' whose expression of 'widespread dissent' belonged in 'an enduring tradition of independent criticism of dominant power and ideology in the cultural public sphere', despite its seeming lack of political impact (2005, p. 440).

Provocatively problematic tenses contribute to this. At the start, we are told: 'We had it coming, a lot of people have said that, but hindsight's a wonderful thing'. Past and future tenses collide: this comes from the text's future (an interview later in the programme) and simultaneously describes the imagined future (the events and what people say about them), the imagined past (in our future) and the actual past that informs the discursive present: we *have* it coming, and this glimpse of the future is not hindsight-as-foresight. Language disavows provisionality; the programme tells us that 'It wasn't a case of *if* it's gonna happen, it was a case of *when*', and ends by predicting that there 'will be another December the nineteenth', seeking to render a fictional date as an icon in the familiar language of landmark dates. Taking the audience's witnessing (of the programme) as social trauma, its call to stop this happening (again) affirms its social function. As Ward notes, the crucial part of the 'this will happen, unless ...' mode of address is the word 'unless': this 'is a call to (social) action' and a 'potentially innovative political edge' (2006, p. 275).

This register was a source of controversy in 2015's *UKIP: The First 100 Days* which formed a potentially interventionist critique of one party's present composition in the year of a General Election. Its disclaimer – 'None of the events that follow have actually happened' – shares the playful qualities of the postmodern and reflexive docudramas covered earlier in this chapter, unless the viewer adds '... yet'.[25] The 'unless' register can place the conditional tense docudrama in the continuity of public service broadcasting. Just as Horrocks saw *Dirty War* as part of the BBC's 'traditional role to put across information to the public' (*Dirty War: Your Questions Answered*), so Mills noted these docudramas' public service function in 'sustaining citizenship and civil society', seeking to 'explore and question government policy, societal changes and the relationships between the personal and the political' and generating debate on helplines, discussion programmes and new interactive options (2011, p. 82).

How deeply this engagement goes is a question for further studies of conditional tense docudramas. Their quality as imitation has led scholars to consider whether 'the most useful way to discuss them is within the [...] mockumentary' (Ward 2006, p. 273) given that 'their simulation of documentary construction' overlaps with that form (Hight 2010, p. 142). Given the association of mockumentary with reflexivity, the question arises whether the foregrounding of construction in conditional tense docudramas makes for 'progressive and politically open texts' (Stewart and Butt 2011, p. 84) that 'alert audiences both to issues *and* their representation' (Paget 2011, p. 272).[26] However, the conditional tense may be reflexive at the level of form rather than only content as they 'make the viewer interrogate [...] their own role in interpreting and anchoring meaning' (Ward 2006, p. 275). The future-oriented conditional tense docudrama shares with mockumentary the reflexive concern with 'how documentary's representation of the past is a generic trope that can easily be adopted by fictional forms' (Mills 2011, p. 83). If the discourse of sobriety is invoked, attention is drawn to it and 'the spectator both looks *at* and looks *through* the highly mediated presentation' (Ward 2006, p. 279). This potential for reflexivity places the conditional tense docudrama at the heart of contemporary practice, and postmodern and reflexive discourses are defining characteristics of recent British docudrama. They mark current developments in the form, the specificity, and the sophistication of the British mode in the European context.

Notes

1. For an account of the development of social realist drama in the context of the development of television policy, see Rolinson (2011). For a primer on British television drama, see Cooke (2015).
2. See Cooke (2012) for a history of regional television drama, including a detailed case study of Granada.

3. For an account of these debates in the context of docudramas, see Rolinson (2011) and Caughie (2000a).
4. For an account of banned and delayed docudramas in this period, see Rolinson (2005) and Hill (2011, 2013).
5. The British 'borstal' was a kind of youth detention centre, abolished in 1982.
6. For a case study of docudrama debates in relation to *Scum*, see Rolinson (2005, pp. 74–93).
7. The 'Birmingham Six' were six men wrongly accused of terrorist bombings in Birmingham in 1975. Their life sentences were quashed in 1991 after a long campaign.
8. Accounts of Kosminsky's contribution to political docudrama in light of debates covered in this chapter can be found in Rolinson (2010) and Paget (2013b). *The Government Inspector* explored the events leading to the death of a weapons inspector caught up in disagreements between the government and the BBC over the latter's reporting of the intelligence justification for the war in Iraq.
9. Pieces like this mark a wider cultural shift: if the 1913 Paris premiere of Stravinsky's *The Rite of Spring* is worthy of re-enactment in *Riot at the Rite* (BBC2, 2006), so are popular forms like video game franchise *Grand Theft Auto* (1997–) in *The Gamechangers* (BBC2, 2015), the start of BBC Television in *The Fools on the Hill* (BBC1, 1986) and the development of comedy double act Morecambe and Wise in *Eric & Ernie* (BBC2, 2011) and situation comedy *Dad's Army* (BBC1, 1968–77) in *We're Doomed!* (BBC2, 2015).
10. This account underplays the intertextual undercurrents. Phoenix/Tanner is played by Jessie Wallace, best known as the not dissimilar Kat Moon in the BBC1 soap *EastEnders* (1985–), often written by Daran Little, this drama's writer and *Coronation Street*'s archivist.
11. In the new deregulated media ecology, Granada made *The Road to Coronation Street* not for ITV but for BBC4.
12. Consistent with industry and academic discourses on television authorship, *The Road to Coronation Street* focuses on the writer, with the director serving his ideas. *An Adventure in Space and Time* does not show the first story's writer. Mark Gatiss, writer of the docudrama but also writer and fan of *Doctor Who*, stressed his personal discomfort at omissions necessitated by compression: 'it's not that I don't understand or appreciate the scale of Donald Wilson as Head of Serials – or of David Whitaker as script editor' but 'I had to just pack away my inner anorak and think: "This is a drama."' He instead nodded to fans with Lambert's diegetic statement that she couldn't list everyone involved because 'we'd be here all day' (Gillatt 2013, p. 33).

13. See Ireland (2012) for details of the use of 1960s production spaces to interpret a 2006 *Doctor Who* episode.

14. Similarly, when Newman allows Hussein and Lambert to re-record the flawed pilot, they visit the Totter's Lane gates that are entered at the start of that episode as if *their* adventure is also beginning.

15. 'The Offer' was a one-off for *Comedy Playhouse* but was subsequently repeated as the first episode of *Steptoe and Son* following commissioning.

16. *This Is Your Life* (BBC 1955–64; ITV/BBC 1969–2003; ITV 2007) was a programme that originated in America on NBC radio in 1948. It attempted to catch celebrities (and occasionally non-celebrities) by surprise, then taking them into a studio to tell their life stories with help from guests.

17. Again, this trope runs more widely: at the start of *The Deal*, reflections in glass show several Gordon Browns (David Morrissey), a moment of abstraction and of multiple possibilities accompanied by the writing credit 'by Peter Morgan', which creates another sense of different Browns: the documented, the impersonated, the private, the authored.

18. For an account of the television debate in the context of changing attitudes to the *Python* film, see Burridge (2015).

19. Similarly, *Smallpox 2002* introduces victim Mark Smits through his surviving partner Rachel (Nadia Cameron-Blakey), integrating home footage (wedding 'film' plus photographs shot with rostrum camera or tracking shots) with hotel video, time-lapse footage of London and a voice-over (Brian Cox) whose constructed markers of verisimilitude – 'At 10.30 a.m. on April the eighth, Mark Smits checked into this hotel in Central London' – are accompanied by tracking shots of empty spaces (the hotel corridor and bedroom) haunted by their (imaginary) past while tonally signposting the programme's presently unfolding and future (imaginary) events.

20. This analysis follows Michael Stewart's lead in applying indexical iconicity to *Death of a President* (2011, p. 256).

21. These docudramas often use real-life news and current affairs formats and newsreaders as if invoking the discourse of sobriety as textual verification of the journalistic base. *Dirty War* is credited as 'A BBC Films Production with BBC Current Affairs in association with HBO Films', an unusual combination of the BBC's Film (not television drama) arm and its in-house Current Affairs unit (reminiscent of *The War Game*'s status as 'a documentary film' made by the documentary department).

22. For example, television drama *Doctor Who* (1963–) has used, amongst others, real-life newsreaders Kenneth Kendall ('The War Machines', 1966) and Huw Edwards ('Fear Her', 2006) in constructions of science-fiction crises hitting London.

23. However, the invocation of the referential code can itself support the programme's evidential base: presenting a 2003 *Newsnight* feature about *The Day Britain Stopped*, Jeremy Paxman asked about its plausibility and whether it could happen 'for real', but noted that 'every traveller' regularly faces disruption. This supports Ward's observation that audiences may refer to their own experience as evidence that 'such events are not only possible, but probable' (2006, p. 274).

24. He questions genuine ASLEF union General Secretary Mick Rix. Earlier, two Sky News presenters reflect on the quietness of the roads at 1.30 p.m.: 'nowhere near the level of chaos we've predicted today. We're all doommongers, aren't we?' This fictional exchange between two real-life Sky News presenters critiques the media's bleak prophecies – in a bleakly prophetic media text – and its tenses are unstable, the present tense of rolling news edging to past-tense reflection, all within a docudrama that has already signposted things to come.

25. Channel 4 surprisingly trailed *UKIP: The First 100 Days* as 'ground-breaking' despite the number of antecedents in this form. It hypothesized UKIP's responses to (imagined, future) problems in footage taken from their (actual) responses to (past) problems. Archive footage of election coverage and politicians' interviews is repurposed to create a UKIP 2015 General Election victory. This follows *The Day Britain Stopped*, in which footage of then-Prime Minister Tony Blair commenting on a tragedy in the House of Commons was deployed as if he is/was commenting on the future tragedy depicted in the programme, though this has the politically loaded inference of circularity.

26. The latter relationship is interrogated in more conventional docudrama – BBC1's *Faith* (2005), depicting the personal lives of fictional characters during the 1984–85 miners' strike, includes a sequence in which actual BBC News coverage is analysed by those who were there to reveal that coverage was transposed so that a police charge was misleadingly depicted as a reaction to action by the miners.

CHAPTER 9

Conclusion: 'Unity in Diversity'?

Tobias Ebbrecht-Hartmann

TELEVISION, DOCUDRAMA, AND EUROPE

Television in Europe has become a complex and entangled net of regional, national, transnational, Pan-European, and global elements. Thus it provides a significant case for studying the interplay and even the collision, between regions, nations and transnational entities. Since the 1980s, television broadcasting has been increasingly liberalized within the European Union (EU), thereby challenging not only the borders of national television broadcasting but also the dominance of the Public Service Broadcasting (PSB) model in Europe. The economically, even ideologically, driven opening-up of the television ecology is something that can be seen clearly currently in the UK in ongoing threats not only to the broadcaster most associated with the PSB model, the BBC, but also to a late twentieth-century PSB variant, Channel 4.[1] In any event, this factor has had the creative effect of forcing Europe's national PSB broadcasters to reorganize their output according to the demands of the developing European market. International co-productions and co-operations at a European level have become a crucial element of producing and programming television. This has had its effect on docudrama, which, as we argue in this book, is an even more focused case for study.

EU programmes such as 'Television without Frontiers' (inaugurated by EU Council Directive 89/552/EEC, of 3 October 1989) provided

© The Editor(s) (if applicable) and The Author(s) 2016
T. Ebbrecht-Hartmann, D. Paget (eds.), *Docudrama on European Television*, Palgrave European Film and Media Studies,
DOI 10.1057/978-1-137-49979-0_9

the necessary logistic, legal, and technical ground for transmitting and distributing television across Europe (Halle 2008, p. 170). Funding mechanisms such as the European MEDIA programme have contributed to the development of content, by funding not only European filmmakers but also television producers. MEDIA 2007 was the fourth such programme to run since 1991. In May 1992 a significant frontier-breaking development saw the launch of the German-French cultural television channel Arte, which was to develop into a Pan-European broadcaster of quality television (Halle 2008, p. 183). All such measures and events addressed two sides of European television culture, the economic and the cultural; both had impacts on, and went hand-in-hand with, the political level of developing unification within the EU.

As understood in the broad definition that informs this volume, docudrama has played a crucial role at both the national as well as the European frame of reference for television broadcasting in Europe. Docudrama, we have argued in the preceding chapters, should be recognized as an important as well as an increasingly influential television format in most, if not all, television cultures around Europe. Nevertheless the chapters in this book show that there are significant differences in regard to the tradition and development of nuanced cultures of docudrama in the different countries under review. In Britain, but also in Germany and Italy, docudrama has played a major role in public broadcasting from the outset, and has also influenced both form and content of a steady stream of programmes. In Spain and France, adoption and development of the genre has occurred rather later. Meanwhile, in the case of Poland, film and programme makers have had to rediscover, even reinvent, docudramatic approaches in the light of that country's complex recent political transitions.

Docudrama as presented in this volume provides an interesting case for the study of European television culture. This is because of its direct relevance to debates about an increasingly hybridized media culture, as well as to key elements of European integration. Two vital current examples of this are the felt need for national identity-building and negotiation of the politics of memory. This latter is a sharply relevant area in the early twenty-first century. In any case it is obvious that docudrama in general, but in regard to Europe and its transnational entanglements in particular, challenges a number of boundaries and thus might be conceptualized as a significant 'European' television phenomenon that can tell us much about the current political health of Europe.

On a stylistic level the genre quite literally challenges boundaries, as the foundational literature on the genre has made clear. Often combining different modes of address derived from television's place in the public *agora*, the mix in particular of the 'factual' of documentary and the 'fictional' of drama, has significantly challenged classical boundaries of 'pure' dramatic and documentary approaches. Interestingly, docudrama has thereby mirrored the output of television in general. Television scheduling, building on developing sophistication in its audiences, is increasingly merging and transgressing factual and fictional elements and segments within its programme flow (Paget 2013b, p. 174). This is even more important regarding the broad definition of docudrama in this book, taking into consideration as it does a wider remit also including the mainly dramatic forms of 'based-on-fact' television drama and 'historical event television'. Those television dramas often constitute significant television events in themselves, and are framed by other, often documentary, segments that constitute extra-textual events and transform the programme schedule itself into a virtual docudrama (as argued in Chap. 2).

At the level of narrative, docudrama significantly challenges the boundaries of classical dramatic genres. The films analysed in the chapters of this book adapt a wide variety of genre patterns. In some countries particular genres have gained special importance and prominence. In French and Swedish docudrama, for example (as illustrated by Georges Fournier in Chap. 4 and Åsa Bergström in Chap. 7), noteworthy events have often been represented in docudrama through crimes and their subsequent court cases. If the crime film genre became popular in these countries, in Germany and Spain (Chaps. 2 and 6) historical dramas have tended to dominate. Yet again, and particularly in the Italian case (see Chap. 4), the biographical docudrama is and remains an important subgenre. It is increasingly evident that none of the available generic variants are likely to appear in pure form. Rather, most docudramas combine patterns and elements from different genres, with the linking factor perhaps to be found in the 'familial' and 'private' mode analysed by Steven N. Lipkin in his work on the influence of melodrama on docudrama (1999: 68). The complex intermixing of genres, however, does not end here, for there are crime and historical drama hybrids, and Chap. 8 even highlights British docudramas' use of science fiction and the creation of possible future scenarios with a basis in research. At the level of historiography, then, television docudrama has even crossed temporal boundaries not only between past and present, but also between present and future. This trans-temporal approach has various implications. Such historical docudramas communicate to younger generations certain aspects of, and incidents in, their national histories and heritage. In this way, it is argued in this book, they contribute to and sometimes provoke intergenerational communication and potentially establish and/or negotiate particular forms and aspects of national memory culture.

At the level of funding and production, we can see that docudrama began at an early stage to transgress existing geographical boundaries within the transforming European media system. If the majority of docudramas are still produced within national frameworks, many have become highly transnational products through burgeoning co-production between leading television broadcasters and production companies.[2] Practically, then, it has become possible for producers to benefit from different regional and national funding streams as well as from EU cultural programmes. 'Creative Europe', the MEDIA-TV sub-programme, for example, sets out its objectives as follows:

> To support European production companies interested in producing a television work demonstrating:
>
> high creative value
>
> cross-border potential
>
> cooperation between operators from different countries participating in the MEDIA sub-programme
>
> increased co-production and circulation of high-profile European television drama series.[3]

Clearly, there is much here of benefit to modern docudrama.

On the level of content, the crossing of geographical boundaries and borders is still the exception rather than the rule. Most docudramas discussed in this volume focus on clearly localized events from the past or present within a regional or national framework. More entangled and European encounters are still mostly the domain of docudramas dealing with traumatic events from the twentieth century still recent enough to have a bearing on the current notion of the 'European'. Here, docudramas dealing with the history of World War II (and the Holocaust in particular) continue to dominate. However, and as discussed in Chap. 2 on Germany, the very border between East and West itself has played a crucial literal and symbolic role, especially in German docudramas about the GDR and the period of Germany's division. Europe as a new reality for European societies and cultures, however, has not as yet constituted an important topic. It remains to be seen whether it will become so in the future, or whether docudrama will focus on, for example, the refugee crisis as a threat to European integration and development.

Still, this book's selective survey of European docudrama culture demonstrates not only the multilayered variety of the genre on European television but also how important docudrama has become for European television culture as a whole. This situation has been achieved in addition to, but also in competition with, American dominance of this particular field of television production. This is equally true of academic writing on the subject and, as pointed out in the Introduction, one objective of this volume was to begin to address the relative lack of writing on docudrama in a broader European context by looking beyond the academic focus of the past 20 years on American and English traditions. It is, of course, always important to note that from the very beginning of European television docudrama its producers and directors were strongly influenced by the Anglo-American docudrama tradition. This is most obviously true for Germany, where the postwar PSB system was significantly modelled on the BBC and its specific objectives and structure. But, as Milly Buonanno notes about Italian fact-based television drama, Anglo-American TV contexts have often been a consideration elsewhere (see her Chap. 4).

THE EMERGENCE OF A 'EUROPEAN DOCUDRAMA'?

The entanglement of national television cultures and the European dimension is also reflected in the framework of this book by a comparative approach that is related to certain constellations, marked by different forms of relations often regarded as binary: separations and boundaries; ongoing tensions between Europe's East and West; and the persistence of, as well as the attempt to overcome division. All this can be traced most significantly in the cases of Germany and Poland, with their obvious East–West implications. But other chapters also address the differences and similarities between North and South, as well as between big and small countries. Likewise there are tensions and comparisons between media systems within our selection of European countries, between highly developed and economically strong systems, and those that can be identified as smaller, younger, or weaker. Through the comparative perspective taken in the chapters, it becomes even more obvious that national contexts make a clear difference. Germany may be argued as an exceptional case, with its two initially competing and finally merged media systems and its developed tradition of docudrama, but it is still a telling one. Chapter 3 also investigates the transitions following the end of the Cold War period in Poland, not only on a social and political level but also in regard to media and broadcasting. There is significant interplay and collision, too, between different systems, models, and traditions—PSB and commercial; American/British and national; formatted television genres and more experimental approaches; and, finally, the interplay of European television culture and post-Socialist television. In short, it becomes more than obvious that both the wider television and the particular docudrama culture in Europe mirrors elements of the broader process of European unification.

Driven as it was and is mainly by economic concerns, the EU as a political entity has only lately begun to regard media and culture as significant aspects of European integration. This cultural dimension goes beyond an economic interest in flexible and liberalized television broadcasting across borders. Similar to the implementation of certain elements of the free market economy in the different European member countries, television culture has been principally defined in terms of open markets and competition. On the other hand European regulation, especially after accepting audiovisual media and television as important aspects of European integration and co-operation, has encouraged increased 'inter-national' co-production. Such collaboration has been especially fruitful for the further development of docudrama and historical television drama. Extended production budgets, either through additional European funding or co-operation with other European countries, has tended to improve quality as well as quantity. This has enabled former Eastern Bloc countries like Poland to revive its docudrama tradition, and it has encouraged other countries, such as Spain, to further develop and cultivate its own docudrama style (see Chap. 6). Thus the European idea of transformation through economic integration has shifted focus to societies in transition. These include not only former Eastern European Socialist countries, but also Southern European countries with histories of authoritarianism and/ or fascism.

Some of this focus has also influenced the domain of docudrama production. Significantly, one of the most dominant discourses in contemporary Europe, the debate about European identity and European memory, has been reflected within the genre. If this has occurred mainly within a national framework, it nevertheless has the potential to participate in the pan-European discussion. In countries like Spain and Italy, but also in Sweden and most significantly in Germany, docudrama and especially its subgenre, historical event drama, has become an important field for the negotiation of national pasts. This applies also to what we identify over the different chapters as the significant increase in historical and biographical docudramas within different national television cultures in Europe. Milly Buonanno in Chap. 4 notes this temporal switch from present to past in the large number of biographical and historical docudramas produced in Italy in the 2000s, and argues that this is a feature impacting on other countries in Europe.

Among the stock subjects with regional and/or national significance, the Holocaust has been a significant transnational topic in many European docudramas since the millennium. It is surely more than coincidence that, following the International Forum on the Holocaust held in the Swedish capital, Stockholm, in 2000, the persecution and murder of the European Jews and other ethnic groups and political opponents became an important aspect of the debate about European history and memory promoted by the EU. This forum inaugurated further important challenges to shared, but also dividing and conflicting, national memories of the recent European past, which collide especially in regard to the history of the Holocaust. Docudrama has participated fully in this process, which develops according to national but also European attempts to canalize, synchronize, and often harmonize the different historical narratives of the European countries. These are significantly shaped by the twentieth-century experience of war, repression, resistance, colonialism, migration, extermination, and collaboration. While in Germany intellectual and public debates frame these controversies—some provoked or triggered by docudramas—other countries have moderated controversy in different ways. Spain passed a 'Law of Memory' in 2006, and as Victoria Pastor-González shows in Chap. 6, this has profoundly influenced the way Spanish history has been presented on the television screen. Contrastingly, in France courts of law have dealt with cases where docudrama has provoked controversy and thereby extended the televisual negotiation of French history into the legal and political spheres, as Georges Fournier shows in Chap. 5. Meanwhile in Poland (see Chap. 3), Wiesław Godzic discusses Poland's so-called 'Institute of National Remembrance'. Most of such debate and legal regulatory activity remains in national public spheres, and therefore references still-existing conflicts and competing perceptions of the past among national societies. But the writers of this book also believe they have to be understood within the framework of a growing interest in the writing of a shared European history as a basis for a democratic culture and the reflexive memory of, and in, a unified Europe.

That this approach, beyond the political and administrative actions of the institutions of the EU, is still a matter of controversial negotiation, again becomes obvious when investigating the degree to which docudrama has given rise to controversial public debates about such political and historical topics within the European public sphere. Docudrama's history as a contested as well as an important genre means it is always likely to have this effect, and the case of the historical German television drama *Unsere Mütter, unsere Väter*, mentioned in Chaps. 2 and 3, provides an interesting example for this dimension. The German mini-series was not only successful when broadcast to its initial German audience; it also became a huge international success. It was awarded with the celebrated Prix Europa, which has been Europe's largest prize for television, radio, and online media since 1987, and it was sold to more than 80 countries. *Unsere Mütter, unsere Väter* was clearly an attempt to articulate and harmonize different generational memories of the war in Germany, but it also had ambitions on a wider European, even international, scale. Accordingly today's president of the European Parliament, Martin Schulz, labelled the production a 'European' film in an 'op-ed' piece in the German newspaper *Frankfurter Allgemeine Zeitung*. He also linked it to the discourse of European memory (Classen 2014, p. 56). But its ambivalent mode, merging fact and fiction, melodrama and war film, German intergenerational dialogue and historical narrative, created controversial feedback because of the collision of unexpectedly conflicting individual and national memories. This is emphasized by Wiesław Godzic in Chap. 3. The film's point of view, warmly received in Germany, was perceived sceptically by the Polish viewing public. The controversy even left the framework of discussion of popular television and transformed this docudrama into an issue of political activism and debate—the mini-series became nothing less than a 'media event' in Poland.

As emphasized by Pastor-González in case of Spain, narratives of consent rather than dissent can also be promoted by docudramas. Not every film in the genre provokes debates and controversies. Pastor-González suggests that far from producing conflicting memories of Spain's past, some of its docudramas seek to defuse conflict. So we can also see reflected in the chapters of this book the fact that 'conservative' modes of docudrama continue to exist alongside more 'experimental' approaches. In the UK, the British tradition now favours more playful and innovative approaches towards the hybrid character of docudrama, as David Rolinson shows in Chap. 8. Within German television both forms exist side by side—although in recent years, here too, the more 'conservative' and 'harmonizing' approach has gained a certain dominance in historical event television. In the narrative and visual strategies adopted in some of the examples examined, it has to be acknowledged that the 'privatization' involved in melodrama provides stylistic inspiration. Accordingly in some countries, especially in those with a history of transition from dictatorship to democracy, the harmonizing approach of docudrama is favoured over the provocation of dissent and examination of conflicting memories. Personalization of history is an important element of the genre, as it also is for documentary. Both very often root their approaches in ordinary peoples' stories and the experiences of everyday life. In this regard docudrama corresponds to television's specific mode of address in general. As Randall Halle puts it, television 'in its history belongs much more strongly to the national, regional, and even local ensemble of production' (2008, p. 171).

European docudrama can be said to be an entangled as well as a contested category. Mostly focused nationally, and bound to a multitude of independent television cultures, it is thus in many ways separated from any concept of 'Europe'. But this book's comparative perspective on different traditions and approaches towards the docudrama genre in seven European countries proves docudrama's significance, and demonstrates many potentially fruitful similarities, relations, and common points of reference. Like the European Union itself, docudrama in Europe can be said to be 'unified in diversity'. Situated as it is within a European media system, which is today based on a 'Television without Frontiers', transnational entanglement is the main feature that emerges. Entanglement, if not unity, is ensured mainly through European funding, co-production, or international co-operation. This is a crucial aspect of the economic dimension of docudrama production and distribution. But, as can be seen in case in particular of *Unsere Mütter, unsere Väter*, nationally rooted docudramas might still contribute to an encounter with the Other within the European community. In this sense docudramas on European television, although not in an organized and interrelated way, also address the 'new citizen [...] for whom mediatised performance is a major factor in their ways of making sense of the world in which they live' (Paget 2011, p. 289). Thus the genre can and does contribute to the transgressing, fragmented, and border-crossing approach of classic docudrama.

Across Europe, docudrama has been used, and will continue to be used, to address conflicts and collisions of interest. It is at the very least an important part of an emerging European public sphere that depends heavily on television and other audiovisual media to tell stories based on fact to Europe-wide audiences.

Notes

1. The UK's Conservative government, elected in 2015, immediately set up a committee to review the renewal of the BBC's Royal Charter (due, if approved, in 2016). Meanwhile, there are persistent rumours of plans to privatize C4, a broadcaster with clear PSB responsibilities in its current form. On the latter issue, see:http://www.theguardian.com/media/2015/sep/24/government-considering-channel-4-privatisation-document-slip-up-reveals—accessed 3 December 2015.
2. The docudramatic work of the British director Peter Kosminsky illustrates this. Docudramas originating with Channel 4 in the UK, such as 2011's *The Promise*, have been co-financed/co-produced with, and broadcast in Europe by, Arte and Canal+.
3. See: https://eacea.ec.europa.eu/creative-europe/actions/media/creative-europe-media-tv-programming_en—accessed 2 December 2015.

SELECT FILMOGRAPHY AND BIBLIOGRAPHY

N.B. Below are the television/film docudramas discussed in this book, arranged in chapter and year of broadcast order.

CHAPTER 1: INTRODUCTION

Churchill's People (BBC1, 1975)
Sex Traffic (C4, 2004)
Generation Kill (HBO, 2008—tx in UK, C4, 2009)
1864 (DR1, Denmark, 2014—tx in UK BBC4, 2015)
Cordon (vtm Belgium, 2014, tx in UK BBC4, 2015)
Kampen om Tungtvannet (The Heavy Water War, NRK, Norway, 2014—tx in UK as *The Saboteurs*, More4, 2015)

CHAPTER 2: GERMAN DOCUDRAMA: WEST GERMANY (PRE-1990)

Besuch aus der Zone (Visit from the Eastern Zone, SDR, 1958, dir. Rainer Wolffhardt)
Mauern (Walls, NDR/SFB, 1963, dir. Egon Monk and Gunther R. Lys)
Ein Tag—Bericht aus einem deutschen Konzentrationslager (One Day—Report from a German Concentration Camp, NDR, 1965, dir. Egon Monk)
Preis der Freiheit (The Cost of Freedom, NDR, 1966, dir. Egon Monk)
Mord in Frankfurt (Murder in Frankfurt, WDR, 1968, dir. Rolf Hädrich)
Die Dubrowkrise (The Dubrow Crisis, WDR, 1969, dir. Eberhard Itzenplitz)

© The Editor(s) (if applicable) and The Author(s) 2016
T. Ebbrecht-Hartmann, D. Paget (eds.), *Docudrama on European Television*, Palgrave European Film and Media Studies,
DOI 10.1057/978-1-137-49979-0

Holocaust (NBC, USA, 1979, dir. Marvin Chomsky)
Flugversuche (Attempts to Fly, ZDF, 1979, dir. Rainer Wolffhardt)
Die Staatskanlei (The State Office, NDR/WDR, 1989, dir. Heinrich Breloer)

EAST GERMANY (PRE-1990)

Nackt unter Wölfen (Naked Among Wolves, DFF, 1960)
Eine Nacht und kein Morgen (Night and No Morning, DFF, 1962, dir. Wolfgang Luderer)
Er ging allein (He Went Alone, DFF, 1967, dir. Hans-Joachim Hildebrandt)
Die Bilder des Zeugen Schattmann (The Images of the Witness Frank Schattmann, DDR-TV, 1972)

UNIFIED GERMANY (POST-1990)

Kollege Otto die Coop Affäre (Colleague Otto, the Coop Affair, NDR/WDR, 1991, dir. Heinrich Breloer)
Todesspiel (Play of Death, ARD, 1997, dir. Heinrich Breloer)
Das Deutschlandspiel (The Germany Game, ZDF/Arte, 2000, dir. Hans-Christoph Blumenberg)
Der Tunnel (The Tunnel, Sat. 1, 2001, dir. Roland Suso Richter)
Der Aufstand (The Uprising, ZDF/Arte, 2003, dir. Hans-Christoph Blumenberg)
Tage des Sturms (Stormy Days, MDR, 2003, dir. Thomas Freundner)
Das Wunder von Lengede (The Miracle of Lengede, Sat. 1, 2003, dir. Kaspar Heidelbach)
Zwei Tage Hoffnung (Two Days of Hope, SWR/WDR, 2003, dir. Peter Keglevic)
Der Untergang (Downfall, 2004, dir. Oliver Hirschbiegel)
Die letzte Schlacht (The Last Battle, ZDF, 2005, dir. Hans-Christoph Blumenberg)
Die Luftbrücke—Nur der Himmel war frei (Berlin Airlift, Sat. 1, 2005, Dror Zahavi)
Speer und Er (Speer and Hitler: The Devil's Architect, WDR/BR/NDR, 2005, dir. Heinrich Breloer)
Die Sturmflut (The Storm Flood, RTL, 2005, dir. Jorgo Papavassilou)
Dresden (ZDF, 2006, dir. Roland Suso Richter)
Die Mauer—Berlin '61 (The Wall—Berlin '61, WDR/Arte/RBB, 2006, dir. Hartmut Schoen) *An die Grenze (To the Border, ZDF, 2007, dir. Urs Egger)
Die Flucht (March of Millions, ARD Degeto, 2007, dir. Kai Wessel)
Die Frau am Checkpoint Charlie (The Woman at Checkpoint Charlie, MDR/BR/ RBB/Arte, 2007, dir. Miguel Alexandre)
Mogadischu (ARD, 2008, dir. Roland Suso Richter)
Das Wunder von Berlin (The Miracle of Berlin, ZDF, 2008, dir. Roland Suso Richter)

Vom Traum zum Terror—München 72 (From a Dream to the Terror—Munich 72, ARD, 2012, dir. Marc Brasse, Florian Huber)
Böseckendorf—Die Nacht, in der ein Dorf verschwand (Böseckendorf—The Night a Village Vanished, Sat. 1, 2009, dir. Oliver Domenget)
München 72—Das Attentat (Munich 72—The Attack, ZDF, 2012, dir. Dror Zahavi).
Unsere Mütter, unsere Väter (Generation War, ZDF, 2013, dir. Philipp Kadelbach—and see 'Poland' below)
Bornholmer Strasse (Bornholmer Street, RBB/MDR, 2014, dir. Christian Schwochow)
Zwischen den Zeiten (Between the Times, ZDF, 2014, dir. Hansjörg Thurn)

CHAPTER 3: POLISH DOCUDRAMA: PRE-1990 POLAND

Kanal (Sewer, 1957, dir. Andrzej Wajda)
Czterej pancerni i pies (Four Tank-Men and a Dog, TP, 1966–70)
Stawka większa niż życie (More Than Life at Stake, TP, 1967–68)
Rok Franka W. (Film documentary: The Year of Franek W., 1967, dir. Kazimierz Karabasz)
Epilog norymberski (The Nuremberg Epilogue, TP, 1969, dir. Jerzy Antczak)
Wanda Gościmińska. Włókniarka (Wanda Gościmińska. The Textile Worker, 1975, dir. Wojciech Wiśniewski)
Personel (Personnel, 1975, dir. Krzysztof Kieślowski)
Człowiek z marmuru (Man of Marble, 1976, dir. Andrzej Wajda)
Z punktu widzenia nocnego portiera (From a Night Porter's Point of View, 1977, dir. Krzysztof Kieślowski)
Próba mikrofonu (Microphone's Test, 1980, dir. Marcel Łoziński)
Człowiek z żelaza (Man of Iron, 1981, dir. Andrzej Wajda)
Alternatywy 4 (4 Alternative Street, TP1, 1983—but tx.1986, dir. Stanisław Bareja)
Sensacje XX wieku (Sensations of the Twentieth Century, TVP1, 1983-2005, dir: Bogusław Wołoszański)*
Ćwiczenia warsztatowe (Workshop Exercises, 1987, dir. Marcel Łoziński)

POST-1990 POLAND (N.B. SEE ALSO * ABOVE)

Takiego pięknego syna urodziłam (Such a Beautiful Son I Gave Birth To, TVP1, 2000, dir. Marcin Koszałka)
Jestem zły (I'm Bad, TVP1, 2001, dir. Grzegorz Pacek)
Wielkie ucieczki (Great Escapes, TVN, 2005–06)
Pan Franciszek (Mr. Franciszek, 2006, dir. Kazimierz Karabasz)

Tajemnica Twierdzy Szyfrów (The Secret of the Ciphers Fortress, TVP1, 2007, dir. Bogusław Wołoszański)
Gra o Nobla (Nobel Game, TVN, 2008)
Historia Kowalskich (The Story of the Kowalski Family, TVP 2, 2008)
Czas honoru (*Days of Honour*, TVP2, 2008–)
Wszystkie ręce umyte. Sprawa Barbary Blidy (All Hands Washed. The Case of Barbara Blida, TVP2, 2010)
Kiedyś będziemy szczęśliwi (We Will Be Happy One Day, TVP HD, 2011)
14 godzin. Pierwsi w walce (14 Hours—The First Ones Fighting, TVP Historia, 2013)
Unsere Mütter, unsere Väter (Nasze matki, wasi ojcowie, ZDF/TVP1, 2013, dir. Philipp Kadelbach—and see 'Unified Germany' above)
Anna German (TVP1, 2013)
Powstanie warszawskie (Warsaw Uprising, 2013)

CHAPTER 4: ITALIAN DOCUDRAMA

I figli di Medea (Medea's Children, Programma Nazionale, 1959, dir. Anton Giulio Majano)
La trincea (The Trench, Secondo Programma, 1961, dir. Vittorio Cottafavi)
I giacobini (The Jacobins, Programma Nazionale, 1962, dir. Edmo Fenoglio)
Grandi processi della storia (The Great Trials of History, Programma Nazionale, 1962, dir. Carlo Lodovici)
Vivere insieme (Living Together, Programma Nazionale, 1962–70)
La vita di Michelangelo (The Life of Michelangelo, Programma Nazionale, 1964, dir. Silverio Blasi)
La vita di Dante (The Life of Dante, Programma Nazionale, 1965, dir. Vittorio Cottafavi)
Teatro-inchiesta (Theatre-Inquiry, Secondo Programma, 1966–71)
La vita di Cavour (The Life of Cavour, Programma Nazionale, 1967, dir. Piero Schivazappa)
Di fronte alla legge (In the Face of the Law, Programma Nazionale, 1967–1974)
Processi a porte aperte (Trials with Open Doors, Programma Nazionale, 1968–71)
Dedicato a un bambino (Dedicated to a Child, Programma Nazionale, 1971, dir. Gianni Bongioanni)
La vita di Leonardo da Vinci (The Life of Leonardo da Vinci, Programma Nazionale, 1971, dir. Renato Castellani)
Socrate (Socrates, Programma Nazionale, 1971, dir: Roberto Rossellini)
Blaise Pascal (Programma Nazionale, 1972, dir. Roberto Rossellini)
Agostino di Ippona (St Augustine of Hippo, Programma Nazionale, 1972, dir. Roberto Rossellini) *Diario di un maestro* (Teacher's Diary, Programma Nazionale, 1973, dir. Vittorio De Seta)

Cartesius (Descartes, Programma Nazionale, 1974, dir. Roberto Rossellini)
Gesù di Nazareth (Jesus of Nazareth, Rete Uno, 1977, dir. Franco Zeffirelli)
Ligabue (Rete Uno, 1977, dir. Salvatore Nocita)
Perlasca. Un eroe italiano (Perlasca. An Italian Hero, RAI 1, 2002, dir. Alberto Negrin)
Papa Giovanni (Joannes XXIII, RAI 1, 2002, dir. Giorgio Capitani)
Karol: un uomo che divenne papa (Karol: A Man Who Became Pope, Canale 5, 2005, dir. Giacomo Battiato)
Gli anni spezzati (The Broken Years, RAI 1, 2014, dir. Graziano Diana)
1992 (Sky Atlantic, 2015, dir. Giuseppe Gagliardi)
L'Oriana (Oriana, RAI 1, 2015, dir. Marco Turco)

CHAPTER 5: FRENCH DOCUDRAMA

Si Versailles m'était conté (Stories About Versailles, ORTF, 1955)
La Camera explore le temps (The Camera Explores Time (ORTF, 1957–66)
L'Affaire Seznec (The Seznec Affair, TF1, 1995)
Facteur VIII (Canal+, 1995)
L'Affaire Gordji: Histoire d'une cohabitation (The Gordji Affair: The Story of 'Cohabitation', Canal+, 2002)
Jean Moulin (France2, 2002)
Le Grand Charles (Charles the Great, France 2, 2002)
L'Affaire Dominici (The Dominici Case, TF1, 2003)
L'Odyssée de l'espèce (The Odyssey of the Human Species, France 3, 2003)
Jean Moulin, une affaire française (Jean Moulin, a French Affair, TF1, 2003)
36, Quai des Orfèvres (TF1, 2004)
Nuit noire (A Pitch-Dark Night, Canal+, 2005)
La Séparation (The Separation, FR3, 2005)
Le Promeneur du Champ de Mars (The Last Mitterrand, Canal+, 2005, dir. Robert Guédiguian)
Marie Besnard (TF1, 2006)
L'Affaire du Rainbow Warrior (The 'Rainbow Warrior Affair, Canal+, 2006)
Opération Turquoise (Canal+, 2007)
L'Embrasement (Flashover, ARTE, 2007)
Notable donc coupable (Famous Then Guilty, France 2, 2007)
L'Affaire Villemin (The Villemin Case, France 3, 2008)
L'École du pouvoir (The School for Power, Canal+, 2009)
La Conquête (The Conquest, Canal+, 2012)
Yann Piat, chronique d'un assassinat (Yann Piat, Chronicle of a Murder, Canal+, 2012)

CHAPTER 6: SPANISH DOCUDRAMA

Crónicas de un pueblo (Village Chronicles, TVE 1, 1971–74)
Vivir cada día (Living Each Day, TVE 1, 1978–82 and 1983–88)
Teresa de Jesús (St Teresa of Avila, TVE 1, 1984)
La Huella de Crimen (Traces of a Crime, TVE 1 1985, 1991, 2009)
Lorca muerte de un poeta (Lorca, Death of a Poet, TVE 1, 1987)
El Lute: camina o revienta (El Lute: Run for Your Life, TVE 1, 1987)
Padre Coraje (Father Courage, Antena 3, 2001)
Amar en Tiempos Revueltos (Loving in Troubled Times, TVE 1, 2005–12)
20-N, los últimos días de Franco (20-N, the Final Days of Franco, Antena 3, 2008)
23F: El día más difícil del Rey (23F: The King's Most Difficult Day, TVE 1, 2009)
23F: Historia de una traición (23F: Chronicle of a Betrayal, Antena 3, 2009)
Días sin luz (Days of Darkness, Antena 3, 2009)
Un burka por amor (A Burqa for Love, Antena 3, 2009)
Tarancón, el quinto mandamiento (Tarancón, the Fifth Commandment, TVE 1, 2010)
Clara Campoamor, la mujer olvidada (Clara Campoamor, The Forgotten Woman, TVE 1, 2010)
La Duquesa I & II (The Duchess Part I & II, *Telecinco, 2010–11*)
Alfonso el príncipe maldito (Alfonso, the Doomed Prince, *Telecinco, 2010*)
Raphael, historia de una superación (Raphael, Against All Odds, *Antena 3, 2010*)
Vuelo IL8714 (Flight IL8714, Telecinco, 2010)
Adolfo Suárez, el presidente (Adolfo Suárez, the President, Antena 3, 2010)
El Ángel de Budapest (The Angel of Budapest, TVE 1, 2010)
14 de abril, La República (14 April, The Republic, TVE 1 2011)
11-M, para que nadie lo olvide (11-M, Never Forget, Telecinco, 2011)
Mi gitana (My Gypsy, *Telecinco, 2012*)
Rescatando a Sara (Rescuing Sara, Antena 3, 2012)
Concepción Arenal, la visitadora de cárceles (Concepción Arenal, The Prison Visitor, TVE 1, 2012)
Carta a Eva (Letter to Eva, TVE 1, 2012)
La Conspiración (Conspiracy, EiTB, 2012)
Vicente Ferrer (TVE 1, 2013)
Operación Palace (Operation Palace, La Sexta, 2014)
El Rey (The King, Telecinco, 2015)

CHAPTER 7: SWEDISH DOCUDRAMA

Vi mötte stormen (Film: We Met the Storm, Sverige, AB Nordisk Filmproduktion, 1943 [SVT1, 2004, 2007, 2012, 2015], dir. Bengt Janzon)

Yngsjömordet (Film: The Yngsjö Murder, Sweden, AB Svensk Filmindustri, 1966 [SVT TV2, 1992; SVT1, 2000], dir. Arne Mattsson)

Kvällsöppet (SVT TV2, 1977)

Magasinet (SVT TV2, 1981)

Veckan då Roger dödades (The Week Roger Was Killed, Filmslussen/Svenska Filminstitutet, SVT TV2 1981; SVT TV1, 1982, dir. Staffan Hildebrand)

Alfred Nobel—Mr. Dynamite (SVT TV2, 1983, dir. Olle Häger and Hans Villius)

Mannen från Mallorca (Film: The Man from Majorca, Sweden/Denmark, Drakfilm Produktion AB/Crone Film Sales ApS/SVT TV2 *et al.*, 1984 [SVT TV2, 1987, 1988; SVT1, 2002], dir. Bo Widerberg)

Jane Horney (SVT TV1/DR/MovieMakers Sweden AB, 1985, dir. Stellan Olsson)

Jane Horney—EPILOG (Jane Horney—EPILOGUE, SVT TV1, 1985)

Yngsjömordet (The Yngsjö Murder, SVT TV2, 1986, dir. Richard Hobert)

Bessingemordet (The Bessinge Murder, SVT TV2, 1986, dir. Leif Krantz)

Esarparen (The Man from Esarp, SVT TV2, 1986, dir. Richard Hobert)

Hurvamorden (The Hurva Murders, SVT TV2, 1986, dir. Jan Hemmel)

Innan skottet föll—Bilder från Gustav IIIs och Bellmans dagar (Before the Shooting – Images from the Days of Gustav III and Bellman, SVT TV2, 1986, dir. Olle Häger and Hans Villius)

Sammansvärjningen (The Conspiracy, SVT TV2, 1986, dir. Per Sjöstrand)

Veberödsmannen (The Man from Veberöd, SVT TV2, 1986, dir. Jan Hemmel)

Fyra dagar som skakade Sverige—Midsommarkrisen 1941 (Four Days That Shook Sweden—The Midsummer Crisis in 1941, SVT TV1, 1988, dir. Olle Häger)

Apelsinmannen (The Man of Oranges, SVT Kanal 1/MovieMakers Sweden AB, 1990, dir. Jonas Cornell)

Sista båten till Jurkalne (The Last Boat to Jurkalne, SVT TV1, 1991, dir. Olle Häger)

G som i hemlig (G as in Secret, SVT Kanal 1, 1994, dir. Olle Häger)

Norrmalmstorg (Norrmalm Square, SVT1/NRK, 2003, dir. Håkan Lindhé)

Lasermannen (The Laserman, SVT1, 2005, dir. Mikael Marcimain)

Lasermannen—Dokumentären (The Laser Man—The Documentary, SVT2, 2005, dir. Gellert Tamas and Malcolm Dixelius)

Lovisa och Carl Michael—En dag i makarnas liv (Lovisa and Carl Michael—A Day of Their Lives, SVT1/NRK, 2005, dir. Leif Magnusson)

Ninas resa (Film: Nina's Journey, Sweden/Poland, East of West Film AB/VILM Production/SVT *et al.*, 2005 [SVT2, 2007], dir. Lena Einhorn)

Skotten i Knutby (A Fall from Grace, TV4, 2005, dir. Phil Poysti and Karin Swärd)

Styckmordet (The Dismemberment Murder, SVT2, 2005, dir. Anders Engström, Claes J.B. Löfgren and Kristian Petri)

August (SVT1/NRK/YLE/Nordvisionsfonden *et al.*, 2007, dir. Stig Larsson)

Selma (SVT1, 2008, dir. Erik Leijonborg)

Vägen hem (The Religious Sect—A Murder Story, TV4, 2009, dir. Karin Swärd)

Vägen hem (Film: The Religious Sect—A Murder Story, Sweden, TV4 AB, 2009, dir. Karin Swärd)

Shtikat Haarchion (A Film Unfinished, Germany/Israel, Oscilloscope Laboratories/Belfilms *et al.*, 2010, dir. Yael Hersonski)

The Arbor (Film: UK, Artangle Media, 2010, dir. Clio Barnard)

Call Girl (Film: Sweden/Norway/Ireland/Finland, Garagefilm International AB/SVT *et al.*, 2012 [SVT1, 2015; SVT2 2015], dir. Mikael Marcimain)

En pilgrims död—Mordet på statsminister Olof Palme (Death of a Pilgrim—The Assassination of Prime Minister Olof Palme), SVT1/Chimney/DRTV/NRK/YLE/ Nordvisionsfonden *et al.*, 2012, dir. Kristoffer Nyholm and Kristian Petri)

Hassel—Privatspanarna (Film: Roland Hassel, Sweden, Anagram Produktion AB/SVT, 2012 [SVT2, 2015], dir. Måns Månsson)

Palme (Film: Sweden, B-Reel AB/SVT *et al.*, 2012, dir. Kristina Lindström and Maud Nycander)

Palme (SVT1/B-Reel AB *et al.*, 2012, dir. Kristina Lindström and Maud Nycander)

CHAPTER 8: BRITISH DOCUDRAMA

The War Game (1965, dir. Peter Watkins—tx BBC1 1985)
Cathy Come Home (BBC1, 1966, dir. Ken Loach)
Days of Hope (BBC1, 1975, dir. Ken Loach)
Three Days in Szczecin (Granada, 1976)
Scum (1977, dir. Alan Clarke—tx BBC2 1991, though a cinema remake was released in 1979)
Invasion (Granada, 1980)
Death of a Princess (ATV/WGBH, 1980)
The Fools on the Hill (BBC1, 1986)
Who Bombed Birmingham? (Granada, 1990)
Hostages (Granada/HBO, 1992)
Cor Blimey! (ITV, 2000)
Gas Attack (C4, 2001)
Surrealissimo: The Scandalous Success of Salvador Dali (BBC4, 2002)
Smallpox 2002: Silent Weapon (BBC1, 2002)
The Day Britain Stopped (BBC2, 2003)
The Deal (C4, 2003, dir. Stephen Frears)
Dirty War (BBC/HBO, 2004)
The Man Who Broke Britain (BBC2, 2004)
If... (BBC2, 2004-5)
The Government Inspector (C4, 2005, dir. Peter Kosminsky)
Faith (BBC1, 2005)
Riot at the Rite (BBC2, 2006)

Fantabulosa! (BBC4, 2006)
Death of a President (More4/C4, 2007)
The Curse of Steptoe (BBC4, 2008)
Hancock and Joan (BBC4, 2008)
The Road to Coronation Street (BBC4, 2010)
Hattie (BBC4, 2011)
Holy Flying Circus (BBC4, 2011)
Eric & Ernie (BBC2, 2011)
Best Possible Taste (BBC4, 2012)
Burton and Taylor (BBC4, 2013)
Blackout (C4, 2013)
An Adventure in Space and Time (BBC2, 2013)
Marvellous (BBC2, 2014)
The Gamechangers (BBC2, 2015)
UKIP: The First 100 Days (C4, 2015)
We're Doomed! (BBC2, 2015)

BIBLIOGRAPHY

ABC. 2012. El biopic sobre la vida de Julio Iglesias se emitirá, aunque su rodaje está paralizado. *Diario ABC*, May 30. http://www.abc.es/20120530/tv-series/abci-biopic-sobre-vida-julio-201205301344.html. Accessed 22 July 2013.

Agger, G. 2013. *Mord til tiden: Forbrydelse, historie og mediekultur*. Aalborg: Aalborg Universitetsforlag.

Anania, F. 2003. *Immagini di storia. La televisione racconta il Novecento*. Roma: RAI-ERI.

Anderson, C., and J. Lupo. 2008. Introduction to the special issue. *Journal of Popular Film and Television* 36(2): 50–51.

Aprà, A. 1995. Itinerario personale nel documentario italiano. In *Studi su dodici sguardi d'autore in cortometraggio*, ed. L. Miccichè, 281–295. Torino: Associazione Philip Morris Progetto cinema.

Aveyard, K., P. Majbrit Jensen, and A. Moran (eds.). New *patterns in global television formats*. Bristol/Chicago: Intellect.

Assmann, J. 2008. Collective memory and cultural identity. *New German Critique* 65: 125–133.

AVM. 2015a. Svensk Mediedatabas. http://smdb.kb.se/(homepage), keyword: 'dokudrama'. Accessed 5 Feb 2015.

AVM. 2015b. Svensk Mediedatabas. http://smdb.kb.se/(homepage), keyword: 'docudrama'. Accessed 5 Feb 2015.

AVM. 2015c. Svensk Mediedatabas. http://smdb.kb.se/(homepage), keyword: 'dramadokumentär'. Accessed 5 Feb 2015.

AVM. 2015d. Svensk Mediedatabas. http://smdb.kb.se/(homepage), keyword: 'drama documentary'. Accessed 5 Feb 2015.

Barg, W.C. 2012. "Hunger nach Realität" oder: Die Geburt des Doku-Dramas im westdeutschen Fernsehen aus Quellen der Aufklärung und der Unterhaltung. In *Spiel mit der Wirklichkeit: Zur Entwicklung doku-fiktionaler Formate in Film und Fernsehen*, ed. K. Hoffmann et al., 279–291. Konstanz: UVK.

Barlozzetti, G. 1988. I Promessi Sposi. In *La televisione presenta...*, ed. F. Pinto et al., 29–34. Venezia: Marsilio.

Barroso, J. 2005. Docudrama y otras formas en el límite de la ficción televisiva española. In *Nada es lo que parece Falsos Documentales, hibridaciones y mestizajes del documental en España*, ed. M.L. Ortega, 171–206. Madrid: Ediciones Ocho y medio.

Baudry, J.-L. 1992. The apparatus: Metapsychological approach to the impression of reality in the cinema. In *Film theory and criticism: Introductory readings*, ed. G. Mast et al., 703–704. Oxford: Oxford University Press.

Bechelloni, G. 2003. Papa Giovanni e Perlasca. Due eroi dell'Italia profonda. In *Storie e memorie*, ed. M. Buonanno, 89–120. Roma: RAI-ERI.

Bell, E., and A. Gray. 2010. *Televising history: Mediating the past in post-war Europe*. London: Palgrave Macmillan.

Bellotto, A. 1996. *Sipario!* vol. III. Roma: RAI-ERI.

Bennett, T., S. Boyd-Bowman, C. Mercer, and J. Woollacott (eds.). 1981. *Popular television and film*. London/Milton Keynes: British Film Institute/Open University Press.

Bergstrand, G. 2007. *Inte bara Knutby: Drömmen om det fullkomliga*. Stockholm: Natur & Kultur.

Bignell, J. 2010. Docudramatizing the real. Developments in British TV docudrama since 1990. *Studies in Documentary Film* 4(3): 195–208.

Bignell, J. 2013. *An introduction to television studies*. London: Routledge.

Bignell, J., S. Lacey, and M. Macmurraugh-Kavanagh (eds.). 2000. *British television drama: Past, present and future*. Basingstoke: Palgrave Macmillan.

Bingham, D. 2010. *Whose lives are they anyway?: The biopic as contemporary film genre*. Piscataway: Rutgers University Press.

Blickpunkt:Film. 2002. Lenze/Blumenberg mit ZDF-Doku-Drama *Der Aufstand*. *Blickpunkt:Film: News*, October 8. http://www.mediabiz.de/film/news/lenze-blumenberg-mit-zdf-doku-drama-der-aufstand/122077. Accessed 24 March 2015.

Bondebjerg, I., and F. Bono (eds.). 1996. *Television in Scandinavia: History, politics and aesthetics*. Luton: University of Luton Press.

Böser, U. 2012. A film unfinished: Yael Hersonski's re-representation of archival footage from the Warsaw Ghetto. *Film Criticism* 37(2): 38–56.

Brooks, P. 1976. *The melodramatic imagination*. New Haven/London: Yale University Press.

Brown, T., and B. Vidal (eds.). 2014. *The biopic in contemporary film culture.* New York/London: Routledge.

Brunsdon, C. 1997. *Screen tastes: Soap opera to satellite dishes.* London/New York: Routledge.

Bruzzone, M. 1984. *Piccolo grande schermo Dalla televisione alla telematica.* Bari: Edizioni Dedalo.

Bundeszentrale für politische Bildung. 2012. "Besuch aus der Zone": Die Bundestagsdebatte zur Ausstrahlung der Sendung. *Deutsche Fernsehgeschichte in Ost und West,* August 30, 1–3. http://www.bpb.de/system/files/dokument_pdf/PuF_FS_05_Besuch%20aus%20der%20Zone.pdf. Accessed 24 March 2015.

Buonanno, M. 1993. News-values and fiction-values: News as serial device and criteria of "fictionworthiness" in Italian television fiction. *European Journal of Communication* 8(2): 177–202.

Buonanno, M. (ed.). 2003. *Storie e memorie.* Roma: RAI-ERI.

Buonanno, M. 2007. *Sulla scena del rimosso. Il dramma televisivo e il senso della storia.* Santa Maria Capua Vetere: Ipermedium Libri.

Buonanno, M. 2012a. *Italian TV drama and beyond: Stories from the soil, stories from the sea.* Bristol/Chicago: Intellect.

Buonanno, M. 2016. Medea's children. The Italian version of *The War of the Worlds.* In *New Patterns in Global Television Formats,* eds. K. Aveyard et al. (pp. 181–194). Bristol/Chicago: Intellect.

Burgoyne, R. 2008. *The Hollywood historical film.* Oxford: Blackwell.

Burridge, R.A. 2015. The Church of England's *Life of Python*—Or "What the Bishop saw". In *Jesus and Brian: Exploring the historical Jesus and his times via Monty Python's Life of Brian,* ed. J.E. Taylor, 19–41. London/New York: Bloomsbury/T&T Clark.

Buß, C. 2009. Republikflucht-Drama auf Sat.1: Strohpuppen in Ossi-Tracht. *Spiegel-Online,* September 22. http://www.spiegel.de/kultur/tv/republikflucht-drama-auf-sat-1-strohpuppen-in-ossi-tracht-a-650501.html. Accessed 24 Mar 2015.

Butler, D. (ed.). 2007. *Time and relative dissertations in space, critical perspectives on Doctor Who.* Manchester: Manchester University Press.

Buzzolan, U. 1973. Un maestro da ricordare. *La Stampa,* March 6, p. 7.

Calcagno, G. 1962. I Giacobini. *Radiocorriere TV* XXXIX(11): 15–16.

Cardinal, M. 1983. *The words to say it.* Cambridge: Van Vactor & Goodheart.

Carrias, P., Y. Thélen, J. Teyssier, and R. Pacaut. 2003. *Dominici: De l'accident aux agents secrets.* Paris: Editions Cheminements.

Carson, B., and M. Llewellyn-Jones (eds.). 2000. *Frames and fiction on television.* Exeter/Portland: Intellect.

Carveth, R. 1993. Amy Fisher and the ethics of "Headline" docudramas. *Journal of Popular Film and Television* 21(3): 121–127.

Casetti, F. (ed.). 1984. *L'immagine al plural.* Venezia: Marsilio.

Castellani, L. 1965. La "Vita di Dante". *Radiocorriere TV* XLII(50): 11.

Castellani, L. 1995. *La TV dall'anno zero*. Roma: Edizioni Studium.

Caughie, J. 1980. Progressive television and documentary drama. *Screen* 21(3): 9–35 [also: Caughie, J. 1981. Progressive television and documentary drama. In *Popular television and film*, eds. Bennett et al., 327–352].

Caughie, J. 2000a. What do actors do when they act? In *British television drama: Past, present and future*, ed. J. Bignell et al., 162–174. Hampshire/New York: Palgrave Macmillan.

Caughie, J. 2000b. *Television drama: Realism, modernism and British culture*. Oxford: Oxford University Press.

Chicharro, Merayo M. 2012. Nuevos formatos y nuevas audiencias para la Guerra Civil televisada. In *La Guerra Civil televisada*, ed. S. Hernández Corchete, 197–209. Salamanca: Comunicación social.

CIS (Centro de Investigaciones Sociológicas). 2014. Barómetro de octubre de 2014, p. 27.

Classen, C. 2014. Opa und Oma im Krieg: Zur Dramatisierung des Zweiten Weltkrieges im Fernsehmehrteiler "Unsere Mütter, Unsere Väter". *Mittelweg* 36(1): 52–74.

Clifford, R. 2013. *Commemorating the Holocaust: The dilemmas of remembrance in France and Italy*. Oxford: Oxford University Press.

Collin, L. 2005. Bellman bortom idyllen. *Svenska Dagbladet*, December 22.

Collin, L. 2007. Strindbergskt drama i jul. *Svenska Dagbladet*, December 23.

Collins, A. 2015. From iron lady to rock star. *Radio Times*, August 29–September 4, pp. 38–39.

Colombo, F., and G. Aroldi. 2003. *Le età della TV. Indagine su quattro generazioni di spettatori italiani*. Milano: Vita e Pensiero.

Colonna, V. 1961. Che cosa chiedono i critici. *Radiocorriere TV* XXXVIII(19): 8–10.

Cooke, L. 2012. *A sense of place: Regional British television drama, 1956–82*. Manchester: Manchester University Press.

Cooke, L. 2015. *British television drama: A history*. London: Palgrave Macmillan/ British Film Institute.

Copple Smith, E. 2009. A form in peril? The evolution of the made-for-television movie. In *Beyond primetime: Television programming in the post-network era*, ed. A. Lotz, 138–155. New York: Routledge.

Corbett, S. 2012. *Harry H. Corbett: The front legs of the cow*. Stroud: The History Press.

Corner, J. (ed.). 1991. *Popular television in Britain*. London: British Film Institute.

Corner, J. 1996. *The art of record: A critical introduction to documentary*. Manchester/New York: Manchester University Press.

Corner, J. 1999. *Critical ideas in television studies*. Oxford: Clarendon.

Corner, J. 2000. What can we say about documentary? *Media Culture and Society* 22(5): 681–688.

Costa, A. 1985. Italian serials: modelli cinematografici e produzione di serialità nella fiction televisiva italiana. In *Lo spettacolo degli italiani*, ed. A. Costa et al., 23–60. Torino: RAI-ERI.

Costa, A., G. Grignaffini, and L. Quaresima (eds.). 1985. *Lo spettacolo degli italiani*. Torino: RAI-ERI.

Cowie, E. 2011. *Recording reality, desiring the real*. Minneapolis/London: University of Minnesota Press.

Cristiansson, T. 2004. *Himmel och helvete: Mord i Knutby*. Stockholm: Bokförlaget DN.

Custen, G. 1992. *Bio/pics: How Hollywood constructed public history*. New Brunswick: Rutgers University Press.

D'Alessandro, A. 1957. *Lo spettacolo televisivo*. Roma: Ed. dell'Ateneo.

Davies, N., and R. Moorhouse. 2003. *Microcosm: Portrait of a Central European city*. London: Pimlico.

Dayan, D., and E. Katz. 1992. *Media events: The live broadcasting of history*. Cambridge, MA/London: Harvard University Press/Princeton.

De Certeau, Michael. 1988. *The practice of everyday life*. Berkeley: University of California Press.

De Fornari, L. 2011. *Teleromanza Mezzo secolo di sceneggiati & fiction*. Alessandria: Edizioni Falsopiano.

Der Spiegel. 1979. Diese Woche im Fernsehen. *Der Spiegel* 48: 287–288. http://magazin.spiegel.de/EpubDelivery/spiegel/pdf/39867472. Accessed 23 Mar 2015.

Diamanti, I. 2009. *La società italiana XXI secolo*. http://www.treccani.it/enciclopedia/la-società-italiana_(XXI-secolo). Accessed 30 Jan 2015.

Díaz, J. 2011. 11-M, una innecesaria TV movie. July 5. http://www.vayatele.com/ficcion-nacional/11-m-una-innecesaria-tv-movie. Accessed 20 July 2013.

Diego, P. 2010. *La ficción en la pequeña pantalla. Cincuenta años de series en España*. Pamplona: Ediciones Universidad de Navarra.

Djurberg, C. 2007. Med tillspetsad teatermustasch. *nummer.se*, December 19.

Doglio, F. 1963. *Il teledramma*. Roma: Edizioni di Bianco e Nero.

Donaldson, L.F. 2014. Performing performers embodiment and intertextuality in the contemporary biopic. In *The biopic in contemporary film culture*, ed. T. Brown et al., 103–117. London/New York: Routledge.

Ebbrecht, T. 2007a. Docudramatizing history on TV: German and British docudrama and historical event television in the memorial year 2005. *European Journal of Cultural Studies* 10(1): 35–53.

Ebbrecht, T. 2007b. History public memory and media event: Codes and conventions of historical event-television in Germany. *Media History* 13(2–3): 101–114.

Ebbrecht, T. 2010. (Re)constructing biographies: German television docudrama and the historical biography. In *Televising history: Mediating the past in postwar Europe*, ed. E. Bell et al., 207–220. Houndmills: Palgrave Macmillan.

Ebbrecht, T. 2011. *Geschichtsbilder im Medialen Gedächtnis: Filmische Narrationen des Holocaust*. Bielefeld: Transcript.

Eco, U. 1984. Tipologia della ripetizione. In *L'immagine al plurale*, ed. F. Casetti, 19–36. Venezia: Marsilio.

Edgerton, G. 1991. High concept, small screen: Reperceiving the industrial and stylistic origins of the American made-for-TV movie. *Journal of Popular Film and Television* 19(3): 114–127.

Edgerton, G. 2001. Television as historian. In *Television histories: Shaping collective memory in the media age*, ed. G. Edgerton et al., 1–16. Lexington: University Press of Kentucky.

Edgerton, G., and P. Rollins (eds.). 2001. *Television histories: Shaping collective memory in the media age*. Lexington: University Press of Kentucky.

Edin, A. 2000. *Den föreställda publiken: Programpolitik, publikbilder och tilltalsformer i svensk public service-television*. Stockholm och Eslöv: Brutus Östlings Bokförlag Symposium.

EFE. 2010. Las cadenas apuestan por el género de las "tv movies". *Diario El País*, April 3. http://elpais.com/elpais/2010/04/03/actualidad/1270277329_850215.html. Accessed 12 Aug 2010.

Einhorn, L. 2005. *Ninas resa: En överlevnadsberättelse*. Stockholm: Prisma.

Ekman, S. (ed.). 1986. *Stormaktstryck och småstatspolitik: Aspekter på svensk politik under andra världskriget*. Stockholm: Liber Förlag.

Ellis, J. 1992. *Visible fictions*. London: Routledge.

Ellis, J. 2000. *Seeing things: Television in the age of uncertainty*. London/New York: I.B. Tauris.

Erll, A. 2008. Literature, film, and the mediality of cultural memory. In *Cultural memory studies: An international and interdisciplinary handbook*, ed. A. Erll et al., 389–398. Berlin/New York: Walter de Gruyter.

Erll, A., and Nünning A. (eds.) 2008 *Cultural memory studies: An international and interdisciplinary handbook*. Berlin/New York: De Gruyter.

España. 2009. Referencia del Congreso de Ministros. Octubre 16. http://www.lamoncloa.gob.es/consejodeministros/referencias/Paginas/2009/refc20091016.asp. Accessed 10 Jan 2014.

España. 2010. Ley 7/2010, de 31 de marzo, General de la Comunicación Audiovisual. Boletín Oficial del Estado, 1 April 2010, núm. 79, 30157–30209.

Essén, C. 2008. *Sektbarn: Ett reportage om de utvalda för paradiset*. Stockholm: Bonniers.

Europa Press. 2014. 19 películas de la República y la Guerra Civil, en el cajón de TVE por los recortes. August 5. https://www.telecinco.es/telemania/televisiones-publicas/TVE-stock-peliculas-no-emitidas-razones-presupuestarias_0_1839075319.html. Accessed 10 July 2015.

Falkowska, J., and M. Haltof (eds.). 2003. *The new polish cinema*. Trowbridge: Flicks Books.

Fernández, A. 2009. "TV movies", éxito de taquilla y público. *Diario El Mundo*, January 10. http://www.elmundo.es/elmundo/2009/10/01/television/1254382982.html. Accessed 6 Jan 2010.

Ferretti, C., U. Broccoli, and B. Scaramucci. 1997. *Mamma RAI: storia e storie del servizio pubblico radiotelevisivo*. Firenze: Felice Le Monnier.

Fisher, J. 2008. *Tony Hancock. The definitive biography*. London: Harper Collins.

Fiske, J., and J. Hartley. 2003. *Reading television*. London: Routledge.

Focardi, F. 2012. Rielaborare il passato. In *Riparare risarcire ricordare*, ed. G. Resta et al., 241–272. Napoli: Editoriale Scientific.

Foot, J. 2009. *Italy's divided memory*. Basingstoke/New York: Palgrave Macmillan.

Formula TV. 2008. Vuelve *Salvados*, ahora con periodicidad semanal. October 16. http://www.formulatv.com/noticias/9133/vuelve-salvados-ahora-con-periodicidad-semanal/. Accessed 2 Mar 2015.

Forsyth, A., and C. Megson (eds.). 2009. *Get real: Documentary theatre past and present*. Basingstoke/New York: Palgrave Macmillan.

Fortunati, V., and E. Lamberti. 2008. Cultural memory: A European perspective. In *Cultural memory studies: An international and interdisciplinary handbook*, ed. A. Erll et al., 127–137. Berlin/New York: Walter de Gruyter.

Furhammar, L. 1995. *Med TV i verkligheten: Sveriges Television och de dokumentära genrerna*. Stockholm: Stiftelsen Etermedierna i Sverige.

Gannon, M.J. 1994. *Understanding global cultures*. London: Sage.

García Hernández, C. 2014. Te lo cuento en dos capítulos: las tv movies más vistas de la última década. March 23. http://www.vertele.com/noticias/te-lo-cuento-en-dos-capitulos-las-tv-movies-mas-vistas-de-la-ultima-decada/#None. Accessed 13 Aug 2014.

Gay, N. 2007. ¿Quién ve los programas del corazón? November 24. http://www.vanitatis.elconfidencial.com/cache/2007/11/24/33_quien_programas_corazon.html. Accessed 11 Aug 2014.

Gentele, J. 2008. Selmas hemliga liv ger mersmak. *Svenska Dagbladet*, December 23.

Gillatt, G. 2013. Ghosts in the machine. *Doctor Who Magazine* 467: 28–35.

Godzic. W. (ed.). 2001. *Podglądanie Wielkiego Brata (Peeping at Big Brother)*. Krakow: Rabid.

Godzic, W. 2004. *Telewizja i jej gatunki. Po 'Wielkim Bracie' (TV and Its Genres. After Big Brother)*. Kraków: Universitas.

Godzic, W. (ed.). 2005. *30 najważniejszych programów TV w Polsce (The 30 Most Important TV Programmes in Poland)*. Warszawa: TRIO.

Godzic, W., and Z. Bauer (eds.). 2015. *E-gatunki* (E-genres), Warszawa: Poltext.

Gordon, R. 2012. *The Holocaust in Italian culture, 1944–2010*. Stanford: Stanford University Press.

Grasso, A. 2000. *Storia della televisione italiana*. Milano: Garzanti.

Guadaño, L. 2009. Representación histórica, crónica negra y legitimación de la democracia: La Huella del Crimen. In *Historias de la Pequeña Pantalla: Representaciones históricas en la televisión de la España democrática*, ed. F. López et al., 273–292. Frankfurt am Main: Vervuert.

Guicheteau, G. 2008. *François Mitterrand: La Résistance et Vichy*. Paris: Jean-Claude Gawsewitch Editeur.

Gustafsson, I. 2012. Familjen Palme anmäler "Call Girl" för förtal. *Aftonbladet*, December 7.

Halle, R. 2008. *German film after Germany: Toward a transnational aesthetic*. Urbana/Chicago: University of Illinois Press.

Hausen, J. 2014. 8,000 Illuminated balloons released for the fall of the Berlin Wall's 25th anniversary. *The Creators Project*: http://thecreatorsproject.vice.com/blog/8000-illuminated-balloons-will-recreate-the-berlin-wall. Accessed 24 Mar 2015.

Hemmel, J. 2010. *Skånska mord*. Malmö: Roos & Tegnér.

Hernández Corchete, S. (ed.). 2012. *La Guerra Civil televisada*. Salamanca: Comunicación Social.

Hickethier, K. 1979. Fiktion und Fakt: Das Dokumentarspiel und seine Entwicklung bei ZDF und ARD. In *Fernsehsendungen und ihre Formen: Typologie, Geschichte und Kritik des Programms in der Bundesrepublik Deutschland*, ed. H. Kreuzer et al., 53–70. Stuttgart: Reclam.

Hickethier, K. 1994. Das Fernsehspiel oder: Der Kunstanspruch der Erzählmaschine Fernsehen. In *Das Fernsehen und die Künste*, ed. H. Schanze et al., 303–348. München: W. Fink.

Hickethier, K. (with P. Hoff). 1998. *Geschichte des deutschen Fernsehens*, Stuttgart: Metzler.

Hight, C. 2010. *Television mockumentary: Reflexivity, satire and a call to play*. Manchester/New York: Manchester University Press.

Hill, J. 2011. *Ken Loach: The politics of film and television*. Basingstoke: Palgrave Macmillan/British Film Institute.

Hill, J. 2013. From *Five Women* to *Leeds United!* Roy Battersby and the politics of "radical" television drama'. *Journal of British Cinema and Television* 10(1): 130–150.

Hills, M. 2014. The year of the Doctor: Celebrating the 50th, regenerating public value? *Science Fiction Film and Television* 7(2): 159–178.

Hills, M. 2015. *Doctor Who: The unfolding event—Marketing, merchandising and mediatizing a brand anniversary*. Basingstoke: Palgrave Macmillan.

Hißnauer, C. 2008. Das Doku-Drama in Deutschland als Journalistisches Politikfernsehen. *MEDIENwissenschaft* 3: 256–265.

Hoffer, T., R. Musburger, and R. Nelson. 1980. Evolution of docudrama on American television networks: A content analysis, 1966–1978. *Southern Speech Communication Journal* 45: 149–163.

Hoffer, T., R. Musburger, and R. Nelson. 1985. Docudrama. In *TV genres: A handbook and reference guide*, ed. B. Rose, 181–211. Westport: Greenwood Press.

Hoffmann, K., R. Kilborn, and W.C. Barg (eds.). 2012. *Spiel mit der Wirklichkeit: Zur Entwicklung doku-fiktionaler Formate in Film und Fernsehen*. Konstanz: UVK.

Hörzu. 1958. Besuch aus der Zone. *Hörzu*, November 1958, p. 49. http://www. zuschauerpost.de/zupo/docs50/1958a.htm. Accessed 23 Mar 2015.

Iglesias, J. 2012. Interview on Cada Mañana sale el sol. *ABC Punto Radio*, June 6. http://www.abc.es/20120606/estilo-gente/abci-julio-iglesias-punto-radio-201206061352.html. Accessed 2 Feb 2015.

Ireland, P.M. 2012. "Conditions of time and space". A re-enactment experiment with the British TV series *Doctor Who*. Ph.D. thesis, University of Bournemouth, http://eprints.bournemouth.ac.uk/20444/1/Ireland_PhD_Exegesis.pdf

Izod, J., and R. Kilborn with M. Hibberd, (eds.) 2000. *From Grierson to the docusoap: Breaking the boundaries*. Luton: University of Luton Press.

Jacobs, J. 2011. The medium in crisis: Caughie, Brunsdon and the problem of US television. *Screen* 52(4): 503–511.

James, C. 1982. *Visions before midnight*. London: Picador.

Jansen, M. 2007. Resurrection and appropriation: Reputational trajectories, memory work and the political use of historical figures. *AJS* 112: 953–1007.

Jansen, M. 2008. Giorgio Perlasca "giusto tra le nazioni" e "eroe italiano". In *Memoria collettiva e memoria privata: il ricordo della Shoah come politica sociale*, eds. S. Lucamante *et al.*

Jansson, B.G. 2006. *Episkt dubbelspel: Om faktionsberättelser i film, litteratur och tv*. Uppsala: Hallgren & Fallgren.

Johansen, J.D., and L. Søndergaard (eds.). 2010. *Fact, fiction and faction*. Odense: University Press of Southern Denmark.

Johnsson, H.-I. 2004. DN:s stora kris. *Dagens Nyheter*, December 11.

Jonquet, T. 2001. *Moloch*. Paris: Gallimard.

Jönsson, M. 2008. Marcimainstream? History in two contemporary Swedish TV series. *Film International* 6(5): 36–41.

Jönsson, M. 2012. "Call girl" är en feg film. *Svenska Dagbladet*, November 12.

Kastner, F. 2012. När fiktionen smutskastar verkligheten. *Svenska Dagbladet*, December 15.

Kezich, T. 1968. Processi celebri. *Radiocorriere TV* XLV(12): 57.

Kilborn, R., and J. Izod. 1997. *Confronting reality: An introduction to television documentary*. Manchester/New York: Manchester University Press.

Kleberg, M. 1996. The history of Swedish television: Three stages. In *Television in Scandinavia: History, politics and aesthetics*, ed. I. Bondebjerg et al., 182–207. Luton: University of Luton Press.

Kończak, J. 2008. *Od Tele-echa do polskiego Zoo. Ewolucja programu TVP (From Tele-Echo to Polish Zoo. The Evolution of TVP)*. Warszawa: WAiP.

Kozieł, A. 2003. *Za chwilę dalszy ciąg programu... Telewizja Polska ostatnich czterech dekad 1952–1989 (To be continued... Polish Television in the last four decades 1952–1989.* Warszawa: ASPRA-JR.

Kozieł, A. 2015. O gatunkach i formatach telewizyjnych (About TV Genres and Formats). In *E-gatunki. Dziennikarz w nowej przestrzeni opowiadania (E-Genres. The Journalist in New Communication Sphere)*, eds. W. Godzic et al., 237–258.

Kreuzer, H., and K. Prümm (eds.). 1979. *Fernsehsendungen und ihre Formen: Typologie, Geschichte und Kritik des Programms in der Bundesrepublik Deutschland.* Stuttgart: Reclam.

Kronbrink, H. 2005. Lovisa träder fram i Bellmanskildring. *Dagens Nyheter*, December 23.

Lacey, S. 2015. Embedded journalism. In *The 'War on Terror': Post 9/11 television drama, docudrama and documentary*, ed. S. Lacey et al., 33–48. Cardiff: University of Wales Press.

Lacey, S., and D. Paget. 2015. *The 'War on Terror': Post 9/11 television drama, docudrama and documentary.* Cardiff: University of Wales Press.

Landy, M. 2000. Cinematic history, melodrama and the Holocaust. In *Humanity at the limit: The impact of the Holocaust experience on Jews and Christians*, ed. M.A. Signer, 376–390. Bloomington: Indiana University Press.

Lapidus, A. 2007. Mord via sms. *Expressen*, December 12.

Larsson, Å. 2013. "Call girl" klipps om efter uppgörelse. *Svenska Dagbladet*, March 13.

Liebman, S. 2011. The never-ending story: Yael Hersonski's "A Film Unfinished". *Cineaste* 36(3): 15–19.

Lindeberg, P. 1999. *Döden är en man: Historien om obducenten och allmänläkaren.* Stockholm: Fischer.

Lipkin, S.N. 1999. Real emotional logic. *Cinema Journal* 38(4): 68–85.

Lipkin, S.N. 2002. *Real emotional logic: Film and television docudrama as persuasive practice.* Carbondale/Edwardsville: Southern Illinois University Press.

Lipkin, S.N. 2011. *Docudrama performs the past: Arenas of argument in films based on true stories.* Newcastle upon Tyne: Cambridge Scholars.

Lipkin, S.N. 2015. Post 9/11 American television drama. In *The 'War on Terror': Post 9/11 television drama, docudrama and documentary*, ed. S. Lacey et al., 49–64. Cardiff: University of Wales Press.

Lipkin, S.N., D. Paget, and J. Roscoe. 2006. Docudrama and mock-documentary: Defining terms, proposing canons. In *Docufictions essays on the intersection of documentary and fictional filmaking*, ed. G.D. Rhodes et al., 11–26. Jefferson: McFarland & Co.

Loe, E. 2009. *Kurt i Kurtby.* Stockholm: Alfabeta.

López, F., E. Cueto Asin, and D.R. George (eds.). 2009. *Historias de la Pequeña Pantalla: Representaciones históricas en la televisión de la España democrática.* Madrid/Frankfurt: Iberoamericana.

Lotz, A. (ed.). 2009. *Beyond primetime: Television programming in the post-network era*. New York: Routledge.

Lowenthal, L. 1944. The triumph of mass idols. In *Literature, popular culture and society*, ed. L. Lowenthal. Englewood Cliffs: Prentice-Hall.

Lowenthal, L. (ed.) *Literature, popular culture and society*. Englewood Cliff: Prentice-Hall.

Lucamante, S., M. Jansen, R. Speelman, and S. Gaiga (eds.). 2008. *Memoria collettiva e memoria privata: il ricordo della Shoah come politica sociale*. Utrecht: Igitur/Utrecht.

Ludvigsson, D. 2003. *The historian-filmmaker's dilemma: Historical documentaries in Sweden in the era of Häger and Villius*. Uppsala: Acta Universitatis Upsaliensis.

Lugato, G. 1963. Spettacoli per tutti i gusti. *Radiocorriere TV* XL(39): 7–8.

Lumholdt, J. 2012. "Visst har vi varit respektlösa". *Svenska Dagbladet*, December 1.

Lundgren, E. 2008. *Knutby-koden*. Stockholm: Modernista.

Lyttkens, Y. 1951. *Yngsjömordet*. Stockholm: Bonniers.

Maciejewski, L. 2005. Byłem Isaurą. 'Niewolnica Isaura', czyli stan wojenny w telewizji' ('I used to be Isaura'. 'Isaura, the Slave Girl', or 'Marshall Law in Television'). In *30 najważniejszych programów TV w Polsce*, ed. W. Godzic, 151–160. Warszawa: Wydawn. "Trio".

Marcus, M. 2007. *Italian film in the shadow of Auschwitz*. Toronto: University of Toronto Press.

Marill, A.H. 2007. *Big pictures on the small screen*. Westport: Praeger.

Mast, G., M. Cohen, and L. Braudy (eds.). 1992. *Film theory and criticism: Introductory readings*. Oxford: Oxford University Press.

Mavise. 2014. TV and on-demand audiovisual services in Spain. http://mavise.obs.coe.int/country?id=12. Accessed 10 Jan 2015.

McArthur, C. 1981. Historical drama. In *Popular television and film*, ed. T. Bennett et al., 288–301. London: British Film Institute.

McBride, I. 1999. Where are we going and how and why? In *Why docudrama? Fact-fiction on film and TV*, ed. A. Rosenthal, 111–118. Carbondale: Southern Illinois University Press.

McGuigan, J. 2005. The cultural public sphere. *European Journal of Cultural Studies* 8(4): 427–443.

Medhurst, A. 1991. Every wart and pustule. Gilbert Harding and television stardom. In *Popular television in Britain*, ed. J. Corner, 60–74. London: BFI.

Miccichè, L. (ed.). 1995. *Studi su dodici sguardi d'autore in cortometraggio*. Torino: Associazione Philip Morris-Progetto Cinema/Lindau.

Mills, B. 2011. Days of future past. Documenting the documentary. *Journal of British Cinema and Television* 8(1): 81–98.

Moine, R. 2014. The contemporary French biopic in national and international contexts. In *The biopic in contemporary film culture*, ed. T. Brown et al., 52–67. New York/London: Routledge.

Monteleone, F. 1999. *Storia della radio e della televisione in Italia*. Venezia: Marsilio.

Moral, J. 2009. Javier Maqua y el docudrama. *Anàlisi: quaderns de comunicació i cultura* 39: 95–112.

Moran, A. 2009. *New flows in global TV*. Bristol/Chicago: Intellect.

Moran, A., and K. Aveyard (eds.). 2015. *Global television formats before Big Brother*. Bristol/Chicago: Intellect.

Moran, A., Aveyard, K., and P. Majbrit Jensen (eds.). forthcoming 2016. *New patterns in global television formats*. Bristol/Chicago: Intellect.

Müller, V. 2003. Ulbricht und der Holzhammer. *Berliner Zeitung*, June3. http://www.berliner-zeitung.de/archiv/spannender-beitrag-zum-17--juni--das-doku-drama--der-aufstand--im-zdf-ulbricht-und-der-holzhammer,10810590,10090748.html. Accessed 24 Mar 2015.

Murado, M.A. 2013. King Juan Carlos of Spain: A fairytale told by politicians. *The Guardian*, April 16. http://www.theguardian.com/commentisfree/2013/apr/06/king-juan-carlos-spain-fairytale. Accessed 13 June 2014.

NE. 2015a. *Nationalencyklopedin*. http://www.ne.se/(homepage), keyword: 'dokumentärdrama'. Accessed 5 Feb 2015.

NE. 2015b. *Nationalencyklopedin*. http://www.ne.se/(homepage), keyword: 'dramadokumentär'. Accessed 5 Feb 2015.

Neale, S. 2000. *Genre and Hollywood*. London: Routledge.

Nelson, R. 2000. Performing (Wo)manoeuvres: The progress of gendering in TV drama. In *Frames and fiction on television*, ed. B. Carson et al., 62–74. Exeter: Intellect.

Nichols, B. 1991. *Representing reality: Issues and concepts in documentary*. Bloomington: Indiana University Press.

Nilsson, M. 2005. *Pastorerna i Knutby: En autentisk kriminalroman*. Uppsala: Succéförlaget abc.

Nordling, J. 2004. *Knutby: Sanningen och nåden*. Uppsala: Hallgren & Fallgren.

Nordström, A. 2013. "Call Girl" klipps ner. *Dagens Nyheter*, March 13.

nummer.se. 2015a. nummer.se. http://nummer.se/(homepage), keyword: 'teatermustasch'. Accessed 5 Feb 2015.

Olsson, S., and J. Moen. 1986. *Jakten på Jane Horney*. Höganäs: Wiken.

Onieva, A. 2012. Isabel Pantoja, la bien pagá de Telecinco retratada en *Mi gitana*. *Vaya tele*, March 21. http://www.vayatele.com/telecinco/isabel-pantoja-la-bien-paga-de-telecinco-retratada-en-mi-gitana. Accessed 10 June 2014.

Ortega, M.L. (ed.). 2005. *Nada es lo que parece. Falsos Documentales, hibridaciones y mestizajes del documental en España*. Madrid: Ediciones Ocho y medio.

Paget, D. 1990. *True stories? Documentary drama on radio, stage and screen*. Manchester/New York: Manchester University Press.

Paget, D. 1998. *No other way to tell it: Dramadoc/docudrama on television*. Manchester/New York: Manchester University Press.

Paget, D. 2000. Disclaimers, denials and direct address: Captioning in docudrama. In *From Grierson to the docusoap: Breaking the boundaries*, ed. J. Izod et al., 197–208. Luton: University of Luton Press.

Paget, D. 2011. *No other way to tell it: Docudrama on film and television*. Manchester/New York: Manchester University Press.

Paget, D. 2012. Docudrama: A format of last resort? In *Spiel mit der Wirklichkeit: Zur Entwicklung doku-fiktionaler Formate in Film und Fernsehen*, ed. K. Hoffmann et al., 241–253. Konstanz: UVK.

Paget, D. 2013a. Dramadoc? Docudrama? The limits and protocols of a televisual genre. In *The documentary film book*, ed. B. Winston, 76–82. New York: Palgrave Macmillan.

Paget, D. 2013b. Making mischief. Peter Kosminsky, Stephen Frears and British television docudrama. *Journal of British Cinema and Television* 10(1): 171–186.

Paget, D. 2015. Ways of telling, ways of showing. In *The 'War on Terror': Post 9/11 television drama, docudrama and documentary*, ed. S. Lacey et al., 11–32. Cardiff: University of Wales Press.

Palacio, M. 2008. *Historia de la televisión en España*. Barcelona: Gedisa.

Palin, M. 2006. *Michael Palin Diaries 1969–1979. The Python Years*, London: Wiedenfeld & Nicolson.

Pérez Ornia, J.R. 1982. La vida y la obra de santa Teresa serán motivo de una serie de seis horas de Televisión Española. *Diario El País*, October 15. http://elpais.com/diario/1982/10/15/radiotv/403484402_850215.html. Accessed 10 Mar 2010.

Pérez-Lanzac, C. 2010. La realidad supera a la ficción... en la ficción. *Diario El País*, November 16. http://elpais.com/diario/2010/11/16/sociedad/1289862001_850215.html. Accessed 10 Jan 2011.

Perlasca, G. 1997. *L'impostore*. Bologna: Il Mulino.

Perra, E. 2010. *Conflicts of memory*. Bern: Peter Lang.

Persson, L.G.W. 1978. *Grisfesten: En rövarroman*. Stockholm: Liber Förlag.

Persson, L.G.W. 2002. *Mellan sommarens längtan och vinterns köld: En roman om ett brott*. Stockholm: Piratförlaget.

Persson, L.G.W. 2003. *En annan tid ett annat liv: En roman om ett brott*. Stockholm: Piratförlaget.

Persson, L.G.W. 2007. *Faller fritt som i en dröm: En roman om ett brott*. Stockholm: Bonniers.

Peyron, U. 1986. *Fallet Jane Horney*. Stockholm: Norstedts.

Pickering, M., and E. Keightley. 2006. The modalities of nostalgia. *Current Sociology* 54(6): 919–941.

Pinto, F., G. Barlozzetti, and C. Salizzato (eds.). 1998. *La televisione presenta*. Venezia: Marsilio.

Pokorna-Ignatowicz, K. 2003. *Telewizja w systemie politycznym i medialnym PRL. Między polityką a widzem (Television under the political and media system of PRL. Between politics and viewer).* Kraków: WUJ.

Potter, I. 2007. The Filipino army's advance on Reykjavik: World-building in studio D and its legacy. In *Time and relative dissertations in space. Critical perspectives,* ed. D. Butler, 161–175. Manchester/New York: Manchester University Press.

Prager, B. 2015. *After the fact: The Holocaust in twenty-first century documentary film.* New York: Bloomsbury Academic.

Przylipiak, M. 2000. *Poetyka kina dokumentalnego (The poetics of film documentary).* Gdańsk: Wydawnictwo Uniwersytetu Gdańskiego.

Przylipiak, M. 2003. Polish documentary film after 1989. In *The new Polish cinema,* ed. J. Falkowska et al., 143–164. London: Studio Vista.

Rapping, E. 1992. *The movie of the week.* Minneapolis/London: University of Minnesota Press.

Rauscher, D., and J. Mattsson. 2004. *Makten, männen, mörkläggningen: Historien om bordellhärvan 1976.* Stockholm: Vertigo.

Resta, G., and V. Zeno-Zencovich (eds.). 2012. *Riparare risarcire ricordare.* Napoli: Editoriale Scientifica.

Rhodes, G.D., and G.P. Springer (eds.). 2006. *Docufictions: Essays on the intersection of documentary and fictional filmmaking.* Jefferson/London: McFarland.

Rolinson, D. 2005. *Alan Clarke.* Manchester: Manchester University Press.

Rolinson, D. 2010. A documentary of Last Resort? The case of *Shoot to Kill. Journal for the Study of British Cultures* 17(1): 47–58.

Rolinson, D. 2011. Small screens and big voices. Televisual social realism and the popular. In *British social realism in the arts since 1940,* ed. D. Tucker, 172–211. New York: Palgrave Macmillan.

Roscoe, J., and C. Hight. 2001. *Faking it: Mock-documentary and the subversion of factuality.* Manchester: Manchester University Press.

Rose, B. (ed.). 1985. *TV genres: A handbook and reference guide.* Westport: Greenwood Press.

Rosenstone, R.A. 2006. *History on film/film on history.* Harlow: Pearson Longman.

Rosenthal, A. 1995. *Writing docudrama: Dramatizing reality of film and TV.* Boston/Oxford: Focal Press.

Rosenthal, A. (ed.). 1999a. *Why docudrama? Fact-fiction on film and TV.* Carbondale: Southern Illinois University Press.

Rosenthal, A. 1999b. *Death of a Princess:* The politics of passion, an interview with Antony Thomas. In *Why docudrama? Fact-fiction on film and TV,* ed. A. Rosenthal, 188–200. Carbondale: Southern Illinois University Press.

Rosenthal, A. 2007. *Writing, directing, and producing documentary films and videos.* Carbondale: Southern Illinois University Press.

Rosenthal, A., and J. Corner (eds.). 2005. *New challenges for documentary*. Manchester/New York: Manchester University Press.

RTVE. 2010. TVE rememora, casi 80 años después, la histórica entrada en el Congreso de Clara Campoamor. December 1. http://www.rtve.es/television/20101201/tve-rememora-80-anos-despues-historica-entrada-congreso-clara-campoamor/378023.shtml. Accessed 10 Jan 2015.

Rueda Laffond, J.C., and C. Coronado Ruiz. 2009. *La mirada televisiva. Ficción y representación histórica en España*. Madrid: Fragua.

Rueda Laffond, J.C., and E. Galán Fajardo. 2014. La duquesa y Alfonso, el príncipe maldito: memoria en la ficción televisiva española. *Bulletin of Spanish Studies* XCI(7): 1019–1042.

Schanze, H., and B. Zimmermann (eds.). 1994. *Das Fernsehen und die Künste*. München: Fink.

Schwab, U. 2007a. Die fiktionale Geschichtssendung im DDR-Fernsehen der 60er Jahre: Forschungsprämissen und Charakteristik. In *Fiktionale Geschichtssendungen im DDR-Fernsehen: Einblicke in ein Forschungsgebiet*, ed. U. Schwab, 9–66. Leipzig: Universitätsverlag.

Schwab, U. (ed.). 2007b. *Fiktionale Geschichtssendungen im DDR-Fernsehen: Einblicke in ein Forschungsgebiet*. Leipzig: Universitätsverlag.

Sciascia, U. 1965. *Vivere insieme*. Torino: RAI-ERI.

SFI. 2015a. Svensk Filmdatabas. http://www.sfi.se/sv/svensk-filmdatabas/ (homepage), keyword: 'dokudrama'. Accessed 5 Feb 2015.

SFI. 2015b. Svensk Filmdatabas. http://www.sfi.se/sv/svensk-filmdatabas/ (homepage), keyword: 'docudrama'. Accessed 5 Feb 2015.

SFI. 2015c. Svensk Filmdatabas. http://www.sfi.se/sv/svensk-filmdatabas/ (homepage), keyword: 'dramadokumentär'. Accessed 5 Feb 2015.

SFI. 2015d. Svensk Filmdatabas. http://www.sfi.se/sv/svensk-filmdatabas/ (homepage), keyword: 'drama documentary'. Accessed 5 Feb 2015.

SFI. 2015e. Svensk Filmdatabas. http://www.sfi.se/sv/svensk-filmdatabas/ (homepage), keyword: 'Vi mötte stormen'. Accessed 5 Feb 2015.

SFI. 2015f. Svensk Filmdatabas. http://www.sfi.se/sv/svensk-filmdatabas/ (homepage), keyword: 'Alfred Nobel—Mr. Dynamite'. Accessed 5 Feb 2015.

SFI. 2015g. Svensk Filmdatabas. http://www.sfi.se/sv/svensk-filmdatabas/ (homepage), keyword: 'Ninas resa'. Accessed 5 Feb 2015.

Signer, M.A. (ed.). 2000. *Humanity at the limit: The impact of the Holocaust experience on Jews and Christians*. Bloomingdale: Indiana University Press.

Silverstone, R. 1999. *Why study the media?* London: Sage.

Sjöberg, T. 2005. *Barnflickan i Knutby*. Stockholm: Wahlström & Widstrand.

Sobchack, V. (ed.). 1996. *The persistence of history: Cinema, television, and the modern event*. New York/London: Routledge.

Sorice, M. 2002. *Lo specchio magico Linguaggi, formati, generi, pubblici della televisione italiana*. Roma: Editori Riuniti.

Spigel, L. 2001. *Welcome to the dreamhouse*. Durham: Duke University Press.

Steinle, M. 2012. Auferstanden als Ruine: die DDR im Nachwende-Doku-Drama. In *Spiel mit der Wirklichkeit: Zur Entwicklung doku-fiktionaler Formate in Film und Fernsehen*, ed. K. Hoffmann et al., 305–318. Konstanz: UVK.

Stenberg, B. 1983. *Apelsinmannen*. Stockholm: Norstedts.

Stewart, M. 2011. Death of a President: Post-9/11 docudrama as shock, trauma and victimhood. *Journal of War and Culture Studies* 4(2): 251–264.

Stewart, M., and R. Butt. 2011. We had it coming. Hypothetical docudrama as contested form and multiple fantasy. *Critical Studies in Television* 6(1): 72–88.

Strindberg, A. 1879. *Röda rummet: Skildringar ur artist—och författarlifvet*. Stockholm: Seligmann.

SVT. 2015a. svt.se. http://www.svt.se/(homepage), keyword: 'Palme fakta fiktion'. Accessed 5 Feb 2015.

Taboada, P. 2013. TVE tiene sin emitir un filme de la conspiración contra la II República. *Diario El País*, November 17. http://ccaa.elpais.com/ccaa/2013/11/17/galicia/1384710119_864640.html. Accessed 10 July 2015.

Tamas, G. 2002. *Lasermannen: En berättelse om Sverige*. Stockholm: Ordfront.

Taylor, J.E. (ed.). 2015. *Jesus and Brian: Exploring the historical Jesus and his times via 'Monty Python's Life of Brian*. London/New York: Bloomsbury/T&T Clark.

Tota, A. (ed.). 2001. *La memoria contesa. Studi sulla comunicazione sociale del passato*. Milano: Franco Angeli.

Trueba, D. 2010. Volar o no. *Diario El País*, September 23. http://elpais.com/diario/2010/09/23/radiotv/1285192803_850215.html. Accessed 10 May 2011.

Trus, H., and Y. Niklasson. 2008. "Det är en falsk sida av Selma"—Lesbisk kärlek och en falsk Nils Holgersson—SVT-serien får hård kritik. *Aftonbladet*, December 23.

Tucker, D. (ed.). 2011. *British social realism in the arts since 1940*. Basingstoke: Palgrave Macmillan.

Vaughan, D. 1999. *For documentary: Twelve essays*. Berkeley: University of California Press.

Vertele. 2014. Evole divide a los famosos: de la indignación a la obra maestra. *Vertele*, February 24. http://www.vertele.com/noticias/evole-divide-a-los-famosos-de-la-indignacion-a-la-obra-maestra/. Accessed 10 Mar 2015.

Vidal, B. 2014a. Introduction: The biopic and its critical contexts. In *The biopic in contemporary film culture*, ed. T. Brown et al., 1–32. New York/London: Routledge.

Vidal, B. 2014b. Morgan/Sheen: The compressed frame of impersonation. In *The biopic in contemporary film culture*, ed. T. Brown et al., 140–158. New York/London: Routledge.

Viklund, L., and T. Nilsson. 2013. Familjen Palme går inte vidare i fallet "Call girl". *Dagens Nyheter*, January 20.

Vincendeau, G. 2014. Chanel on screen: Female biopics in the age of global branding. In *The biopic in contemporary film culture*, ed. T. Brown et al., 176–194. New York/London: Routledge.

Vitiello, G. (ed.). 2012. *In nome della legge*. Soveria Mannelli: Rubbettino.

Von Festenberg, N. 2003. Raserei, die alles mitreißt. *Der Spiegel* 19: 92–94.

Waldau, Å.M., and B. Karlsson. 2007. *Kristi brud: Vem kan man lita på?* Skara: Heja Sverige.

Ward, P. 2006. The future of documentary? "Conditional tense" documentary and the historical record. In *Docufictions: Essays on the intersectionality of documentary and fictional filmmaking*, ed. G.D. Rhodes et al., 270–283. Jefferson: McFarland & Co.

Welzer, H. 2005. *Grandpa wasn't a Nazi: The Holocaust in German family remembrance*. New York: American Jewish Committee. http://www.ajc.org/site/apps/nlnet/content3.aspx?c=7oJILSPwFfJSG&b=8449863&ct=12485707. Accessed 4 July 2015.

Wheatley, H. (ed.). 2007. *Re-viewing television histories*. London/New York: I.B. Tauris.

Whitaker, T.R. 1977. *Fields of play in modern drama*. Princeton: Princeton University Press.

Winnock, M. 2015. *François Mitterrand*. Paris: Gallimard.

Winston, B. (ed.). 2013. *The documentary film book*. London: BFI/Palgrave Macmillan.

Woodhead, L. 1999. *The Guardian* lecture: Dramatized documentary. In *Why docudrama? Fact-fiction on film and TV*, ed. A. Rosenthal, 101–110. Carbondale: Southern Illinois University Press.

Wróblewski, B. 2014. Jak na Małej kręcili powstanie (How the Warsaw Uprising was filmed on Mała Street). *Gazeta Telewizyjna*, supplement to *Gazeta Wyborcza*, August 1–7, p. 3.

YouTube. 2015a. youtube.com. https://www.youtube.com/(homepage), keyword: 'Call Girl—official trailer'. Accessed 5 Feb 2015.

YouTube. 2015b. youtube.com. https://www.youtube.com/(homepage), keyword: 'Kvällsöppet Palme MacLaine'. Accessed 5 Feb 2015.

Zawiśliński, S. 2005. *Kieślowski. Ważne, żeby iść... (It is important to go...)*. Izabelin: Skorpion.

Zetterberg, K. 1986. Den tyska transiteringstrafiken genom Sverige 1940–1943. In *Stormaktstryck och småstatspolitik: Aspekter på svensk politik under andra världskriget*, ed. S. Ekman, 97–118. Stockholm: Liber Förlag.

Index

© The Editor(s) (if applicable) and The Author(s) 2016   265
T. Ebbrecht-Hartmann, D. Paget (eds.), *Docudrama on
European Television*, Palgrave European Film and Media Studies,
DOI 10.1057/978-1-137-49979-0